Los Angeles Kings

Hockeywood

Rick Sadowski

Sagamore Publishing
Champaign, IL

Book design: Brian J. Moore
Dustjacket and photo insert design: Michelle R. Dressen
Editors: Susan M. McKinney and Russ Lake
Proofreader: Phyllis L. Bannon

Library of Congress Catalog Card Number: 93-86780
ISBN: 0-915611-87-2

To my wonderful wife, Pamela, and our precious daughter, Rebecca.
You are my shining, shooting stars.

Contents

Acknowledgments

The words on these pages could not have been produced without the help of a great many people, to whom the author is deeply indebted. The following deserve special mention:

The folks at Sagamore Publishing, especially Joe Bannon Jr. and Michelle Dressen, who gave me the opportunity to write this book in the first place.

My editors at the *Los Angeles Daily News*, for allowing me the time to hook, hold and slash my way through this project. A blast of the Chicago Stadium organ to my former boss, Rick Vacek, who encouraged me from the beginning.

The staff and players of the Los Angeles Kings, who after all these years finally got it right. A special thanks to Rick Minch and everyone in the media relations department, who always get it right.

My colleagues on the hockey beat, in particular Frank Brown of the *New York Daily News*, Keith Gave of the *Detroit Free Press* and Dave Molinari of the *Pittsburgh Post Gazette*. That's a hat trick in any league.

Wayne Gretzky and Bob Miller, for their outstanding contributions to this book. They really are kings, on and off the ice.

My parents, Edward and Charlotte, for all their love, support, guidance and wisdom. They truly are Great Ones.

Foreword

When I was asked to express some of my thoughts about our 1992-93 season, my immediate reaction was: Which one, which season within the season? It was such a complex year for me and for my teammates, for Kings management and for all of our great hockey fans in Los Angeles.

We experienced just about every emotion possible in professional sports. It was a year I'll never forget—the satisfaction, the camaraderie, the leadership we had, as well as the support we received from our fans. But it also brought a bittersweet ending.

When we started in September, all the guys believed we could take a serious run at the Stanley Cup. The success the club enjoyed while I was recovering from my back problems was even more evidence that our team had great talent and depth.

Although we hit some rough spots midway through the season, we had so much experience in the dressing room and it became clear that the veterans were planning to peak for the Stanley Cup playoffs.

As everyone knows, all cylinders have to be firing for a team to succeed in the playoffs, and that's exactly what happened with us. You need great goaltending, and we definitely had that from start to finish, from the early minutes of our first series with Calgary all the way through the Stanley Cup final with Montreal.

And even though we had to open all four of our playoff series on the road, we all looked at it as an opportunity to quickly steal back home-ice advantage. We actually believed the pressure was on the home clubs, and our intensity on the ice increased that pressure.

We motivated each other as a group while our head coach, Barry Melrose, marvelously motivated us on an individual basis with his own unique beliefs and techniques. To a man, we knew that everyone was prepared to pay a price. It reminded me of my early days in Edmonton, when we lost to the New York Islanders in the Stanley Cup final in 1983; the Islanders were willing to pay any price to win, and they did.

Ten years later, I watched my Kings teammates do the same. All the players found a way to push ailing arms, shoulders and legs out of their minds and found a way to push their sore and tired bodies back onto the ice. I've never been more proud of a group of guys.

It was amazing how our youngsters played with the courage and poise of veterans. They were an inspiration to the older players. In the dressing room before Game 7 of our Campbell Conference championship series in Toronto, I looked around the dressing room and couldn't find a single player who didn't look like a confident 10-year veteran. We were relaxed and focused. It was our turn.

In the Stanley Cup final, we faced an equally-prepared club in the Montreal Canadiens. It's very possible the Kings and Canadiens were hockey's best prepared teams the entire season. Unfortunately, we weren't able to do what the Canadiens did— and they did what we didn't do. That's how championships are won and lost.

The Canadiens won the series, four games to one, with three of our defeats coming in overtime. To advance that far and lose probably hurt me and the rest of the veterans more than if we had been beaten in an earlier round. You realize how very close you got, and that you may never get that close again. Such are the thoughts of a veteran.

And then you look at how many youngsters we had, some of them only a matter of months removed from junior and European hockey. Hey, they played in a Stanley Cup final! You realize that these players are the Kings of the future. I am happy to say that we went a long way last year in solidifying that future here in Los Angeles.

—Wayne Gretzky

One

Crowning Achievement

The big blue scoreboard that hung from the Forum ceiling was blank, and the sideboards were bare. The lines, circles, and stencils had been removed from the ice, which was melting, slowly turning into slush. Maintenance workers would begin scraping the stuff off the concrete floor soon, then a bulldozer could finish the job.

Nothing unusual about that. The ritual took place every year.

Only now it was June. June 11, 1993, to be more precise. Usually the ice was taken out in April, when the Los Angeles Kings maintained their tradition of exchanging hockey sticks for golf clubs and tennis rackets. For a quarter-century of mostly lousy hockey, the Kings had always been gone before the May flowers bloomed. No big deal. The early exits from the Stanley Cup playoffs were a convenience, really, a blessing for long-suffering fans who were freed to turn their attention to more pleasurable pursuits. Like filling out forms for the Internal Revenue Service.

See, the Kings had never advanced beyond the second round of the playoffs before. Not ever, not in any one of their 25 previous seasons, too many of them marked by buffoonery in the front office, comical strategical moves that translated into incompetence on the ice and indifference in the community at large.

They traded first-round draft picks that other teams turned into stars — Ray Bourque, Tom Barrasso, Steve Shutt, Ron Duguay, Phil Housley. They kept first-round picks and wasted them on flops — Craig Duncanson, Dan Gratton, Craig Redmond. They drafted potential stars — Kevin Stevens — and then they traded them, too. They even drafted a baseball player—Tom Glavine.

They devoured head coaches like piranha chew meat and discarded goaltenders like yesterday's trash. They lost a lot of games and were embarrassed often. They missed the playoffs frequently and were knocked out in the first round repeatedly.

The Kings even lost 23 of 39 playoff games following the arrival of megastar Wayne Gretzky, who was snared by Kings owner Bruce McNall in 1988 to put hockey on the map in Southern California and hang a Stanley Cup banner onto the Forum's north wall. Four years later, except for a banner they put up after a first-place regular-season finish in 1991, the wall was bare.

Kings' playoff history was a chronology of missed opportunities and embarrassing moments. There had been 18 postseason appearances and 11 first-round exits, seven second-round appearances and seven second-round exits. Seven times they missed the playoffs entirely, in a league where a playoff berth was a given for most teams.

In 1975, after the Kings rolled to a club-record 105 points behind the goaltending of Rogatien Vachon, they were driven out in the opening round by the Toronto Maple Leafs.

In 1981, the high-scoring Triple Crown Line of Marcel Dionne, Charlie Simmer, and Dave Taylor led the Kings to 99 points. Then came the playoffs, and out went the Kings. They were trounced by the New York Rangers in the first round, dropping a 10-3 heartbreaker in the decisive game.

In 1987, all-time penalty king Dave "Tiger" Williams scored a key goal when the Kings surprised the Edmonton Oilers in the opening game of a first-round series. They were edged in the second game, 13-3, and lost every subsequent playoff game but one over the next two years.

The Kings did advance to the second round three years in a row starting in 1989 after Gretzky came in from the cold and McNall replaced the team's purple and gold uniforms with the black, silver and white ones they wear today. But it was just like old times in 1992 when they stumbled to a lifeless first-round loss to the hated Oilers. The pratfall so enraged McNall that he shook up the front office, brought in a new head coach — Barry Melrose became the 11th in a 13-year period — and took away the team's luxury airplane.

And that is why 1992-93 was so special, not that it began that way. Gretzky missed half the year with a career-threatening back injury; the team suffered through winless streaks of seven and 10 games; high-scoring defenseman Paul Coffey was included in an unpopular trade with the Detroit Red Wings; management, concerned with its goaltending, brought in a career minor leaguer; and the roster was gutted by injuries to almost every front-line player.

Melrose, whose positive attitude spread to every nook and cranny in the organization, squeezed 88 points out of this team in the regular season, but even that was only good enough for third place in the division and 11th overall in the league.

Then the Kings pulled together and defeated the Calgary Flames, Vancouver Canucks, and Toronto Maple Leafs in the playoffs. Smythe Division and Campbell Conference championship banners were hung. The Kings advanced to the Stanley Cup final and won over a new legion of fans. They turned Hollywood into Hockeywood.

Except for a bounce here or a different rule interpretation there, the Kings might have upset the Montreal Canadiens and carted home hockey's most cherished prize. They won the opening game, then lost four games in a row, three of them in overtime. But what a ride it had been.

"Personally, I would kill for (the Cup) and it would mean even more for hockey if we could win in California," Gretzky said during the surprising march to the final. "I fantasize about it a lot. I want to win so desperately now." When the Kings didn't, he considered retiring.

Melrose was disappointed, not crushed. "This team gave me a lot of blood, guts and courage," he said. "It's very tough because we lost. It's bittersweet. We took some giant steps, but I lose hard. Now we have to take the next step. The losing part always hurts, but we have to feel pride for what we accomplished."

Pat Conacher felt a mixture of emotions as he watched teammates clean out their lockers, some for the final time as Kings, though he couldn't have known it at the time.

"Of all the pro teams I've ever played on," Conacher, a 14-year veteran, said, "this has been the closest team, the best bunch of guys. That's why I try not to think about disbanding. People move on, go to other places. It happens all the time, but you're always sad to see guys go. This team was special, I think. We got to play in a final, and that's what you live for. Who knows if we'll ever get back. It's a bitter pill to swallow because we were so close to winning."

Nine months earlier, they seemed closer to losing it all.

Two

99 Fears

Wayne Gretzky hadn't looked this happy in four years, since the Kings knocked out the defending Stanley Cup champion Edmonton Oilers in the first round of the playoffs. Gretzky had spearheaded the Oilers' attack the season before, winning his second Conn Smythe Trophy as playoff MVP. His thank-you gift from Edmonton owner Peter Pocklington came in the form of a trade, followed by Pocklington's insensitive "crocodile tears" remarks, a reference to Gretzky's emotional display during a farewell news conference in Alberta, Canada.

Unfortunately, things hadn't gone so well since then. Not in the playoffs. Edmonton had eliminated the Kings in the playoffs three consecutive springs, even won a Stanley Cup in 1990. And Gretzky's 1991-92 season was simply the pits. He scored just 31 goals, the lowest of his extraordinary career, failed to produce 100 assists for the first time in 12 years, and finished with a career-low 121 points. Gretzky could do no better than third in the NHL's individual scoring race, finishing behind Pittsburgh Penguins stars Mario Lemieux and Kevin Stevens. Concerned he might not be capable of reaching his own lofty expectations any longer, he even hinted at retirement.

But Gretzky also was disgusted with the play of his team. The Kings' regular-season points total plummeted from 102 to 84 and the club was upset by his nemesis, the Oilers, in the very first round; Los Angeles hadn't gone out that early since the Great One's arrival.

That wasn't the worst of it. Gretzky's father, Walter, was stricken with a life-threatening brain aneurysm in October 1991, while painting a house at the family farm in Brantford, Ontario. He was rushed to a hospital and eventually underwent delicate surgery. Gretzky missed five games to be at his father's side and spent the better part of the season worrying about his condition. Walter's progress was painstakingly slow, but, almost miraculously, he improved so much that a year later he was exchanging quips with his famous son and was allowed to travel. Wayne's spirits soared.

"It was such a blow to me," Gretzky said. "It really hit me hard. My dad is my best friend, and I was always able to lean on him. Every athlete goes through tough times. We all have down times and I used to lean on him whenever I played poorly. Now, we just feel so lucky that he is alive."

There were other reasons for the extra bounce in Gretzky's stride as he reported for training camp at Lake Arrowhead, California — a breathtaking mountain resort that sits 90 minutes from smog-ridden Los Angeles — in September 1992. His wife, Janet, was due to give birth to the couple's third child any day now, and Gretzky was planning to be present for the happy event. Gretzky also seemed pleased with the team's new head coach, Barry Melrose. Just 36, Melrose had coached the Adirondack Red Wings to the American Hockey League championship the year before. Even better, Melrose believed in playing a fast-paced, aggressive style of game that was missing under Tom Webster, who coached the previous three seasons. "I think he's going to be good," Gretzky said of Melrose. "He's talking about winning a championship, and that's why we're here."

No one could have predicted it at the time, but Gretzky wouldn't be there for much longer. He spent two days at camp, then left September 13 for home following a late afternoon session. Janet gave birth to a healthy boy, Trevor Douglas, the couple's second son, the following morning. The plan was for Gretzky to remain at home for two days and then drive back to Lake Arrowhead for an evening scrimmage on September 16. Instead, he checked into Centinela Hospital Medical Center. Pain in his chest that had surfaced the previous spring was flaring again, and he wanted to be certain the condition was of no consequence. According to the Kings, Gretzky had a strained upper back and would remain in the hospital to undergo a battery of tests.

Two days later, as the Kings opened exhibition play in Vancouver, the Kings released a statement from Dr. Robert Watkins, a back specialist whose patients included Mario Lemieux and baseball's Darryl Strawberry. Watkins said Gretzky was experiencing "significant pain" and would remain hospitalized through the weekend. "Our goal is to reduce the amount of pain Wayne is experiencing," he said. "We will continue to evaluate the multitude of tests that have been taken. In the meantime, Wayne will remain under our care so that he receives the proper treatment and therapy." Suddenly, Gretzky seemed to be suffering from a back ailment that was probably a lot more serious than a strain.

He was. The Kings called a news conference September 22 to announce that the 31-year-old center had a herniated thoracic disk, an excrutiatingly painful condition that threatened to end Gretzky's career. Gretzky had felt pain in his chest because the problem disk, which was located in his upper back, protruded into the spinal canal and put pressure on a nerve running between two ribs. Five months earlier, within minutes of the Kings' first-round playoff exit in Edmonton, Gretzky revealed his ribs had been bothering him for some time. Sure, some observers snickered then. Gretzky, while being shadowed by 210-pound Kelly Buchberger, was held to two goals in six games; by using rib pain as an excuse, the belly-aching Gretzky had sunk to a new low. Well, no one was snickering now.

"The only thing I'm worried about is getting rid of the pain so I can walk down the street with you guys," Gretzky said at the news conference inside the Forum Club. He also would like to be able to bend over and scoop up any of his three children. "I feel I'm in the best hands possible and I'm a very positive person," he said. "Maybe I'm being egotistical, but I think I've been extremely positive from day one in trying to handle this. This is not a time to drown in my sorrow." Gretzky forced a smile. Janet, sitting at her husband's side, looked crushed.

Gretzky said his ribs had troubled him for several months the previous year. "March, April and May," he said. "I had no idea when I had gotten hit. I remember talking to (broadcaster) Bob Miller on our last flight home (after the playoffs) and telling him that I couldn't remember how or when it happened. I thought it was torn (rib) cartilage." The pain eventually subsided, then it reappeared during a summer vacation trip to Hawaii. Gretzky visited a clinic there, but he didn't find any answers and felt well enough to report to training camp.

Dr. Watkins, a spine consultant from the Kerlan-Jobe Orthopaedic Group in Inglewood, California, expressed optimism that Gretzky eventually would recover and be able to play. "There has been a small amount of calcification but no significant evidence of spinal cord injury," he said. But he also said the chances of a person suffering such an injury were "one in a million" and he wouldn't speculate on how long it might take for Gretzky to regain his health. "It's a most unusual spinal injury," he said. "I've never treated a lesion exactly like this one . . . there is a possibility he could return this year."

According to Gretzky, his pain had subsided significantly from the previous week and Watkins was recommending a conservative approach that would include anti-inflammatory medication to eliminate the pain. Physical therapy would follow, but Watkins refused to speculate on when that might start. "Many times time is on your side. Just because a lesion doesn't heal in three months doesn't mean it won't heal in six months," he said.

For his part, Gretzky was willing to do whatever it would take to save his career. Retirement, he said, hadn't crossed his mind. "I don't think I want to get into that," he said. "(Hockey) is my life. I love to play. It excites me. It cranks me up. I don't have anything else on my plate. But am I frightened? No. I've got a great wife and a great family with three beautiful kids. I don't know what the future holds, yet I'm optimistic and positive with the people I have around me. Hey, I feel great right now because after spending six days in the hospital, I'm going to go out and have a nice dinner with my wife."

Watkins emphasized that it was not possible to determine precisely when the injury took place, but Gretzky blamed the cumulative effect of "getting pounded" over the years. "Those people who say Wayne Gretzky never gets hit, I guess I'm living proof that that's a lie," Gretzky said. He and Kings owner Bruce

McNall said the injury was further evidence that the league needed to do something about players who check from behind. A rule that allowed referees to eject players who hit from behind was instituted in 1991-92. "It's a serious problem and we have got to stop it," McNall said. "Wayne had pain for several months. To imagine that he played hockey with this injury is absolutely remarkable."

Gretzky had suffered two previous back injuries, a hyperextension on March 22, 1990, when he was checked from behind by Alan Kerr of the New York Islanders, and a similar ailment on September 15, 1991, when Calgary's Gary Suter cranked him into the boards during a Canada Cup tournament game between the United States and Canada. Neither hit was believed related to the herniated thoracic disk, but the checks should have been enough to dispel the notion that Gretzky, in the eyes of NHL referees, was a sacred cow who couldn't be touched under any circumstances.

For sure, Gretzky knew better.

Kerr had driven him into Ken Baumgartner, a 200-pound defenseman and a former King who tried to cushion Gretzky's fall. Gretzky's upper body went in opposite directions and then he crashed to the ice. "I'm surprised he was able to get up," Dr. Steve Lombardo, the team physician at the time, remarked. Gretzky said, "I didn't even know (Kerr) was there. He didn't hit me that hard and Kenny tried to catch me. Hitting Kenny's chest was like hitting a wall. The ironic thing is that I'd probably be absolutely fine if I hadn't run into Kenny. It's like when a guy gets checked into the boards. That's when you can get hurt. It was accidental. Kerr didn't mean to hurt me, but maybe they should change the rules. The game is so fast now . . . maybe it should be like football, where you can't hit from behind." Gretzky, who suffered back spasms, said the whiplash effect of Kerr's check was similar "to getting rear-ended in a car. I really thought I broke my back."

Gretzky would miss the final five games of the regular season and the first two playoff games of his career when the Kings met Calgary in the opening round. "The pain part of it doesn't bother me, I'd have no problem with that," he said at the time. "It's not a question of getting hit and having it affect me for the rest of my life. That's not going to happen. But I have absolutely no strength in my back muscles. It bothers me when I try to bend over and pick up my daughter."

Gretzky returned wearing a back brace and helped the Kings defeat the Flames to advance to the Smythe Division final. Then he wrenched his back in a collision with Edmonton shadow Esa Tikkanen in Game 1 of the division final and suffered another hyperextension in Game 3 when Oilers defenseman Steve Smith checked him in the same spot as Kerr did. The injury forced Gretzky out of Game 4, which the Oilers won to complete a series sweep.

Ironically, in April 1992, coach Tom Webster ripped the Oilers for putting shadows — Tikkanen and Kelly Buchberger — on Gretzky in the playoffs. The pair literally sat on Gretzky at times, a practice that Webster condemned. "Every time Wayne goes on the ice, he's carrying a 200-pound weight on his shoulders for 30 minutes a game. There could probably be a penalty called on every shift," Webster said. Gretzky hated being shadowed. "It's the easiest job in the world. Anybody could follow a guy around the ice," he said. Gretzky never suggested the incessant checking tactics he has endured throughout his career contributed to the herniated disk, but they couldn't have helped much.

Gretzky missed all but one preseason game in 1991 after he was flattened by Suter at the Montreal Forum in the Canada Cup tournament. "I didn't think he was trying to hurt me," he said. Rogie Vachon, who was general manager of the Kings, lit into Suter. "A very nasty hit. He just crushed him," Vachon said. "Wayne couldn't protect himself. Suter came in from nowhere. Wayne was four feet from the boards when he got cross-checked from behind. Suter kept hitting him. Wayne fell and Suter fell on top of him. I thought for sure he broke his back. It looked worse than (Kerr's hit)." Suter, who isn't regarded as a dirty player, said he thought his check was "a clean hit."

The point is, Gretzky was getting cranked as often as the next guy, and a league that was dying for attention could hardly afford to lose one of its few recognizable names. Another, Mario Lemieux, has been in and out of the Pittsburgh lineup in recent years because of serious back problems.

"People who play this game are getting bigger, faster, and stronger," Gretzky said. "Hitting from behind is a serious situation. We can't afford to lose a Mario Lemieux or a Brett Hull. I hope this (herniated disk) shows people there is a lot of hitting from behind. To me, this injury is not from one hit. It's the culmination of getting pounded night after night."

The news that their meal ticket would be out indefinitely — this was the best-case scenario — shook the Kings. They were in the Pacific Northwest, getting ready to play an exhibition game against the Penguins in Tacoma, Washington, when coach Barry Melrose delivered the stunning information. He met with the players at the team's hotel at about the same time Gretzky was addressing the media at the Forum. "It was a good meeting," he said. "It was somber, but it was also upbeat and positive. I think they were relieved to finally know what was going on. Not knowing was harder than knowing. They all expressed that they were happy to finally know."

But not pleased to know that Gretzky might have skated his last lap around a rink with them. "We're all concerned," Tony Granato said. "The most important thing is that Wayne gets healthy. I saw him before we left L.A. and everyone was real worried that it was going to be something serious. We'll be okay. We just can't panic and put ourselves in a situation where we say, 'Wayne's not here, we'll wait until he gets back before we start playing.' "

Melrose, who has never met a problem he considered unconquerable, realized there would be no point in requesting NHL officials to postpone the start of the season until Gretzky returned. If he was going to return at all. So he decided the Kings had to make the best of a bad situation and get on with business.

"We lost Wayne Gretzky, but I'm the coach and I still have to find a way to win," Melrose said. "I don't dwell on problems, I dwell on solutions. Sitting on the bus and crying because I lost Wayne Gretzky isn't going to do the Kings any good. I mean, we lost a good friend. The guys are worried about Wayne that way. They want to help him get through it. But we're focused on solutions, not problems. We've got to make a positive out of it. If you sit in the bus and say, 'Oh, we lost Wayne, we lost Wayne, it's terrible' . . . we've got to handle the situation. If you handle it right, there's no problem."

Some players acknowledged they hadn't handled adversity especially well in previous seasons. Generally speaking, the Kings usually caved in at the first sign of distress. And if this wasn't a stressful situation, what was? But Melrose's ability to look cool when the world was crumbling around him had a calming effect on the team.

"We've got a system we believe in," Granato said. "We've got a coach we believe in. I think a fresh start in that way is really going to help us through this time. I think we're going to respond in a very positive way. Certainly last year we had a lot of adversity and we didn't handle it very well, didn't play very well. So this is a situation where we can learn from last year and use it as a positive thing. It's going to give someone else a chance to play, going to give other players a chance to see a lot more ice time."

Robert Lang, a highly-touted draft pick who had starred for Czechoslovakia in the Olympic Games the previous winter, was one of the players the Kings were counting on to fill the huge void at center. With Gretzky, the Kings had a decent stable of players at the position. Without him, there was little depth. Corey Millen and John McIntyre were the only returning veterans, so Pat Conacher, picked up from the New Jersey Devils a week before camp opened, would probably have to make the team. That left Bob Kudelski, who was better suited for the wing; Scott Bjugstad, a journeyman who couldn't be counted on to make an impact; and a bunch of untested kids led by Lang, Mike Vukonich, and Shawn McCosh.

Melrose said he would use the remaining five preseason games to experiment with his line combinations. Maybe Jari Kurri, whose first season in Los Angeles was a disaster, could fill in the middle for a while. "Wayne's a great athlete, a great competitor. He'll be back," Melrose said. No one asked him where he went to medical school. In the meantime, Granato would shift from left wing to center, a position he once played at the University of Wisconsin. That's where he was later that night when the Kings tied the Penguins, 3-3. The Tacoma Dome was half-empty; only 9,286 bothered to brave a rainstorm to see an exhibition game that wouldn't include Gretzky.

After the game, general manager Nick Beverley denied a report out of Detroit that said he was interested in acquiring a center from the Red Wings. The center's name was Jimmy Carson.

Three

A New Attitude

This training camp was going to be a lot different than any the Kings had experienced in recent seasons. While Wayne Gretzky's absence was a significant contributing factor, so was the presence of another man: Barry Melrose. On June 25, Melrose became the 17th head coach in the 26-year history of the franchise, the 11th in 13 years. Yes, it was accurate to conclude the Kings spent a good chunk of their time hiring — and firing — head coaches.

Melrose's predecessor, Tom Webster, was let go in May 1992, even though his three-season record of 115-94-31 translated into a .544 winning percentage, the best-ever by any Kings coach. In 1990-91, Webster's second at the helm, the Kings registered 102 points and finished in first place in the Smythe Division; it remains the only first-place finish the Kings have ever had.

So why did Webster fall out of favor with management and lose the respect of too many of his players, even though most of them genuinely liked him as a person? First and foremost, the management team of owner Bruce McNall, business executive (and soon-to-be club president) Roy Mlakar, and then-general manager Rogie Vachon was angered by the first-round playoff loss to Edmonton. The Kings had advanced to the division final in each of the preceding three seasons, but they barely looked motivated against the Oilers, and McNall couldn't believe he had just paid these guys nearly $14 million; his payroll was among the

NHL's highest. "I felt like firing everybody, and I felt like getting rid of all the players, too," McNall said. "It was by far the most disappointing season we've had."

Fair or not, Webster was seen as incapable of lighting a fire under his well-heeled troops. "It certainly was not our best effort," Vachon said after a flat 3-0 defeat in the series finale in Edmonton. Of the 35-31-14 regular season, Vachon said, "Some games we played really hard, and some others we didn't."

In fairness to Webster, no one could recall a single game when he laced on a pair of skates and gave the puck away. "The players have to be held accountable, too," Vachon pointed out. "With all the money we pay them and the way we treat them . . . you look at all the big names we've got and still we never challenged for first place in the division. You can't just blame the coaches."

Webster had helped seal his own fate by missing 31 games during a sometimes bizarre tenure that was marked by illnesses and suspensions. An inner-ear problem that required surgery cost Webster 15 games in 1989-90 after he slipped while taking a shower in his Edmonton hotel room. Much worse, he was suspended by the league in each of his last two seasons, once for exchanging punches with then-Calgary Flames center Doug Gilmour, and also for throwing a hockey stick, javelin-style, at referee Kerry Fraser to protest a call.

The latter penalty, 12 games, was an NHL record for a coach. The $10,000 fine the Kings had to pay, presumably for failing to keep Webster away from the stick rack behind the bench, wasn't a record, but McNall surely could have found a more productive way to spend such a sum. And the players wondered privately how Webster could expect discipline from them if he couldn't control himself. "When Tommy threw the stick . . . you can't do that and then tell the guys not to badger the officials. It's kind of contradictory," winger Bob Kudelski said.

Webster managed to escape with ejections for two other incidents — throwing a stick onto the ice in anger when referee Ron Hoggarth made a decision he didn't like, and asking another referee, Bill McCreary, if his "helmet was on so tight that it was squeezing his brain cells." Webster's antics seemed almost comical in the beginning, but they soon became a source of utter embarrassment to the organization.

"It boils down to accountability," Webster, who was hired to coach the Detroit Junior Red Wings in the Ontario Hockey League, said after he was dismissed by the Kings. "Certainly I was accountable for my sicknesses and for my suspensions. I blame no one but myself for them. But don't point fingers at me for everything."

Besides all the games he missed, Webster often sat in the stands and bantered with reporters as assistant coaches Cap Raeder and Rick Wilson ran the practices. Rest assured the reporters didn't mind; Webster was an engaging fellow and hanging out with him during practices gave the writers quicker access to the players in the dressing room. Essentially, this meant they could begin to write their stories earlier and be finished by a decent hour. This did not displease their editors. Not that the players complained *on the record* until well after Webster was handed his pink slip. Some felt the practices should have been tougher, others said they were held back by a conservative philosophy. A few even accepted a share of the blame for the mediocre season.

This much is certain: The perception around the NHL was that Kings coaches were not permitted to call their own shots, that they had to answer to a higher authority, namely Wayne Gretzky. It was an accusation that surfaced after coach Robbie Ftorek was fired in 1989, even though the Kings were coming off a 91-point season, their best in some time; Ftorek had benched Gretzky during a game in Detroit, an incident that generated gobs of publicity on both sides of the 49th parallel. It was a charge Gretzky repeatedly denied, and Vachon came to his support. "Ridiculous. No one has ever said to a coach, 'Play this guy or that guy,'" Vachon said. He conceded the Kings are not an easy team to coach.

Enter Melrose, a wise-cracking 36-year-old who was everything Webster is not, a hands-on coach who at first had a difficult time delegating authority to Raeder (Wilson left to join Bob Gainey's staff in Minnesota). A disciple of pop psychologist Anthony Robbins — the late-night pusher of self-help videotapes eventually became a very visible part of the traveling entourage — Melrose had an air about him that bordered on arrogance. Yet his attitude, for the most part, impressed the players. "He said we're going to attack teams, let them worry about us," all-star winger Luc Robitaille said. "He doesn't care how many goals we score or how many we give up. He said, 'Just win the Stanley Cup.' I like that a lot." Management was relieved when its new coach promised not to heave any sticks.

Melrose wasn't much of a player before he decided to enter the coaching fraternity in 1987-88, when he guided the Medicine Hat Tigers of the Western Hockey League to a Memorial Cup championship, which is the equivalent of the Stanley Cup in junior hockey.

A 6-foot, 205-pound defenseman in his playing days, he spent three seasons with Cincinnati in the World Hockey Association and didn't accomplish a whole lot there except to meet his wife, Cindy. Then he moved on — and on and on — to the NHL, stopping in Winnipeg, Toronto and Detroit. He wound up with the Adirondack Red Wings of the American Hockey League, a minor-league team based in Glens Falls, New York. Melrose wasn't exactly the second coming of Bobby Orr; including the 170 games he spent in the minors, he scored 25 goals and piled up 1,644 penalty minutes in 648 professional games over an 11-year career that ended in 1987 because of a knee injury.

But Melrose was successful every place he coached and he was considered such a hot prospect that the Kings needed to give him $1.2 million over four years and a $100,000 signing bonus — these were big bucks for a rookie NHL coach — to lure him to the Left Coast. Melrose had spent the previous three years coaching Adirondack, the Detroit Red Wings' top farm club, and he was supposed to be the heir apparent to Detroit coach Bryan Murray. Melrose guided Adirondack to the AHL championship in 1991-92, and Detroit wanted to keep him in its organization. Even Melrose fully expected to stay. But the Kings tendered an offer he couldn't refuse and the Red Wings decided against matching it. "There were no other options," Murray said. Melrose was on his way to Los Angeles. "The players will know I'm here for the long term," he said of the deal.

Melrose was a little nervous about moving his family, which includes two young sons, from the sleepy village of Glens Falls to sprawling Los Angeles. The city was rocked by riots shortly before he started contract negotiations with Nick Beverley, who succeeded Vachon as general manager, and natural disasters like earthquakes are always a possibility. "With what's gone on in the last couple of months, L.A.'s a scary place to move to. It'll take a little time to adjust," Melrose admitted. Glens Falls, he said, "is kind of like Mayberry." So far as anyone knew, there weren't any Barney-Fife-type police officers in the LAPD. Melrose probably was disappointed to learn that Jed Clampett didn't really exist, either. "All I knew about L.A. when I was growing up came from watching The Beverly Hillbillies," he joked.

Not that he had much idle time to waste on television while growing up in Kelvington, Saskatchewan, a farming community of 900 in Canadian prairie country. "There were pigs to take care of, and cattle. I drove a tractor and worked the fields, too," he said. "In the summers, I was up at 5 a.m. and we worked until dark, which usually was sometime around 10. It definitely was a working environment."

Melrose made certain the same kind of atmosphere existed when he traded in his pitchfork for a hockey stick. Los Angeles wouldn't be any different in that regard, no matter what had happened there in the past. "You know the old saw about a country-club atmosphere?" Beverley said. "I wouldn't necessarily use that to describe the situation that existed. But maybe it was a little lax. Certainly a huge part of addressing this issue is Barry and his attitude. He's a leader and he motivates. I guess the biggest accolade I can give him is that his teams play hard and they play to win."

Melrose didn't disagree with Beverley's assessment. He had definite ideas about the team he inherited and pulled no punches in discussing them. One thing about Melrose, he didn't believe in sugar-coating things. Not only were the Kings too old and too small, he said, but they also played soft. Playing "soft" is about the worst charge that can be leveled against a team.

"I must have seen them on television 20 times and my impression was you could play against them all night long and never get touched," he said. "I just don't think they played hard enough. My way isn't an easy way to play, and it's going to be my will against theirs. This is a talented team, but it's got to decide which way it wants to go. It can play soft and go nowhere or it can play my way. It's human nature to want to do things the easy way. This team has been doing that for some time. The overriding thing with me is how hard you play. You'll probably hear me talk about that a hundred times in the first month alone." In reality, the subject was probably mentioned a thousand times before the Kings played a regular-season game.

Melrose suggested fans might want to at least think about bringing neck braces to games in order to keep up with the fast tempo he promised the Kings would play. Come to think of it, opponents might want to bring braces as well because the Kings were going to hit anything and everything that moved as long as it wasn't wearing black, silver and white. He vowed the Kings eventually would become bigger, stronger, and meaner.

No surprise there. Members of Melrose's Adirondack teams spent hours in AHL penalty boxes, serving fighting majors. Already he was glowing about a 202-pound winger named Warren Rychel who was coming off a 29-goal, 376-penalty minute season in the minors. Rychel, a free agent who had been in the Chicago, Winnipeg and Minnesota organizations, was willing to do anything for the sake of the team. In other words, he was Melrose's type of player.

But Melrose made it clear he intended to make proper use of a stable of skilled players that included Luc Robitaille, Tomas Sandstrom, Tony Granato, Corey Millen, Mike Donnelly and Paul Coffey. Melrose took an immediate liking to the emotionally-charged Robitaille, who could be counted on to score between 40 and 50 goals. He expected Jari Kurri, who once was the most feared winger in hockey, to bounce back from a disappointing first season in Los Angeles. Young defensemen Rob Blake, Darryl Sydor, and Alexei Zhitnik would be given ample opportunity to grow. Bruising Marty McSorley, who could play on the wing and defense, was going to skate on a forward line with John McIntyre and either Rychel or big Jay Miller. Even without Gretzky, Melrose said, the Kings were going to be a potent club. "We can win the Stanley Cup," he would say a zillion times. As long as his players believed him, it didn't matter if outsiders thought he was crazy.

Guess what? All the players were believers. "He coaches the way I think the game should be coached," said Coffey, who was acquired from Pittsburgh the previous season. Coffey, whose end-to-end rushes would have left Melrose the player gasping for oxygen, arrived in midseason but was limited to 10 games because of injuries to his back and wrist. The highest-scoring defenseman in league history, Coffey is close to Gretzky, a relationship that began when they were teammates in Edmonton. The Kings were hoping the two could rekindle some of the magic they made during the Oilers' glory days, and they were also hoping he would jump-start a power play that often had little juice. Neither happened with Coffey missing as many games as he did. Now he was healthy and Gretzky wasn't.

Still, Coffey was enthused about playing under Melrose, whose brashness and aggressive approach to how the game should be played reminded him of his highly-successful coach in Edmonton, Glen Sather. "This is the '90s and Barry is a '90s coach," Coffey said. "He likes to attack, play aggressive and not give (opponents) a second to react. He's young, hungry and determined. I've been impressed with him since the first day. Look, none of us were happy with the way things turned out last year, but life is too short to look at the downside. Maybe our losing in the first round was a blessing in disguise because now we've got Barry Melrose as our coach."

Not every player was quite that passionate about the new coach. Millen scored 23 goals in only 42 games during the previous season, after the Kings got him from the Rangers in exchange for Randy Gilhen. It was one of the best trades Vachon ever made. But Millen is 5-feet-7 and 168 pounds, one of the smallest players in the league. He used breakneck speed to make up for his lack of size, but Millen became alarmed when Melrose talked about bringing in big forwards. Millen is a center and should have felt reasonably comfortable about his situation. Gretzky was out of the picture, after all, and the Kings weren't up to their ankles in people who could play the position.

Yet, Millen wasn't assuaged. "They claim they're going to bring in some stronger, bigger, tougher people, so you never know what's going to happen," he said. "We've got a new coach and you just hope they will appreciate some of the things you can provide, like speed and quickness. I hope L.A. has some plans for me. I think this team has unbelievable potential. I mean, I don't want to sound like I'm afraid of getting cut. I just never take anything for granted." He was also worried about his contract; his $200,000 salary was a pittance even by NHL standards, and he had filed to play out his option. So when Millen wasn't fretting about one thing, he had the other to fall back on.

Word got back to Melrose and he insisted anyone is capable of fitting into his hard-hitting system, that the size of one's heart is more important than physical stature. "Heart" and "courage" are Melrose buzzwords, as much a part of his vocabulary as "a" and "the." Tony Granato, a winger who was being tried at center, stood 5-feet-10 and weighed maybe 185 pounds, but he is willing to muck it up in the corners and accept physical abuse, and he soon became one of Melrose's favorite players. "Small men can play the way I want if they've got courage," Melrose said.

He has a reputation for being a taskmaster and a disciplinarian, but it wasn't as though Melrose walked around with a whip secured to his belt. "You can't come in and kick garbage cans every night," he said. "You've got to come up with different ideas. I know there are going to be nights when I want to have 12 beers after a game and bitch for two hours, but what's that going to accomplish? I'll have to slap myself in the face to get out of those moods. Dwelling on problems doesn't do anybody any good. My job is to find solutions."

Gretzky wasn't the only regular Melrose would have to do without. Millen found more reason to worry when he strained his lower back, an injury that caused him to miss six of eight preseason games. Blake and Sandstrom had undergone off-season shoulder operations and weren't allowed to participate in contact drills. Blake, a big-hitting defenseman who is going to be a star some day, missed 15 games the year before with a recurring shoulder problem. Sandstrom, an abrasive power forward who always seems to get hurt, had missed 26 games with a partially dislocated shoulder. The encouraging news was that both were expected to be ready for the October 6 regular-season opener in Calgary. The news wasn't so good for Miller, who was being treated for a bacterial infection and was in danger of losing his job to Rychel.

Beverley acknowledged he had shopped for goaltending help. Kelly Hrudey played in 60 of 80 games the year before and was expected to be the No. 1 goalie again, but the Kings were in need of a back-up. The only goalies in camp with a shot at the No. 2 job were Robb Stauber and David Goverde, both rookies. "But I can have some patience and still not end up in a bind," he said.

Melrose didn't mind giving Stauber, 24, and Goverde, 22, long looks, because he knew it was important for the Kings to find roster spots for some young players. And he was especially looking forward to working with defensemen Darryl Sydor and

Alexei Zhitnik. Sydor, 20, was a Kings rarity, a bonafide first-round draft pick (in 1990) while Zhitnik, 19, had played for the famed Central Red Army team in the former Soviet Union. Right winger Jim Hiller, 23, was another young player who was making a splash. "One of the things they asked me before I took this job was, 'What do you think about playing some kids?' " Melrose said. "I guess that's been a bone of contention here, but I love working with kids."

Many observers around the league felt the Kings mortgaged their future when they sacrificed draft picks and young players to acquire marquee names like Gretzky, Coffey, Kurri, and defenseman Charlie Huddy, all of them now in their 30s. The Kings were mockingly called "Edmonton South" because these four players established their careers with the Oilers. Even the harshest of critics acknowledged it had been well worth the expense to land Gretzky because he is hockey's greatest ambassador and fills seats. But the Kings hadn't come close to winning a Stanley Cup while stockpiling veterans and were hard-pressed to find ways to inject some youth into the organization. Their high draft picks were gone and free-agency in the NHL is pretty much a joke.

So when rumors persisted that the Kings were in the market for a center, Melrose wondered what they would have to give up in order to get one. "I would like to get some more depth at center, but we're not going to give up a bunch of kids to get an aging center to tide us over for half a year," Melrose said. "That's not the way to build a good team. If we can make a deal that will help us, great. But we're not going to panic." Melrose and Beverley were inclined to hold fast, at least for the time being. Melrose was willing to endure tough times in October if the experience gained meant better times in April. He understood teams were judged on what they did in the playoffs and said the President's Trophy, which is awarded to the team that finishes first overall in the regular season, was little more than a "big cheeseplate" to him.

In the meantime, Stauber was making a strong bid to make the team. He made 48 saves in a 3-3 tie in Vancouver and 32 saves in a 5-2 win over Pittsburgh in Portland, Oregon. The Penguins held Mario Lemieux and Jaromir Jagr out of the lineup, but Stauber needed to be sharp, and he came through. He wasn't supposed to play against Pittsburgh but was pressed into service when Goverde, his main competition, couldn't go because of sore ribs.

"The writing's on the wall, there's a job open," said Stauber, whose career had been plagued by injuries since he left the University of Minnesota a year early to sign in 1989. The Kings made him available in the June expansion draft, but the Ottawa Senators and Tampa Bay Lightning passed. "I've had some tough years," Stauber said, "but Barry has been so positive. He called me this summer and expressed probably more positive things than I had heard from anybody in a long time. It meant a lot."

The Kings took the wraps off Zhitnik in the Pittsburgh game and he responded with two power-play goals and an assist. Management thought a lot of Zhitnik, enough to sign him to a four-year, $1.7 million contract. Not bad for a fourth-round draft pick.

Imagine the surprise when Hiller continued to turn heads. He was a lowly 10th-round pick in 1989 who had grown so frustrated while waiting for a team to take him on draft day that he walked out of his parents' house in British Columbia rather than stay by the phone. He claimed to have learned the Kings finally grabbed him by reading the small type in the newspaper the next morning. Hiller scored 31 goals and managed to pick up 119 penalty minutes in 41 games at Northern Michigan University — fighting is banned in college hockey — in 1991-92, his junior season. He left school to sign a three-year, $800,000 contract, proof that he needed only two classes to complete his degree in economics.

A strong winger who used his 6-foot-2, 200-pound frame to hang around the net and score "garbage goals," Hiller looked like a guy who could compete for the Calder Trophy as the NHL's best rookie. Fairly impressive when you consider the leading candidate figured to be Eric Lindros of the Philadelphia Flyers; Lindros had gotten as much ink for sitting out a season rather than play for the Quebec Nordiques, who made him the first pick in the 1991 draft, as Gretzky and Lemieux had for electrifying fans with their work on the ice.

Anyway, Hiller scored a goal and set up another in a 7-2 defeat to the Rangers in San Diego. He now had four goals and seven points in four preseason games, best on the club. "He's a force every time he touches the puck in the offensive zone,"

Melrose raved. "He's a good kid, too." Hiller was a natural right winger, but he was shifted to the left side to accommodate Granato's move to center. Kelly Hrudey went the distance in goal, but the Kings had stacked their lineup with future members of the Phoenix Roadrunners, their affiliate in the International Hockey League, and the Rangers outshot the Kings, 50-21.

The Kings' performance in a rematch with New York two nights later in Phoenix wasn't much better. Goverde's ribs were fine, which is more than could be said of the support he received in a 6-2 defeat. "Obviously, Robb and I do know what's going on," Goverde said. "Management has been patient in not making a trade for a goalie and in giving us an opportunity to win a spot. But I can only control what happens on the ice when I'm out there. Barry told me not to give up. At least they think one of us can step in and back up Kelly. Whichever one doesn't get the job, at least he'll still be considered a prospect by management."

The game wasn't a complete loss, though, because Melrose watched Jari Kurri play center and score two power-play goals. "He made some nice plays and checked guys in our end," said Melrose, who decided Granato was better suited as a winger. Experimenting with Kurri in the middle came about as something of a fluke. When the Kings needed an extra center for one of their drills, assistant coach Cap Raeder suggested using Kurri. What the heck, Kurri played quite a bit of center for the Milan Red Devils in the Italian League in 1990-91. Cynics hinted Kurri didn't play much wing, left or right, in Los Angeles in 1991-92, when he posted career-lows for goals (23) and points (60) after signing a four-year, $3.75 million contract.

Kurri had been a free agent whose rights still belonged to Edmonton, and the Kings parted with defenseman Steve Duchesne, center Steve Kasper and a fourth-round draft pick to get him in a three-way trade with the Oilers and Flyers in May 1991. True, defenseman Jeff Chychrun also came to the West Coast, but the wrist he broke his last year in Philadelphia hadn't healed, requiring unexpected bone graft surgery that put him on the shelf for the first 20 games. Nice trade. Chychrun eventually was shipped to Pittsburgh in the Coffey deal.

The 32-year-old Kurri's desire to play with the Kings was tied mainly to his wish to be reunited with Gretzky. The two were the scourge of the NHL for nearly a decade as Oilers, a dynamic duo that helped Edmonton win four Stanley Cups in eight years. Kurri, who was born in Helsinki, Finland, and returns there in the summer, once scored 71 goals for the Oilers, but he didn't look comfortable as a King. He was called the Finished Finn by some, the Stealth Winger by others.

"You can't always look to go back and expect the magic to be there," Beverley said. "Jari maybe came in a little heavy. I think he sort of thought that things would just fall into place and away we go. Then some problems cropped up, he began to press and it had a snowball effect. I think (the poor season) was somewhat of an eye-opener for him. Now, I think he's taking it much, much more... I don't want to say he didn't take it seriously, (but) I think he's taking it even more seriously than he did last year."

It was a strange twist indeed that Kurri might be asked to replace Gretzky at center. "Oh, please. Don't start *that*," Kurri pleaded. What exactly was Melrose seeking in a center, anyhow? "A guy with vision, a guy who can see the whole ice," he said. "Someone who can win draws, make some plays, and throw some checks in his own end."

Bob Kudelski could do all of those things reasonably well and play all three forward positions, too, but he was having a hard time making an impression. A Springfield, Massachusetts native, Kudelski joined the Kings in 1987 after he graduated from Yale, but he didn't exactly set the league on fire at the start. His rookie season consisted of 26 games, during which he managed to score zero goals. His second season in the bigs, one goal in 14 games, was spectacular in comparison. Eventually, he would prove to be a valuable commodity, a sort of "Mr. Fix-it" in that when a player went down with an injury, Kudelski could plug in the hole and do more than an adequate job.

He scored 23 goals in just 62 games in 1989-90, some of them coming on a line with Gretzky while filling in for winger Mike Krushelnyski, who broke his wrist in that season's opener. "With a hard shot like he's got, I can't understand why he didn't score before," Gretzky said. Kudelski added 23 goals in 1990-91 and 22 goals in 1991-92, when it seemed like he played a different position or on a different line on a nightly basis. Kudelski was smart, strong in his own end, and able to kill penalties. By the looks of things, the Kings would be killing a lot of penalties this year. But Melrose barely knew who he was. "Bob's been a pleasant surprise," Melrose said. "He was a total unknown to me. When people talk about L.A., you never hear them talk about Bob Kudelski."

The things people were saying about the goalie situation weren't very nice, especially in light of the 6-2 shelling the Canucks administered to Hrudey in the next-to-last preseason game. A crowd of 10,092 at the Forum watched Vancouver score five goals in the second period, three in a four-shot flurry a little over two minutes apart. Hrudey's only other preseason game had come a week before and he didn't receive much support, but neither did he do much to help himself.

Hiller and Luc Robitaille each scored goals for the Kings, who got their first game action from Sandstrom and Blake. Kurri centered a line with Sandstrom and Granato, and, barring a trade for a center, it was obvious he would begin the season there. "He's been excellent," Melrose said. "He handles the puck a lot, and he sees the ice so well. Any time a man in the middle sees the ice, he's going to make plays and be effective." Gee, didn't they used to say that about Gretzky? Oops, now don't start *that*.

Beverley announced before the game that Miller's services were no longer wanted, proof positive that Rychel was going to make the team. It made sense as well as cents. Miller was 32 years old and had two years to go on a contract that would cost the Kings $640,000 if they didn't buy him out. Rychel was seven years younger and probably could be signed for half Miller's salary. He was represented by Tom Laidlaw, a former Kings defenseman who had recently moved to the Detroit area to become a player agent. Laidlaw wanted a one-year contract for Rychel so that he could become a free agent again the following summer. Rychel got it, a deal that would pay him $150,000 with an additional $25,000 deferred.

With one preseason game and three days remaining before the games would count, Melrose was toying with the idea of keeping three goalies. There isn't a coach on any level who enjoys carrying three goalies, for no other reason than it's impossible to keep them all sharp in practice; last time anyone looked, a rink can handle no more than two nets. Hrudey was going to be the No. 1 guy, despite what all the critics said, but Melrose claimed to be torn between Stauber and Goverde.

"The kids keep making it hard on us," he said. "Keeping three may be tough for everybody, but they've both played great and deserve to start the season with us. I'm really proud of them, happy about the way they have played under pressure." Well, Stauber was unbeaten with a 2-0-1 record and a splendid 2.27 goals-against average, but Goverde was 0-1-1 with a 4.32 average. His numbers weren't great by any stretch of the imagination, Melrose's included.

There were other decisions to make, not the least of which concerned Dave Taylor, who is one of the classiest people in all of professional sports. He and Robitaille were the only Kings left who had worn the old purple and gold uniforms. Taylor was 36 years old and embarking on his 16th NHL season, all with Los Angeles, and Melrose had the upmost respect for him. But a head coach can get into trouble when he gets too sentimental, and Melrose had made it clear he intended to give young forwards like Hiller, Rychel, and Robert Lang ample opportunity to grow. He already was committed to playing Pat Conacher, the 33-year-old handyman whom Beverley had plucked from New Jersey, so where did that leave Taylor?

"Davey knows the situation," Melrose said. "I'll get him in there when I can." Taylor didn't sound overly concerned. Every year he was told his playing time would be cut, and every year his impeccable work habits kept him in the lineup. He played in 77 games the year before, the fifth-highest total on the team. Once an all-star, his role had changed considerably. He went from the first line to the third unit, and sometimes the fourth; went from being a prolific scorer to a checker who would chip in an occasional goal.

But Taylor could still bang people around in the corners and he rarely, if ever, made a glaring mistake. The younger players looked up to Taylor, who served as team captain for four years and unselfishly stepped aside in 1989-90 so Gretzky could sew the coveted "C" on his sweater. He was a fixture in Southern California, where he lived year-round with his wife, Beth, and two children, and would rather be a part-time player with the Kings than a full-timer someplace else. Couldn't blame him. He was as much a part of the L.A. scene as the palm trees that sway outside the Forum.

Finally, the preseason came to an end when the Kings scored four power-play goals, just enough to overcome some sloppy defense and Stauber's erratic goaltending, in an 8-5 victory over the dreadful San Jose Sharks. Robitaille led the way with three goals and an assist, while Lang and Blake each provided a goal and two assists. The Kings outshot the Sharks, 51-27, and closed out the exhibition schedule with a 3-3-2 record. It was possible they would need to score like this on a regular basis because opponents lit them up for 34 goals in the eight games and scored five-plus goals in half of them.

Ah, but optimism abounded, as it does for just about every team at this time of year. It was October 4. In two days, the real season would begin in Calgary's Olympic Saddledome.

Four

Leave Your Troubles Behind

Some unfinished business remained for Barry Melrose as the Kings filed off the Forum ice and, still wearing skates, clop, clop, clopped on a red carpet down a hallway and into the dressing room following the final practice session of the preseason.

The Kings were going to leave soon for Calgary, where they were scheduled to open regular-season play the next night, and Melrose hadn't yet announced who he had picked to succeed Wayne Gretzky as captain.

Speculation centered on Tony Granato, a 28-year-old winger who spilled his guts on the ice every shift. Born in Downers Grove, Illinois, a couple of slap shots from Chicago Stadium, Granato surely exhibited the kind of "heart" and "courage" Melrose would expect from his captain. Not only that, Granato is well spoken, a good communicator who served as assistant to NHL Players Association representative Marty McSorley during the strike-torn year before.

Melrose didn't disagree, but he threw reporters and even a few players a looping curveball when he said Luc Robitaille was going to wear the "C" and join the likes of Gretzky, Dave Taylor, Terry Ruskowski, Dave Lewis, Mike Murphy, Terry Harper, and Bob Pulford, all of whom had been Kings captains. Granato and Paul Coffey would serve as assistant captains.

"I'm a big instinct guy, a hunch guy," Melrose said in explaining his selection of Robitaille. "Luc's a guy who grabbed me right from the start. I think it's time he emerged as a leader. He's a young guy, he plays very hard and he hates to lose. So he fits right in with the direction I want to go in."

Robitaille, 26, is one of the best left wingers in the NHL, a status he has enjoyed since 1986-87, when he scored 45 goals and beat out Philadelphia Flyers goaltender Ron Hextall for the Calder Trophy as the league's best rookie. His nickname is "Lucky," but fortune has had little to do with his emergence as a perennial all-star. The friendly French-Canadian was a lowly ninth-round draft pick, the 171st player taken, in 1984 because most scouts doubted he would ever be able to score enough goals to make up for the manner in which he skated. Poorly.

Robitaille has shown that no scouting system is infallible. He has worked his short pants off to become more than an adequate skater and at his present clip he eventually will glide right into the Hockey Hall of Fame. No one has questioned Robitaille's talent level recently, and he has always had an obsessive desire to win, one that sometimes rears an ugly side in angry outbursts and ill-timed penalties.

But Melrose likes to see emotion in a player, and he felt he could help Robitaille channel his in a positive direction. "This is going to be a new way for him to envision himself," Melrose said. "I don't think anyone has ever thought of Luc in this vein before. I've already told him I expect a lot from our leaders."

Robitaille relished the chance to prove Melrose had made a clever move. He was married over the summer and, shortly after reporting to camp, vowed to take on as much responsibility as a player as he has in his personal life. "Nobody can replace Wayne." he said. "Certainly I can't. This is just for now. When he comes back, he'll be the guy."

In anointing Robitaille, Melrose also seemed to be trying to reinforce the stark reality that the season would need to go on without Gretzky and enable him to lessen the identity crisis that was created when No. 99 went down with his herniated thoracic disk. "Barry will make a new identity," said Gretzky, who was visiting the dressing room. He looked a little sad watching players prepare for the bus ride to the airport. "It's going to be an extremely aggressive team, a team that plays with a lot of emotion," he said. "Lucky's a good choice. He plays with a great deal of enthusiasm and he's really coming into his own. I'm excited for him."

Gretzky's aching back was in absolutely no condition for him to even contemplate playing. He was taking cortisone injections to feel more comfortable, and he sounded prepared to miss the entire regular season. "I'll be around," Gretzky said, "but I don't want to get in the way. I'm focusing on being at full stride come playoff time. Anything before that would seem like a bonus. I don't know where I'm at right now, and I have no idea how long it's going to be. I wish I was playing, but at least the pain is going away. It's nowhere near where it was."

It didn't seem right for the Stanley Cup's centennial season to start without Gretzky, especially now that NHL games were going to be carried by the ESPN cable network in the United States, where for too long frustrated fans were denied television access. The league's previous deal, with SportsChannel America, had been a failure. The network did a bang-up job, but creatures in outer space had better access to the games than Americans. Kings owner Bruce McNall had been elected in June to the powerful post of chairman of the NHL's Board of Governors, replacing the retired Bill Wirtz of the Chicago Blackhawks, and he engineered a five-year deal with ESPN that would net the league $80 million. More important, ESPN would provide exposure for a league that was desperate to expand its horizons.

There were other changes. Gil Stein replaced John Ziegler as league president and the search was on for a commissioner. Two teams, the Tampa Bay Lightning and the Ottawa Senators, were set to begin their inaugural seasons. Also, a player who instigated a fight would be subject to an ejection in the form of a game misconduct, and the league put in a rule to clamp down on players who check from behind. Referees could assess a major penalty and a game misconduct if the victim of such a hit was not in a position to protect himself. Gretzky approved of that one.

Several new players were aboard the Kings' flight to Calgary, six of them rookies: Defensemen Darryl Sydor and Alexei Zhitnik; center Robert Lang; right wingers Jim Hiller and Warren Rychel; and goaltender Robb Stauber. Melrose had junked his three-goalies idea, so David Goverde was dispatched to Phoenix. The other newcomer was Pat Conacher.

NHL prognosticators weren't impressed. A few predicted

the Kings would squeeze into the playoffs by finishing fourth in the Smythe Division but the majority relegated them to fifth. Melrose claimed not to care. "It's great," he said, "when everybody thinks you're no good."

Melrose didn't even mind that the Kings would have to take commercial flights rather than use the Boeing 727 McNall bought for the team three years earlier. The Kings log approximately 60,000 air miles in the regular season, which is much more than most teams, and McNall figured a private jet would go a long way in easing the burden, maybe even help them win a few more games. The plane cost him $5 million, and that was before it was outfitted entirely with first-class seats, television monitors with videotape machines and individual headsets, an extensive galley and a trainer's room. McNall hired a flight crew, pilots and all, and players were served gourmet meals that included Caesar salad and expensive ice cream treats for dessert.

The plane was luxurious enough that McNall leased it to then-Arkansas Governor Bill Clinton for a while during his bid for the Democratic nomination for president. But the Kings weren't going to be flying it in 1992-93, not after that first-round playoff defeat to Edmonton. "Why should I pay $2 million (in additional expenses) if we're not going to advance any further than that?" McNall said. "All the fans care about is winning and the players have yet to prove (the plane) will help them win. It was a nice thing and they didn't respond to it. If they win 10 in a row, it'll prove they don't need it. And I'm not going to reward them for losses. Well, maybe if we lose 10 in a row I'll give them the plane — without pilots."

"Air McNall," as the plane was affectionately called by the players, was grounded. Melrose, always looking for an edge, said spending extra time standing in lines at airports would help bring the team closer together. Granato didn't disagree. "Instead of flying out of a city immediately after a game, we can go out and get something to eat because we're staying overnight," he said. "That might not seem like much, but it's good to hang out with one another every once in a while. It's something that just doesn't happen much in L.A., if for no other reason than it's so spread out and the guys live pretty far from one another."

So who needs a private plane? The Kings might not have required wings to soar home after stealing a 5-4 decision from the

Flames, who took a 4-3 lead with 93 seconds remaining when a puck shot by Sergei Makarov hit Gary Roberts' skate and caromed into the net. But Jari Kurri, the new center, set up Granato for the tying goal with 39 seconds to play and passed to Tomas Sandstrom for the winner at 3:40 of overtime. Kelly Hrudey, who didn't look good in either of his two preseason starts, made 15 of his 33 saves in the third period.

"It'll sink in later," Melrose said of his first NHL win. He heaped praise on Sandstrom, the feisty winger who missed most of training camp to recover from off-season shoulder surgery. Melrose wasn't so pleasant a week earlier, when Sandstrom looked rusty in a preseason game. "Sometimes you've got to get on Tomas a little bit," he said. Long-time King Dave Taylor didn't even dress for the game. "Barry told me before the game that there were no guarantees because they think the future of the club is with the younger guys," Taylor said.

When the Kings arrived at the Forum the next day for practice, they found this message scrawled on the blackboard: "Great game, boys. Congrats. Gretz."

News leaked that Kings general manager Nick Beverley spoke with Detroit Red Wings general manager-coach Bryan Murray about the possibility of acquiring center Jimmy Carson. The Kings also were said to be interested in a couple of wingers who had played for Melrose at Adirondack, Marc Potvin and Gary Shuchuk. "Carson was in it and we were interested," a Kings source was quoted as saying in the *Los Angeles Daily News*. "But Detroit is dealing from a position of power. They wanted too much." Murray told the *Detroit Free Press* the Kings "backed out." Carson wondered if the deal was dead. "We have a lot of centers and they don't," he said.

Even without Gretzky, the atmosphere for the October 8 home opener was festive. Melrose was excited because the Kings were going to play Detroit, the team for which he once was groomed to coach. The sellout crowd of 16,005 gave Gretzky the loudest ovation in pregame ceremonies that included multi-colored spotlights and fireworks, but Taylor's reception was longest. He even got to play, if only because Granato was out with a sore back.

"To hear that cheering when I skated out there meant a lot," Taylor said. "It's always nice to be acknowledged. I've been here a long time and I guess people respect me for that. I've never been flashy like Marcel (Dionne) or Luc, but I think I have been pretty consistent. I'm sure there were some people sitting out there who were over 30 who liked seeing an older guy playing."

But nothing much positive transpired after referee Andy van Hellemond dropped the puck. A first-period hit by Red Wings rookie Dallas Drake sent Sandstrom to the hospital with a concussion and the Kings lost, 5-3. Detroit's best center, Steve Yzerman, scored twice. "We were crap," Melrose snapped. "We made them look good."

He didn't stay steamed for too much longer, however, as the Kings closed out the homestand by rattling off four consecutive wins. Maybe they weren't going to be so awful after all. "I've heard people say how pleasantly surprised they are by our play, that it's okay if we lose as long as we play hard and the games are close," Corey Millen said. "Well, that isn't okay. We're paid to win."

Victories would be easier to pocket if the goaltending—a subject of scorn nearly every year—continued to hold up. Stauber was sharp in a 6-3 win over the Winnipeg Jets, while Hrudey was outstanding in 2-1 and 4-0 victories over the San Jose Sharks and the Flames, respectively. He stopped 36 shots to pick up his 14th career shutout and second decision over Calgary in a span of nine days. "I'm not a shutout master," Hrudey said. "I like the wins, though."

Sandstrom only missed one game with the concussion — he once scored a playoff goal while playing with a broken bone in his leg — and Granato sat out three with what was diagnosed as a relatively minor back problem. Not that the symptoms were minor. "The same things Wayne had, they were happening to me," Granato said. "I was nervous. Everything was all knotted up, and I had been having some spasms. My whole side ached." Granato used the time off to needle Kurri. "I told him, 'Wayne played with you all last year and he got hurt. Now it's me and Tomas.' "

And Millen. He shrugged off back pain to play in the first four games, but now, he said, "My back's killing me." Brent Thompson, another of the young defensemen, was just getting ready to return after missing all of camp with a strained hip flexor, which is related to the abdomen. With Thompson on the verge of playing, veteran Tim Watters was shipped to Phoenix.

The rash of back and abdominal injuries would result in a new approach to off-season training, according to Melrose. "One thing we're going to have to do is really get the players to work on their stomach and trunk areas," he said. "Players are getting so big and strong. If there's a weak link, it's in the stomach area. The abdominal muscles aren't strong enough to handle all that upper-body strength and it winds up putting a strain on the back." Sounded good. Maybe Melrose really did go to medical school.

Except for the injuries, things were going extremely well. Okay, attendance was a disappointment. In 1991-92, the Kings became the first team in Los Angeles history to sell out every home game, but they hadn't had a full house since the Detroit game; that was their 75th sellout in a row over parts of three seasons. The average of 14,992 through four home games was 1,013 below capacity. Crowds were down throughout the league, even in Pittsburgh, where the two-time defending champion Penguins reside. But the baseball Pirates were involved in the playoffs, so the decrease there was understandable. The Kings couldn't use baseball as an excuse; the Dodgers and Angels had provided more comic relief than solid baseball and didn't qualify for the posteason.

Team president Roy Mlakar cited the loss of Gretzky, the rotten California economy, and the riots of the previous spring that spilled into Inglewood, site of the Forum, for the Kings' disappointing attendance figures. Mlakar acknowledged the first-round playoff loss to the Oilers also hurt. "People don't forget," he said. "We didn't play well in the playoffs and, quite frankly, we weren't an exciting team to watch. We knew going in it was going to be tough. We're disappointed, but we expected this. When all is said and done, we've got to win and be entertaining. Those are givens."

The Kings were fun to watch and victorious in their next home game, too, a wild 8-6 decision over the Boston Bruins. Not only was the Forum rocking, it was sold out. The big crowd got a kick out of seeing Stauber skate 20 feet up the slot to check 6-foot-3, 212-pound Vladimir Ruzicka off the puck, the kind of play they would come to expect from the rookie goalie. The loudest howls were saved for Kurri, who became the 18th player in league history to reach the 500-goal plateau in a career. The converted center scored into an empty net with 54 seconds left after the Kings twice blew five-goal leads. He now had three goals and eight assists in six games, and the Kings were 5-1.

"I wish I could adopt him," Melrose said of Kurri. "He's saved our necks with Wayne Gretzky being out. We would have been forced to make a trade from a position of weakness." Melrose was miffed at the team for allowing the Bruins back into the game, though. He looked like he wanted to wring a few of those necks. "I told the team we'll talk about it tomorrow because this is Jari's night," he said. "We played selfish hockey, it's as simple as that. Guys were cheating, trying to score goals when we already had big leads."

Kurri was playing like a kid again, skating between Luc Robitaille and Jim Hiller as if it were the most natural thing in the world. He was hustling, playing well defensively and winning his share of faceoffs. The best compliment of all had come from management when it decided against dealing for Jimmy Carson, but Kurri was being extra cautious about critiquing his play. He had gotten off to a flying start the year before, only to crash-land at the end.

"Things have gone fairly well," he said. "Adjusting hasn't been that bad, but we've only played six games. The biggest difference is I've got two wingers after having someone feed me the puck all those years. Now I've got to get the puck to them. Also, a winger can take off sometimes and look for openings, but I've got to focus on being close to the puck. I have to be more patient."

Despite his troubles of the previous year, when expectations were so high, Kurri said he never lost faith in himself and was using the criticism hurled his way as a motivational tool. "I don't know how to put it into words. It was just really frustrating," he said. "It got to the point where I was running around, playing out of character. As you get older, you've got to play smarter. You want to do so well and things didn't go right. Definitely it was a tough year."

At least the pressure to produce now wouldn't be so overwhelming. Or would it? "What people wanted from me last year was almost unreasonable," he said. "But as a player you've got to be smarter and not let it get to you. At this level, with all the years I've played, that shouldn't happen."

The Kings were about to find out if they really were any good, hitting the road for their first extended trip, a grueling six-game, 12-day excursion through Calgary, Winnipeg, Minnesota, Long Island, Boston, and Hartford. Securing as few as six of a possible 12 points on a trip such as this would be acceptable; there's nothing wrong with playing .500 on the road as long as you win most of your home games. The year before, the Kings were a so-so 20-11-9 at home and 15-20-5 on the road.

Besides, Melrose was relishing the chance to get away from the Forum. Something about too much of a good thing making you stale. He was still hot about the collapse in the Boston game. "It's human nature to ease up after you've won two or three in a row. You win and complacency sets in," Melrose said. "So we need to get out on the road now, go through some hardships."

Melrose was prepared to spend a great deal of time answering questions about Gretzky, especially in Canada. He was getting tired of that routine already but was more concerned about players being distracted by inquisitive reporters. "We're handling it the way we have to," he said. "We're not looking for excuses and we're not talking about it. We don't have him and we're going to have to get into the playoffs without him. I told them, 'Wayne's not here, but we've still got some great players.' We can win without Wayne, and we're going to.

"I just hope everybody keeps putting us down. I don't even think other teams think we're for real. They don't think we can keep it up. That's okay. It doesn't bother me. I kind of like it."

Defenseman Charlie Huddy also said predictions of the team's demise had been premature and looked at the trip as a challenge. "Almost everybody has been writing us off," he said. "Just about every article I've read says we won't even make the playoffs. I mean, people are entitled to have an opinion, but some of the stuff you read can really tick you off. I guess it makes you want to work a little harder. We've been doing that and we're getting rewarded. It was important for us to get out of the gate strong, to give us some momentum to take on the road."

Poof! Where'd the momentum go? Luc Robitaille opened the scoring with his team-leading sixth goal, then Calgary rattled off four goals in the second period on the way to a 6-2 rout. Little Theoren Fleury, a 5-foot-6 pest, burned the Kings for a goal and three assists. "It's like we didn't have any desire," Mike Donnelly said. Melrose didn't see anything he liked. "I guess we can't handle success," he snapped.

Robert Lang was having a tough time handling his chores in the NHL. A 21-year-old rookie who led Czechoslovakia in scoring in the Olympic Games the previous winter, Lang was supposed to help fill the void at center. But he still hadn't scored a goal in seven games and had taken only three shots. It was likely he'd be on a plane to Phoenix unless he started producing. "Robert is not used to playing in intense games night after night," Melrose said. "He's used to gearing up for international tournaments, not the every-day NHL grind."

The Kings claimed winger Lonnie Loach from the Ottawa Senators, who were attempting to send him to the minors. If Loach couldn't crack Ottawa's pathetic lineup, why in the world would the Kings want him? Well, he played for Melrose at Adirondack and scored 37 goals. It would soon become apparent that anyone who stopped to make a telephone call in Glens Falls, New York, was a candidate to join the Kings.

They turned a 2-0 first-period lead and a 1-for-9 performance on power plays into a 4-2 loss in Winnipeg, where Jets goalie Bob Essensa was spectacular and an unknown winger named Darrin Shannon scored twice in three minutes. The ineffective Lang was benched in the third period, and Millen missed his fourth straight game because of a sore back. Millen made the mistake of taking an anti-inflammatory pill on an empty stomach and became ill.

Watching the power play sputter all over the ice was enough to make anybody else sick. The Kings were in a 1-for-28 slump on it and a laughable 6-for-54 with an extra skater for the season. Unfortunately, it isn't possible to decline penalties in the NHL. "We're making it too easy for teams to ice it," Paul Coffey said. "We've got to have two or three black sweaters on the puck, not just one. We're the ones with the extra guy, right?"

The honest truth was it was hard to tell. Melrose complained the Kings stood around too much and were reluctant to shoot, but they couldn't even set the power play up in the attacking zone most of the time. "The league is cracking down on holding and high-sticking and teams are getting more power plays than ever," Rob Blake said. "If you don't cash them in, you're going to get beat."

Finally, the Kings picked up a point with a weird 5-5 tie with the North Stars at the Met Center, which, hard to believe, was in danger of losing professional hockey. According to a story in the *St. Paul Pioneer Press*, North Stars owner Norm Green was interested in moving the team to Anaheim, where an arena was under construction. It was hard to imagine the NHL with two franchises in Southern California and none in the Land of 10,000 Lakes. Green was credited with saving the team when he bought it two years before and the North Stars were drawing nearly 13,500 per game, up substantially from 1991-92, but Green didn't like his lease.

Kings owner Bruce McNall, who was scheduled to preside over a league Board of Governors meeting in a few days, said talk of such a move had not gotten past the rumor stage. McNall would know, considering he would have to be compensated if Anaheim was going to ice a team.

"I'm not opposed to the concept, but no one has come forward with a specific proposal," he said. "I think (an Anaheim team) would hurt us (at the gate). But certainly, if a second team came in, it would be helpful in further selling our sport."

Wouldn't the loss of a franchise in a state like Minnesota hurt the sport? "I'm for whatever is best for the league. If it was determined that having a team in Minnesota would not be good over the long term, then (moving the North Stars) would be fine with me. If the feeling is we should try and retain it . . . I think Norm Green has tried very hard to do that. I'm sort of 50-50 on it."

A capacity crowd of 15,174 saw Minnesota's Todd Elik score 16 seconds into the game on a 40-foot slap shot, and the Kings were in a 3-0 hole before the first period was seven minutes old. Maybe they were still groggy from the 5 a.m. wake-up calls that rang in their Winnipeg hotel. The team assembled in the lobby 45 minutes later and, after clearing U.S. customs at the airport, took a 7:20 flight to Minneapolis, 80 minutes away. Alarm clocks sounded in the third period, when Mike Donnelly scored two goals and Tomas Sandstrom another to salvage the tie.

Robb Stauber, a Duluth native who spent three years at the University of Minnesota, recovered from a shaky start to finish with 45 saves before 14 family members and friends. Stauber couldn't understand how Elik had managed to beat him to the short side until assistant coach Cap Raeder looked at videotape between the first and second periods. He concluded Elik's shot went through the side of the net and shouldn't have counted. "We found it by accident. Cap wanted to get a look at Robb's angle," Melrose said. When told his first goal of the year really wasn't a goal, Elik said, "As long as I get to keep it." He did.

The Kings found encouragement in the comeback and in Stauber's play. Sure, he tended to act like a forward at times, leaving the net vulnerable in order to charge after an onrushing skater. His style was, well, unconventional. But he owned a 2-0-1 record and was performing at the level expected of him when he was drafted in 1986. Stauber won the Hobey Baker Award, collegiate hockey's version of the Heisman Trophy, as a Minnesota sophomore the following season and his three-season record was an impressive 73-23 when he left to sign a five-year, $1 million contract with the Kings in June 1989.

Stauber immediately was anointed Kings goalie of the future, but he soon became a goalie without one. His career was nearly wrecked by a rash of injuries that affected his groin, knee, back, and shoulder. Weary of his constant injuries and wary that he would ever be of much help, the Kings made him available in the 1992 expansion draft. Fortunately, it turned out, the Kings didn't lose him.

"There's nothing wrong with having tough times," said Stauber, whose bold, competitive nature was formed while growing up on the western shores of Lake Superior. "It makes you more appreciative of the good times. I've learned a lot about myself the last few years, learned that I'm pretty strong mentally. Half the battle is winning the games upstairs, the ones in your head. I'm not the kind of person who allows life to be ruined by an injury."

Once again, the Kings needed to put on rally helmets to beat the New York Islanders, 4-3, with goals by Pat Conacher, Corey Millen, and Bob Kudelski in the third period wiping out a 2-1 deficit. Melrose credited Warren Rychel's third-period fight with Islanders tough guy Mick Vukota for inspiring the Kings, who still had to kill off John McIntyre's foolish major elbowing penalty to preserve the win. "He's got to have more control," Melrose said of McIntyre, who smashed Brian Mullen's head into the boards with 4:23 left and the Kings nursing a one-goal lead.

Kelly Hrudey, a former Islander, raised his arms to the Nassau Coliseum ceiling and leaped onto Donnelly in the goal crease when the game ended. "I guess I got a little excited," he said. Hrudey didn't even notice dozens of plastic megaphones distributed to fans were being hurled in his direction. "I don't think they like me here anymore," he said.

The Kings needed more than rally helmets two nights later in the matchbox known as Boston Garden. They needed to throw an occasional check, make a semi-intelligent pass and skate into a corner to hunt down a loose puck against a Boston Bruins team that hadn't been home in 17 days. The Kings didn't do any of those things. Nor did they cover Bruins center Adam Oates, who broke loose for three goals and an assist in the 8-3 bludgeoning that ran the Kings' miserable Garden record to 2-15-1 since 1981. "There's no room for error in this place," Charlie Huddy said. The Kings made about a hundred of them.

Marty McSorley's mistake was to cross-check Darren Banks in the face five minutes into the final period. McSorley was given a match penalty by referee Dan Marouelli, which almost guaranteed a suspension. Fortunately for the Kings, league president Gil Stein's disciplinary policy was to "suspend" players for non-game days, so McSorley probably wouldn't miss any games. Unfortunately for McSorley, he would not be paid while serving such a suspension. "I get no pleasure in taking a player's money," Stein said, "but we need to deter any conduct that can cause an injury to another player." McSorley claimed his hit on Banks was "accidental." He also said, "We were down and not playing well. Sometimes you have to try and make a statement. You don't give nobody nothing."

McSorley's worst fears came to pass, fittingly enough, on Halloween after the Kings arrived in Hartford for their final game of the trip. Stein suspended McSorley for six non-game days and tacked on a $500 fine. The suspension would cost him $14,130 in salary. "I don't want to miss practices, but I'm just going to take it," he said while maintaining his innocence. Travel days didn't count as non-game days, which meant it would take 20 actual days for McSorley to complete the six-day suspension. No wonder players around the league were referring to the president as "Einstein."

In what amounted to a stroke of genius, Melrose put Kurri, Sandstrom and Robitaille on a line in Hartford, and the three combined for four goals and two assists in a 7-1 laugher over the Whalers before an intimate Civic Center gathering of 9,244. Maybe the North Stars should stay in Minnesota and the Whalers should leave Connecticut.

The Kings were leaving for home in good spirits. And just one point behind first-place Calgary. The 2-3-1 trip gave them an overall record of 7-4-1, and they were going to play four of the next six games at the Forum. Stauber extended his record to 3-0-1 by stopping 28 shots as the Kings limited an opponent, or a facsimile thereof, under three goals for the first time since October 15, a seven-game stretch. "The only things I worry about are wins and losses," Melrose said. "We're an attacking team, so we're going to give up some chances. We'll get better at playing the way we want to, and you'll see the goals-against go down. But as long as the goals for are better than the goals against, I'll be happy."

The suspension continued to bother McSorley, who also had a sore nose. Hartford's John Cullen whacked him there with his stick in the second period and was tossed from the game. "I think my nose is broken," McSorley said. "My (match penalty) looked worse than his, but I think they were both accidental."

The nice thing about the Kings' strong start was that they were getting contributions from almost every player on the roster. Without Wayne Gretzky, it was the only way they could be successful over the long haul. Pat Conacher was definitely a donor to the cause. Nick Beverley raised eyebrows in September when he plucked Conacher off the New Jersey Devils roster, even though he didn't have to part with much to get him. But weren't the Kings looking to get younger and bigger? Conacher is 5-feet-8 and he was 33 years old.

"I guess you could say he had two strikes against him," Melrose said. "He's been fighting that his whole life, but he always beats the odds. Patty's just a good guy to have on your team. He's added a work ethic and a professionalism that we needed."

Conacher can play all three forward positions and kill penalties. He is stocky, 190 pounds, but owns deceptive speed. A checker throughout a career that began in 1980 with the New York Rangers, Conacher won a Stanley Cup with Edmonton in 1983-84. He'd never played in more than 49 games in any NHL season, and the seven goals he scored with New Jersey the previous year was a personal best, but he already had seen action in 11 games with the Kings and chipped in a couple of goals.

"New Jersey was a dead end for me, and I was happy to get out of there," Conacher said. "(Devils general manager Lou) Lamoriello told me he didn't have any room for me." Conacher was on a termination contract, which meant this could be his last hurrah. For the time being, he and his wife and three children were living in former assistant coach Rick Wilson's home. "All I can control is what I do on the ice. I never take anything for granted," he said.

The Kings were off for four days after returning home, which gave rookie Jim Hiller plenty of time to contemplate his lot in life. It had been better. Hiller took the league by storm with four goals and eight points in the first six games, now he was mired in a six-game slump and wondering if a one-way ticket to Phoenix was in order. He began the year skating with Kurri and Robitaille, but in Hartford was relegated to spot duty on a Gang Green line with fellow rookies Robert Lang and Lonnie Loach.

"Everywhere I've played, I've always been able to score," Hiller said. "I've never been through anything like this. It seems like a lifetime since I scored. I've tried to put it out of my mind, but I've lain in bed at night and thought about it over and over."

Hiller didn't score November 5 when the Kings defeated New Jersey, 5-2, and again there were a lot of empty seats inside the Forum. Only 14,592 watched Robitaille collect his 10th and 11th goals to support the fabulous goaltending of Hrudey. The Kings were outshot, 48-25, an indication they were simply awful in their own end. Perhaps defenseman Jeff Chychrun, who was reacquired from Pittsburgh after the game, could help. The Kings parted with defenseman Peter Ahola in exchange for Chychrun, a 6-foot-4, 215-pound banger who had gone to the Penguins in the Paul Coffey trade.

The November 7 news was mixed. The Kings actually scored two power-play goals — Robitaille had one, stretching his goal-scoring streak to four games — and they defeated the Buffalo Sabres, 5-2, for their sixth consecutive home win before a full house. McSorley scored a shorthanded goal in the third period for a 4-2 lead after Granato took a major high-sticking penalty and was kicked out.

That was the good news. The bad was provided by Wayne Gretzky, whose back apparently was worse than ever. During an interview on the Canadian Broadcasting Corporation's *Hockey Night in Canada* telecast that evening, Gretzky seemed depressed and he sounded pessimistic about his chances of playing again. The pain-killers he was taking contained cortisone and caused him to gain weight, so he looked bloated.

"I hope I can come back to play, (but) reality is telling me maybe that is not possible," Gretzky said. "I don't know what the future holds. In time I believe I'll be able to exercise and do the things I want to do. But the physical side of the game and what it takes to play . . . I don't know. A lot of people think the pain is in my back. The pain is in front. Basically, it stops me from doing any kind of physical exercise. The reality of it is I can't really do anything because of the pain. I've had a couple of injections. From what I've been told, if I still have this pain in my chest, we'll try a nerve block next."

Gretzky wasn't even ruling out a complicated surgical procedure that could keep him sidelined for as long as two years. "They'd have to go through the chest and maybe take out a rib or move a rib," he said. "This isn't like taking tonsils out. We don't have a lot of time. I'm not 22 years old anymore. They tell me (recovery time) for a lower back (operation) is four to six months. The upper back is basically double that. We'd be looking at nine or 10 months. I might be out two years. We have a lot of big decisions to make in the next couple of weeks."

Dr. Ron Kvitne, the Kings' physician, didn't paint such a bleak picture. He said Gretzky was "frustrated" by the two-month-old battle with his herniated thoracic disk, but that some progress was being made. "He has good days and bad days, but we're not losing ground," Kvitne said. "What we're trying to achieve in therapy is for the good days to outnumber the bad days. A situation like this is always hard on the patient. A disk problem won't just miraculously disappear."

Kvitne said Gretzky's pain wasn't severe enough to use a nerve block, which is the injection of an anesthetic to deaden the nerve. He said surgery was a last resort that wasn't being considered. Gretzky's failure to perceive progress, which Kvitne said can be infinitesimal, was absolutely normal.

The same couldn't be said for the manner in which the Kings gutted the Sharks at the Cow Palace the next night. Mike Donnelly scored three goals in the 11-4 win and wasn't even voted one of the game's three stars. Top billing went to Robitaille, Kurri, and Sandstrom, who combined for seven goals and 10 assists. Sharks fans usually serenade the Kings with a "Beat L.A." chant, but hardly a peep was heard from the sellout crowd of 11,089. "We're just trying to enjoy this for as long as we can," said Kurri, who scored two goals to move past Jean Beliveau into 16th place on the all-time list with 508. A few more periods against Sharks goalie Arturs Irbe might have made Kurri a threat to pass Gordie Howe.

The biggest beneficiary of the onslaught was Robb Stauber, now 4-0-1. He didn't feel a smidgen of sympathy for Irbe. "I've been there and nobody felt sorry for me," Stauber said. "It goes with the territory." The 11 goals matched a franchise high for a road game. "Some nights you've just got to let them go," Melrose said. "When the doors are open and the horses are out, you can't pull in the reins."

The Kings were unable to reel in what should have been a sure two points in Winnipeg on November 10 as they blew a two-goal lead in the final five minutes of regulation and settled for a 4-4 tie. Ed Olczyk scored with 6.8 seconds to play, marking the second time in as many trips to Manitoba the Kings squandered a two-goal advantage. They also were outshot badly again, 49-32. The Jets had lost five in a row and led the Sharks by just a point in the Smythe Division. "It was a joke. We gave it to them," Rob Blake said with disgust. The scariest part of the game took place in the first period when Winnipeg's Teppo Numminen took a slap shot that hit Hrudey on the mask, deflected over the glass and broke through a plastic sign 20 feet behind the net. It's hard to believe there was a time when goalies didn't wear masks.

Chychrun was wondering when Melrose planned on using him. He was in the press box for all three games the Kings played since the trade with Pittsburgh. "Sometimes you get in a situation where the coach doesn't use you and doesn't plan to," he said. Chychrun was talking about Penguins coach Scotty Bowman, who benched him for all but one game. He was confident Melrose wouldn't let him rot like that.

The Kings soared to 12-4-2 with big divisional wins over Vancouver (7-4) and Edmonton (6-2) at home, victories that stretched their Forum winning streak to eight games and overall unbeaten streak to 6-0-1. Melrose was sky-high for another reason, his first face-to-face meeting with Anthony Robbins, who writes self-help literature and hawks videotapes on television and at seminars. Melrose said he has read Robbins' best-selling *Unlimited Power* at least a dozen times. "It was great," he said of the hour-long session. "He'd heard I talked about him in the papers and he got in touch with me. He's the one guy who's really grabbed me."

The team's hot start had gotten Bruce McNall's attention. He was ecstatic. The gang that couldn't shoot straight a year ago was giving him reason to smile even as he was forced to watch it play while accompanied by the ailing Gretzky in his private box. Except for the Kings, it would be a terrible year for McNall's athletic enterprises. The Toronto Argonauts of the Canadian Football League had gone from Grey Cup champions to pot in one year. McNall, Gretzky, and actor John Candy owned the team, which played like the New England Patriots and missed the playoffs.

"I had no idea we'd be playing like this," McNall said. "I truly felt the team would play very well, with some intensity, after the way last season ended. But I had no idea we would play like *this*. I thought we'd be good, but this is phenomenal. It's become obvious to me that we have a lot of character on this team. Needless to say, I'm thrilled about it."

But the Kings still weren't getting the plane back.

Not that it would have made much difference in the next two road games, both losses. A 6-3 defeat in Vancouver that snapped the Kings' unbeaten streak at seven games was, in the scheme of things, acceptable. The Canucks are a very good team and two of the goals they scored deflected into the net off skates. But the 6-0 waxing administered by the pitiful Sharks 24 hours later was downright humiliating. The "Beat L.A." chant at the Cow Palace rang in their ears for three embarrassing periods. Irbe, whom the Kings had riddled for 11 goals November 8, was impenetrable. He made 39 saves to post the first shutout in the Sharks' mostly miserable 99-game history. "I am wall," boasted Irbe, who in 1991 quit the Soviet Union's national team to protest the invasion of his hometown of Riga, Latvia.

None of the Kings threatened to quit, even though the Chicago Blackhawks were going to pay them a visit in two days. The Hawks were Melrose's kind of team, armed with wide bodies who enjoyed plastering people to the boards. "At least we're home," Blake said. "We've played really well at home. I think we're about to learn something about ourselves because we've got some tough games coming up."

Robert Lang wouldn't be playing in any of them and neither would Dave Taylor, apparently. Lang couldn't shake out of his slump, was benched for six consecutive games, and finally assigned to Phoenix. "He's young and he's having trouble getting acclimated," Beverley said. "A lot of players go through it. He certainly understands that he needs to play in order for him to get his confidence back. It doesn't do him any good to just sit around."

Taylor, as his luck would have it, suffered a concussion in the November 14 game with the Oilers when Edmonton's Louie DeBrusk drilled him. Taylor's helmet came off during the collision, and his unprotected head slammed against the ice. Not only did he suffer a cut near his left eye, there was some bleeding behind it. The eye itself apparently wasn't damaged, but he was suffering from dizzy spells and vertigo. Taylor was playing regularly and this setback didn't seem fair.

Talk about a schizophrenic week. The Kings pounded the Blackhawks, dominated them, 4-1, to remain in a first-place tie with Calgary. Robitaille scored his 18th and 19th goals, and Stauber turned aside 23 shots against a Chicago team that seemed bent on self-destruction. A double-minor to Chris Chelios late in the second period led to goals by Robitaille and Corey Millen, the latter's seventh in eight games. Marty McSorley fought with Stu Grimson twice and Warren Rychel exchanged punches with Bryan Marchment. "It was an unbelievable game," Melrose chirped.

Not only that, Gretzky surprised everyone by saying his back felt so much better he hoped to start skating by March and resume playing before the playoffs. The Kings were 13-6-2 at the one-quarter mark of the season and seemed a shoo-in for the playoffs. Twelve days earlier, Gretzky seemed almost devoid of hope. But a magnetic resonance imaging test showed a significant reduction in the inflammation surrounding his herniated disk. The pressure the disk was causing on a nerve between two ribs had eased and Gretzky said he was pain free. He was working with ankle weights and riding an exercise bike every day to strengthen his abdominal muscles, and back specialist Dr.

Robert Watkins was designing a protective vest similar to a flak jacket for Gretzky to wear in games.

"If I have a setback, everything I'm saying now is out the window and they'd probably have to operate," Gretzky cautioned. "But I don't think that's going to happen. I really feel optimistic this time. It seems like we've turned the corner. Watching the guys play now is actually worse than it was before because I feel so much better and I wonder why I'm not out there playing."

The way the Kings were going, everybody wanted to get into the act.

Five

Kings of
Pain

The Kings weren't just defeating teams at the Forum, they were pulverizing them. Since the home-opening loss to Detroit, the Kings had rolled to nine consecutive wins in Inglewood, one shy of the franchise record, and were scoring twice as many goals as they were allowing.

The balmy climate, once viewed as a disadvantage, was being used to give the Kings an edge. Teams arriving fresh from the snow belt are often so giddy about catching a few rays of sunshine that they forget about the business at hand.

"Weak people want to spend time at the beach or with their friends and they can lose focus," Barry Melrose said. "The L.A. atmosphere can eat you up if you don't have character. Fortunately, we've got guys with character. One of the things we wanted to do was establish ourselves as a good home team. In the old days, teams would come in here and not have to play all that well to win. I think our fans give us a big boost. The building is loud. When we score a goal, they play that 'I Love L.A.' song and it pumps people up even more."

The Kings were particularly strong in the first periods of home games, when a visiting team is most vulnerable, scoring 15 goals and permitting just three. "Being a goalie," Kelly Hrudey said, "the thing I always try to do on the road is weather the storm in the first 10-15 minutes. Home teams are notorious for coming out firing. The idea is to try to get out of the first period relatively unscathed and then get on with the rest of the game."

A simple pleasure for Bob Kudelski was to merely get into a game. He played in only nine of the first 21 games and sat in the press box for six in a row after being just one of four Kings to play in all 80 games the previous year, when he scored 22 goals. Melrose insisted he didn't have a spot open for the 28-year-old winger and would ask Nick Beverley to make a trade if he could. "Bob's been great for the organization and what's going on here isn't fair to him, so we're going to try and accommodate him," Melrose said. A deal would suit Kudelski fine. He liked Los Angeles, but would rather go elsewhere if it would mean playing regularly.

A simple pleasure for Jim Hiller was to bank a puck off a half-dozen skates into the net, anything to break out of a point-scoring skid that reached 15 games against Chicago. But Melrose said there still were no plans to send him to Phoenix. "Being here is good for him. We see him as an NHL player, and he's seeing what it takes to be successful at this level."

A simple pleasure for Lonnie Loach—not that escaping Ottawa shouldn't have provided more than enough—was to leave for his home in Ontario to be with his wife, Janice, who was expecting to give birth to their second child any day now.

The Toronto Maple Leafs were about to skate into the Forum when a hot rumor began circulating. The Leafs were so enamored with rookie goalie Felix Potvin that they were considering trading Grant Fuhr to the Buffalo Sabres in a three-team deal involving the Edmonton Oilers. The Leafs would get Esa Tikkanen and disgruntled Joe Murphy from the Oilers, with Buffalo's Dale Hawerchuk heading to Edmonton. The Kings would just as soon it didn't happen; the Oilers would be a better team with Hawerchuk and anything that was good for the Oilers was bad for the Kings.

If only Toronto had made good on a deal that included sending Doug Gilmour away, preferably to the moon. That's what the Kings were thinking after they extended their home winning streak to a club-record-tying 10 games with a 6-4 win over the Leafs that was going to cost them dearly. Winger Tomas Sandstrom fractured his left forearm and would be sidelined four to six weeks. Actually, Gilmour did the fracturing with a second-period slash that referee Andy van Hellemond called a minor high-sticking infraction. "It should have been a five-minute penalty," Melrose said. "Andy said he didn't see it. We were lucky to get the two (minutes). He felt he had to call something."

The incident took place 29 seconds after Sandstrom burst past loafing Toronto defenseman Jamie Macoun to gain possession of the puck deep in the Leafs zone and avoid an icing call. Contact was made and Macoun slid heavily into the boards. Macoun was stretched on his back when Sandstrom passed to Mike Donnelly, who chipped the puck behind Fuhr for his second goal of the game and a 4-0 lead. The Kings viewed Gilmour's slash as payback for Sandstrom's bump of Macoun and a deliberate attempt to injure. "I'm sure it had something to do with that play," Tony Granato said. Macoun was shaken, but able to continue playing.

"It was a stupid thing by (Gilmour) to do," Sandstrom said after returning from Centinela Hospital Medical Center, where his arm was placed in a cast. "I didn't even hit (Macoun). We kind of ran into each other, He stopped and I went by him, then he slipped. My arm is pretty sore."

For all the health problems he had to put up with, Sandstrom must have felt cursed. His shoulder injury the year before forced him out for 26 games and his goal production plummeted to 17. He scored a career-high 45 goals in 1990-91, despite missing 10 games with a fractured vertebra in his back and played in two playoff games against Edmonton after an Oilers defenseman Craig Muni caused a fractured bone near his right knee with a submarine check. In 1989-90, after the Kings acquired Sandstrom from the Rangers, he missed five games with a facial fracture and bleeding behind an eye, courtesy of a Glenn Anderson punch in a brawl with Edmonton.

Now this. "I tried to forget about all that and just have a good year," he said. When asked for his feelings about Gilmour, Sandstrom said, "It's up to the league, but whatever they do won't help us. Even if guys get suspended this year it doesn't hurt their team because they still play the games. The guy that's hurt is me."

Sandstrom was referring to league president Gil Stein's policy of suspending players without pay for non-game days. "It's ridiculous. It's a joke," Luc Robitaille said. "I have a question, how could (van Hellemond) call that high sticking? I can't believe it."

The Kings sent a videotape of Gilmour's slash to the NHL office for further review, but Melrose said, "Nothing will happen. All I know is we lost a great player for a long time." Sandstrom was playing the best hockey of his career with 12 goals and 31 points in 21 games. The Sandstrom-Robitaille-Jari Kurri line was on fire with 29 goals and 73 points in 11 games since Melrose put it together October 31 in Hartford. "It's like the puck is on a string when those guys are out there," Mike Donnelly said. Gilmour severed that string. "It's a big blow," Granato said. "Tomas has been playing so well. Obviously that line has carried us to where we are right now. To have it broken up by an injury is a shame."

The Kings also lost rookie defenseman Darryl Sydor to a strained left shoulder when he was hammered into the boards late in the game. "It hurts. How much depends on how much I move it," Sydor said. "I think I've been playing well and this is the kind of thing that can set you back. You never want to get out of the lineup." Dave Taylor was still out with a concussion and vertigo, and Loach remained away waiting for his wife to give birth.

The big winner of the night, if you could call him that, was Hiller. He drew an assist in the opening period for his first point in 16 games and finished the game on the big line with Robitaille and Kurri. Uh, check that. Hiller suffered a back strain and would miss the next four games. Injuries were beginning to take a toll, and the Kings summoned youngsters Guy Leveque and Sean Whyte in order to give them enough bodies to fill four lines for the November 25 game in Edmonton.

While the Kings were en route to Alberta, Maple Leafs head coach Pat Burns was carving them up in the Toronto newspapers. He couldn't understand why they were making such a big deal of Gilmour's slash. "I looked at the tape and I didn't see anything," Burns told the *Toronto Sun*. "Why does everyone want to hang Doug Gilmour by a rope until he's dead? That's hockey, part of the game. Guys get whacked all the time, get broken arms. The Kings are always crying about something. We were getting run from behind left and right. They ran into our goalie twice. This is hockey. Los Angeles and Pittsburgh, you can't touch them without getting suspended."

The teams were going to be meeting again in only a few days.

Marty McSorley got into trouble again in the 3-1 win over the Oilers when van Hellemond gave him a penalty for spearing Martin Gelinas with just two seconds remaining. The Northlands Coliseum crowd of 13,636 jeered McSorley, just as it did when he fought Louie DeBrusk five seconds after the opening faceoff. Not that the fans were pleased when he scored a goal while filling in for Sandstrom on power plays. Strangely, even Gelinas questioned the spear. "It happened so fast, I didn't even see it," he said. Apparently he didn't even feel it. When asked where McSorley's stick blade made contact, Gelinas replied, "I don't know."

McSorley pleaded innocent again, but he seemed genuinely flabbergasted. At least van Hellemond had nailed Gelinas for cutting him near his right eye with a high stick. "I'm not faulting Andy, but I'd like to see a replay. A spearing call has to be pretty obvious. It has to be pretty blatant, doesn't it?" McSorley wondered. "I'm out there playing, I catch a stick in the eye, and I get spearing. If I speared him, how does he drop his gloves and jump me?"

Loach rejoined the team in Detroit and celebrated the birth of a son with an assist in the Kings' 5-3 win. Corey Millen scored twice and Robitaille snared his 20th goal. The Kings were 2-0 without Sandstrom and 16-6-2 overall. "Teams were wondering if the wheels were going to fall off," Melrose said.

The jalopy pulled into Toronto just in time for the Kings to learn that Stein, relatively speaking, had come down hard on Gilmour. He was suspended for eight non-game days, a penalty that would cost him $28,984 of his $1 million salary, and fined another $500. Gilmour was the seventh player to be suspended by Stein and the penalty was the stiffest one yet.

Gilmour was livid. "It was an accident. It was not intentional," he claimed. "I get 10 whacks like that a game, but because I injured a guy I get crucified. This is a game where you're going to get bumps and bruises. I can't change my game, and I won't." *Hockey Night in Canada* broadcaster Don Cherry, whose dislike for non-Canadian players is well known, ripped Sandstrom on the air. "He's a back-stabbing, chicken Swede who got what he deserved," Cherry barked. Replied Sandstrom: "I don't worry about what he says. He's had the same line for five years. That's what his show is all about. He doesn't like Europeans, that's all."

Sandstrom has been called worse. A columnist in the *Winnipeg Sun* once compared him to Saddam Hussein. A swift winger who stands 6-foot-2 and weighs 200 pounds, Sandstrom long has had a reputation as a fellow who breaks all the rules, as a mean player who would gain nearly as much pleasure from wrapping a stick around an opponent's neck as scoring a goal. Ironically, he attended carpentry school in his native Sweden after the Rangers drafted him in 1982. "I consider myself a hard worker," he said. "It doesn't matter to me what people say. I know it's not going to stop."

Just as Stein's disciplinary action wasn't going to prevent Gilmour from playing against the Kings at Maple Leaf Gardens while Sandstrom sat at home with a cast on his arm. But Gilmour wasn't going to go for a leisurely skate in the park on this night. The Kings later denied it, but they seemed more interested in running Gilmour through the boards than honing in on the Leafs, who won the game, 3-2. Granato tattooed him to the boards a couple of times and McSorley roughed him up enough in the second period to draw a penalty.

"You've got to play him hard because he's always in the thick of things," McSorley said. "I didn't want to take a penalty there, but he gave me a shot in the chops." According to Melrose, "The only people who made a big deal out of this was the press. I can live with it. I would have liked to have had him out for one game instead of getting a fine, but he was a distraction only because he's a good player."

Gilmour, Toronto's top scorer with nine goals and 36 points in 23 games, all but dared the Kings to hit him with their best shots before the game. "You think somebody else wants to pay 29 grand? If somebody wants to come after me that badly, go ahead," he said. The fine didn't sting enough to prevent Gilmour from taping a $100 bill on a message board in the Leafs dressing room, to be given to the player who scored the winning goal. It went to Mark Osborne; he hadn't scored a goal in the previous 23 games.

The Kings remained in Toronto the next day rather than fly to Milwaukee, where they would play the Blackhawks December 1 in one of their two neutral-site games, an arrangement the NHL Players Association approved as part of the collective bargaining agreement that was banged out during the previous year's strike.

The Grey Cup game to determine the Canadian Football League championship was being played between the Calgary Stampeders and the Winnipeg Blue Bombers at Skydome, home for Bruce McNall's Toronto Argonauts. The Argos, who are partially owned by Wayne Gretzky and actor John Candy, had finished in the Eastern Division basement one year after capturing the title, but McNall decided the football game might serve as a pleasant diversion for his hockey team. Gretzky attended with his father, Walter.

As Doug Flutie led Calgary to an easy win, McNall discussed the upcoming NHL meetings. He was hoping the Board of Governors would get around to selecting a commissioner, even though the job description wasn't yet defined. The leading candidates were believed to be Stein and Gary Bettman, the National Basketball Association's senior vice-president and general counsel. Bettman had worked with NBA commissioner David Stern on labor negotiations, and the NHL's collective bargaining agreement was set to expire in September 1993. McNall was believed to be in Bettman's corner, while it seemed Stein had the backing of a faction led by Philadelphia's Ed Snider.

The diplomatic McNall wouldn't tip his hand. "The search committee has pretty much gone through the process," is all he would say. "It's come forward with some candidates and I think there'll be a vote. I think we'd all like to have the issue behind us. I think Gil has done a good job, so we're not in a desperate situation, but it is important to get the issue resolved."

Some pile-driving checks from the Kings and four points, including two goals, from Granato fueled a 4-1 win over Chicago before 16,292 at the Bradley Center. The Granato-Millen-Donnelly line took off where the Robitaille-Kurri-Sandstrom line left off, amassing 29 goals and 59 points in 14 games, 10 of which the Kings won.

Flu symptoms prevented Robb Stauber from doing anything more strenuous than working the gate on the bench, but Kelly Hrudey played at a fever pitch, stopping 46 shots. The Kings got a good laugh out of Blackhawks coach Darryl Sutter, who claimed he was poking fun at Melrose when he called the Kings the "hardest-working team in the NHL" after the team's previous meeting. "It ticks me off that they've played 20 games and everybody's saying they're the hardest-working team," Sutter said. "I think we are."

There would have been no point in Sutter arguing about the degree of difficulty of the Kings' travel schedule. The Chicago game completed a stretch in which the Kings played 14 of 20 games on the road. They spent 29 of 43 days on the road, only six full days at home. "You know it's going to be hard, but until you go through it you don't really appreciate how tough it can be," Melrose said. Some teams had it tougher than others. The Montreal Canadiens had yet to play a single game outside their time zone, while the Kings already had played 12.

Not that they needed many breaks the way they were playing, but the Kings were handed a big one on December 3 when Pittsburgh superstar Mario Lemieux was scratched because of a sore heel. Granato and Millen each scored two more goals in the 5-3 win. "It's been bothering me for a while," Lemieux said of his foot. It was the Penguins' only regular-season visit to the Forum, so Los Angeles fans would be denied a Gretzky-Lemieux matchup unless both teams advanced to the Stanley Cup final. The Penguins were certain to get there, but the Kings?

Hrudey was having the time of his life. "The guys on this team are really committed to each other. It's not like each of us has his own agenda," he said. "I feel like I'm playing with a bunch of friends again rather than with a group of businessmen who show up for a couple of hours a night. We used to go out in separate groups, but there aren't any cliques on this team now. It's just a whole lot of fun."

The fun continued December 5 when the Kings bombed the Whalers, 7-3, for their 12th consecutive home win, breaking the club record for the longest home unbeaten streak (10-0-1) originally set in 1990-91. Paul Coffey had four assists and Stauber made 39 saves to run his record to 8-0-1. The Kings were 19-7-2 and their .714 winning percentage was the best in the league.

Certainly the Kings would not have been perking at such a pace without the inspired play of Coffey, the 31-year-old defenseman who has never shaken his reputation for being a one-dimensional player. People rave about his skating, pinpoint passing and precise shots, then quickly mumble something about his needing the explosive speed to overcome all those glaring defensive lapses. Yet the welts and bruises on his arms and legs, punishment absorbed from diving in front of shot pucks, showed he occasionally visited the patch of ice that sits inside his own blue line.

"Any time a guy racks up a lot of points, people think that's all he can do," said Coffey, who began his 13th NHL season with 318 goals and 1,114 points, more than any defenseman in league history. "I've always played this way. Skating is the biggest part of my game, but I broke my jaw two years ago blocking a shot when I was with Pittsburgh. I broke my wrist blocking a shot after I got traded here last year. I've always been willing to do whatever it takes to win. I'd trade in a hundred points for a Stanley Cup any day."

Melrose said he heard "some negative things" about Coffey's work habits before he became Kings coach but was impressed with his attitude in training camp. "I've always loved to practice," Coffey said. "Last year it seemed like we had nothing but days off and I was pushing for more practices. I don't know where you hear this stuff. I want to be a leader. Barry had confidence in me to be that kind of guy. When a coach shows confidence in a player, he will go through the boards for the team."

Millen, his face a living, breathing and ever-changing road map, looked like a guy who had been checked through the boards more than once. Head first. He had a gash on the bridge of his nose, a nick beneath his right eye and a cut near his swollen lip. Millen was one of the fastest skaters on the team, but even he couldn't always outskate the stickblades that were being swung in his direction, painful if futile attempts at slowing him down.

The Kings' little big man compensated for his lack of size with speed and a willingness to play in traffic despite the inevitable hooks, hacks and slashes that were used to impede his progress. He was on a tear with 11 goals and 16 points in 10 games, and had 16 goals and 25 points in 24 games overall despite his sore back. Sure, Millen was small, but Melrose didn't care because he was productive. "Corey makes up for his limitations with speed and a work ethic," Melrose said.

Of course, as well as he was playing, Millen still didn't have a new contract. He was playing out his option and resigned to becoming a restricted free agent when the season ended. "I'm not looking to break the bank," he said. "But Europe is an option. I've got decent connections there. It's not something I'm concerning myself with now, though. Things are going well and the team is winning. You can't ask for much more than that."

Gretzky's name popped up again and the news was somewhat surprising. He skated, stickhandled and shot pucks under doctors' supervision on December 7 at the Culver City Ice Rink after the team left for its neutral-site game with the Montreal Canadiens in Phoenix. "There was a time when he couldn't lift his baby and now he's skating," Dr. Ron Kvitne said in amazement. "Skating puts tremendous pressure on the entire spine and we have to remain very cautious. It's one of the milestones he wanted to reach, so it's a good sign."

The Kings wouldn't be practicing in Culver City for much longer. Construction had begun on dressing rooms and other training facilities at the Iceoplex Arena in the San Fernando Valley, and the team would move there as soon as the work was completed. Coaches and players throughout the NHL complained about the bumpy ice and uneven boards in Culver City. A Kings player once joked the ice he scraped off his car windows when he lived in Canada was in better condition than the surface in Culver City.

"Well, the ice is crooked and there are dips along the boards," Robitaille said. "The puck flies all over the place, you never know where it's going. But the people who work there aren't at fault. They do the best they can." Robitaille was happy about the pending move for another reason, his 25 percent interest in the newer building.

It had been nearly a month since Dave Taylor played anywhere. The hammering inside his head was easing, as were the bouts with vertigo, an eerie spinning sensation. But Taylor was still feeling some effects of the Louie DeBrusk hit that resulted in a concussion and a bruised brain stem. "I'm starting to feel pretty decent," he said. "The dizzy spells are becoming less frequent and less severe. But I need to be especially careful when I bend over, look up or move my head to the left. The feeling can almost knock you down. You feel nauseous. I still get the vertigo every so often, but it goes away if I keep my head straight."

Taylor wasn't angry at DeBrusk, who received a two-minute penalty for charging. But he was concerned that the force of the blow pulled the chin strap away from the side of his helmet. The helmet flew off before Taylor crashed to the ice.

"The ends were still attached at the buckle," he said. "I've got to find a way to tighten the strap where it attaches to the helmet. I'm certain I wouldn't have been hurt so badly if the helmet hadn't come off. (DeBrusk's) shoulder or elbow must have popped my helmet off and you can see (on videotape) that I don't get my arm down to brace the fall and protect myself, which to me means I must have lost consciousness before I hit the ice. Putting my arm down would have been the natural thing for me to do, but I didn't do it. That's why I landed on the side of my face."

The magnitude of Taylor's injury made it seem even more ridiculous that the NHL was permitting players to play without a helmet provided they signed a waiver absolving it of any responsibility. "You'll never see me attempt to play a game without a helmet," Taylor said.

The Kings should have known trouble was brewing when they played the Canadiens before 12,272 — about 1,500 below capacity — in Phoenix's Veterans Memorial Coliseum. Vincent Damphousse played for the Canadiens and he absolutely killed them as an Oiler in the playoffs. "You've got to pay special attention to him," Charlie Huddy said. "If you let him get loose, he's going to do some damage." It took Damphousse most of the game to get warmed up, then he scored three goals in the final 7:40 of regulation to turn what appeared to be a certain Kings victory into a disappointing 5-5 tie. Hrudey described his own play as "horrible," but Melrose didn't let anyone off the hook. "We quit hitting, quit finishing our checks," he said.

Melrose was unable to charge the Kings with either of those crimes after a 5-4 loss to the Quebec Nordiques snapped their 12-game winning streak at the Forum. Logic tells you that quitting cannot take place until after a project has been started. "We were awful," he said, spelling the word for those without dictionaries. Melrose also used a few words that didn't appear in dictionaries.

Bob Kudelski wasn't happy, either. Fed up with his inability to crack the lineup, he said it was long overdue for Nick Beverley to trade him. Kudelski played in only 13 of the team's first 30 games, just four of the past 14, and his patience was running out.

"It's frustrating," he said. "I've been sitting around for over a month. It's gotten to the point where the only way I'll ever play is if there are a ton of injuries and they're forced to dress me. Nick has told me he's working on it and I've tried to handle this as professionally as I can. I'm glad the team is winning and I really can't go in and demand to play because the guys are doing so well, but I really need to go somewhere else for the sake of my career. It's evident to me I never fit into their plans from the beginning."

Earlier in the day, during a break in league meetings in Palm Beach, Florida, Gil Stein announced the awarding of conditional expansion franchises to the Walt Disney Co., which would ice a team in Orange County, and to Blockbuster Entertainment Corp. owner H. Wayne Huizenga, who would put a team in the Miami area. The moves caught many hockey people by surprise. Stein said the teams would pay $50 million each and begin play in 1993-94 or 1994-95, creating a 26-team league.

Getting a team in Orange County was quite a coup for McNall. He picked up an instant archrival for the Kings and $25 million, half of Disney's franchise fee, in one fell swoop; the money was in return for waiving his territorial rights in Orange County, where between 15 and 20 percent of Los Angeles' season ticketholders live.

"I definitely think there is room for two hockey teams," said McNall, who aggressively pitched the idea of placing a team in Orange County to Disney chairman and chief executive officer Michael Eisner. "My view is that hockey has sold in Southern California mainly because of Wayne Gretzky's arrival, but even though he is injured now, our attendance has not appreciably changed. Let's see what develops as a rivalry between us."

Disney was negotiating for use of an arena that was being built in Anaheim and Eisner suggested calling the team the Mighty Ducks, the title of a Disney film that chronicles life on a youth hockey team. The image of a scar-faced hockey player and the sport's inherent violence didn't bother Disney officials, according to Eisner. "I could show you a couple of Goofy cartoons where he's playing hockey pretty aggressively," Eisner said.

There wasn't a single King who disliked the idea of busing to a road game. Not counting the Sharks, the closest NHL destination was Vancouver — 1,080 air miles away. "I think this will be good for the city of L.A.," McSorley said. "The population base here is so big and hockey has caught on so well over the last four, five years. Hockey is becoming a popular sport here. You don't have to have a team in a northern climate to be successful."

The Kings played poorly against the St. Louis Blues, but Stauber put on a spectacular show in a 6-3 win that enabled the Kings to join Pittsburgh as the league's only 20-game winners. Stauber matched Hrudey's club record for consecutive victories by a goalie at seven and remained unbeaten for the year at 9-0-1. He made 44 saves, 21 in the second period when the Kings grabbed a 4-1 lead, and moved 20 feet from the crease to separate the breaking Craig Janney from the puck. "Everyone here has got to finish their checks," Melrose quipped.

It was December 12 when Gretzky skated for the fourth time in a six-day period and then reported he had been pain free for about a month. "The biggest thing right now is that there's no pain," he said. "As time goes by and we start working a little harder, we'll get a real test of where I'm at. Right now it's rather casual and light, like summer skating. But I have to take my time to get back into it."

Monday is medical day, when players visit with their individual doctors. Gretzky was meeting his spine specialist; Sandstrom, his orthopedic surgeon; and Taylor, his neurologist. Taylor was taking part in non-contact drills even though he continued to experience some dizzy spells and vertigo that were caused by a bruised brain stem. "It's lasted a lot longer than I thought it would," said Taylor, who had missed 13 games since Louie DeBrusk decked him.

Melrose shouldn't have been surprised when Lonnie Loach was found to have broken his left thumb in a collision with Huddy at practice. Warren Rychel tried to skate on a tender ankle and couldn't, and Kurri was nursing a sore groin. "We play very hard, very physical," Melrose said. "Teams that don't play hard are the ones that stay healthy. We know we're going to have injuries so we might as well go through them now."

Lightning struck down the Kings, 3-2, and ended Stauber's unbeaten streak when Tampa Bay's Mikael Andersson scored on a penalty shot with 33 seconds remaining as the less-than-capacity crowd of 15,753 watched in stunned silence. The penalty shot was called when Stauber threw his stick at the puck Anderson controlled. The season wasn't even half over and already referees had called the once rare shot 10 times; Anderson was the eighth player to convert.

Jeff Chychrun was beginning to sound like Kudelski. He dressed for 12 of 20 games since his acquisition from the Penguins, but actually played in just eight of them, spending the rest of the time stapled to the bench. "I'm not the first guy who has ever gone through this," he said. "I really can't give you an answer, but I don't want to sit here and complain."

McNall won out when Bettman was elected NHL commissioner in a vote that became unanimous as Stein, in a gesture of unity, bowed out of the race. Bettman was immediately subjected to some good-natured ribbing from his former NBA cohorts. "I sent him a puck," Orlando Magic general manager Pat Williams said. "I heard he spent all day at his desk trying to figure out how to open it up."

Gretzky was skating for an hour every day now, still handling a stick and shooting pucks. His only complaint: he couldn't keep up with the fleet Sandstrom, who had missed 10 games with his broken arm. "The biggest concern is pain," Gretzky said. "God forbid if I get any." Gretzky was "two, three months" ahead of his own schedule and hoped to begin practicing with the team in two or three weeks.

Gretzky's revelation was nearly as stunning as Melrose's decision to elevate Kudelski to the top line alongside Robitaille and Kurri for the Kings' December 18-19 trip to Edmonton and Calgary. The decision was prompted by injuries to five forwards and the demotion of Hiller to Phoenix. "Boy, I better practice extra hard today. I guess it means I won't have to go to the movies three times this trip," Kudelski said. Melrose smirked when he was apprised of Kudelski's comments. "Bobby's practiced well all year," he said.

It's about all Kudelski had done. He hadn't dressed for six games after getting two first-period shifts in the December 1 game against Chicago. "The first (shift) was all right, but they scored a goal against us on the other one, and that was the end for me," he said. Kudelski, his comments laced with sarcasm, was answering questions as his teammates filed past him through a gate leading to the ice. "Easy, Marcus," a smiling player advised, a reference to disenchanted Raiders running back Marcus Allen, who was having problems with the football team's top executive, Al Davis.

Kudelski continued, "I want to get traded now. As each day goes by, I get more frustrated and angry. I'm at the point where something has to be done immediately. We've got a lot of guys who are hurt and as soon as they come back, I'll be back in the stands."

Guess who scored in the third period to trigger a two-goal rally and salvage a 5-5 tie with the Oilers? "It felt great," said Kudelski, who took Robitaille's pass down the middle and snuck a backhanded shot by goalie Bill Ranford. Kudelski's only other goal came October 27 against the Islanders. "It's tough to get going when you haven't been playing. It's hard to jump in there from right out of the stands."

Robitaille was happy for Kudelski. "He's a great goal-scorer. I think he should get a chance with another team if he isn't going to get one here," Robitaille said. His smile turned into a frown when referee Rob Shick's name was mentioned. "(The Oilers) aren't angels, you know? We get a 5-on-3 and they can slash you and break your arm and it's okay. It's ridiculous," he complained.

Finally, Kudelski was free of Melrose. He scored another goal in a 5-3 loss to Calgary that earned the Flames a share of the Smythe Division lead with the Kings, then he was traded in the wee hours of the morning to the Ottawa Senators. Kudelski was so happy to have the ball and chain removed from his legs that he actually was looking forward to playing for the Senators, who were 3-29-3. It was reasonable to think the Kings would have gotten more in exchange than a couple of journeymen wingers, Marc Fortier and Jim Thomson, if Kudelski hadn't been in the slammer all season. On the other hand, there would have been no need to give him away if he'd been getting regular ice time.

The downside of the deal for Kudelski was that Christmas was only six days away and he might not be able to spend the holidays with his wife, Marie-France´, who already had left California for the couple's condominium in Florida. A quirk in the schedule would prohibit Kudelski from heading south; the Senators had two home games and one in Quebec City sandwiched around Christmas Day. "The timing could have been better, but at least I'm going to a place where I'm wanted," he said.

Ottawa, Canada's capital, borders the mostly French province of Quebec, but Marie-France´ is of French-Canadian heritage and bilingual. The adjustment would be further eased because her family lives in a Quebec village 90 minutes from

Ottawa. It seemed fitting that Kudelski's roommate on the road was Chychrun, another Kings spare part who needed a map to locate the ice. "I feel sorry for him. Chych's a good guy," Kudelski said.

Melrose didn't perform figure-eights at practice after the Kings returned home to face the Canucks when he found out Blake was going to miss perhaps two weeks with a broken rib. Blake apparently suffered the injury in a collision with Montreal's John LeClair in Phoenix. Thinking his ribs were merely bruised, Blake put on a flak jacket and played in five games. But the pain became unbearable and he was forced to leave in the second period in Calgary. "I guess it's better than having cartilage damage," Blake said.

At the same time, Melrose finally was able to rip the pages marked "Sandstrom" from his medical report, which was beginning to resemble a thick reference book. Sandstrom missed 12 games with his broken arm while Gilmour sat out eight practices. The Kings went 6-4-2 without Sandstrom but were currently in a 1-3-2 skid and happy to have him back. When asked if he was concerned about getting slashed again, Sandstrom tapped the plastic protective sleeve he would wear and said, "I think a stick would break on this before my arm would."

Gretzky was wearing a wide grin after the morning skate the next day, the first time he wasn't relegated to skating by himself or with injured players. It had been six weeks since he last winced in pain and he expected to take part in a full-blown practice in about a week. "Once I start practicing with the team, that basically means I've been given the green light by the doctors," Gretzky said. "Once that happens, I'm in the hands of the coaches and it's just a matter of me being ready to play. I don't think it'll take long. My excitement and adrenaline will carry me for a while."

If only he had been able to play that evening. Virtually none of the Kings did in a 6-2 loss to Vancouver that kept them two points behind first-place Calgary. The third-place Canucks were on a 7-1-1 tear and closing fast on the Kings, to within one point. Worse, Sandstrom fell heavily on his arm in the second period and didn't return. Corey Millen didn't play at all because of a groin strain.

Hrudey struggled in the first period, giving up four goals on 12 shots, and the sellout crowd attempted to embarrass him with mock cheers when he made routine saves. A cascade of boos, jeers and taunts became a roaring crescendo of ridicule as the Kings left the ice. "I thought I was at a Raiders game," Melrose said later. "I've been booed so many times, it's something that happens. I always told my mom I wish she had named me Lou. When your name is Barry, it's easy to figure out what (the fans) are saying. Lou Boudreau, now that would have been the perfect name. I'd like to have 20 guys named Lou on my team."

Hrudey didn't appreciate being booed, but he was grateful to Melrose for sticking with him the whole game. "It was an opportunity to battle back, to show that I'm not a quitter," he said. "It tears your heart out, but I'll survive."

As badly as the Kings were playing, combined with their injury-depleted roster, the four-day Christmas break couldn't have come at a better time. It would give them a much-needed chance to lick their wounds and gear up for what figured to be two relatively easy games with San Jose and Philadelphia, teams that also were struggling.

The unconventional Melrose said he planned to play nine holes of golf on Christmas Eve with assistant coach Cap Raeder. "I've never done it before," he explained. "This time of year, up in Canada, you can't play. I've always liked to do things I've never done before. I'll go to a fancy restaurant and order something that's different even if I don't like it."

Shark was supposed to be on the menu when the season resumed at the Cow Palace. San Jose had lost 13 consecutive games, nine at home, since Arturs Irbe's shocking shutout of the Kings in November and coach George Kingston was being lambasted in the Bay Area newspapers. But the Kings, their quick start turning into a distant memory, were shelled again, 7-2, despite launching a club-record 59 shots at goalie Jeff Hackett. Stauber was awful in losing his third consecutive game and the Kings' penalty-killing units were burned for four power-play goals. "We're going through a tough time right now," Tony Granato said.

Gretzky traveled with the team for the first time and witnessed the execution from the Cow Palace press box. He insisted he still wanted to play. "I feel the worst is over," Gretzky said of himself, not the nosediving Kings. A fourth magnetic resonance imaging test looked good and his doctors had cleared him to take part in contact drills. "Now it's a matter of taking some hits, getting into game-conditioning drills," he said. "It's not like they're going to line up and hit me."

Melrose was tempted to turn No. 99 loose December 29 when the Flyers visited the Forum, not that the visitors were soaring, even with rookie sensation Eric Lindros. There had been a time when the mere thought of Philadelphia's orange and black uniforms caused the Kings to tremble in harrowing fear. The Kings once went nine *years* between victories over the Flyers, a 32-game stretch from October 22, 1974 through February 5, 1983 that included 27 defeats and five ties. Rumor had it the Kings partied all night after the ties.

But these Flyers, even with the 19-year-old man-child Lindros, could barely get off the ground. They were in a 1-8-1 slump and threatening to miss the Patrick Division playoffs for the fourth year in a row. When a sprained left knee prevented Lindros from dressing, the odds of a Kings' victory increased immeasurably. They skyrocketed when John McIntyre and Robitaille scored goals in the opening three minutes, and then, suddenly, it was 1975 all over again. Or 1976. Or 1977.

Nearly every puck the Flyers shot eluded Hrudey, who was torched for four goals in the first period again. This time, Melrose hauled out his hook. The Flyers, smelling blood, proceeded to light up Hrudey's replacement, Stauber, for six more goals. When the ice chips cleared, the Kings had been pillaged, 10-2. Dave Taylor's first appearance in 19 games didn't even help. "It's ugly right now," Hrudey said. "A slump is one thing, but losing as bad as we've been losing is something else. It eats at you inside."

The worst home loss in their history prompted an immediate players-only meeting. If only the Kings had been as protective of the slot area as they were the dressing-room doors. "It's obvious we're going through a tough stretch," Granato said. "We're not performing up to our own expectations or anybody else's. Believe me, it's tough. We have to step forward, find out how much character we have. We're playing tentative instead of aggressive. We're back on our heels. We're not sharp mentally."

The Kings had lost four games in a row, were winless in six, and a sorrowful 1-6-2 since December 8. The penalty-killing percentage dropped from fifth in the league to 14th. "I can't beat my brains out," Melrose said. He neglected to say the Kings needed a huge game from Hrudey or Stauber because play in every other area had deteriorated. "This isn't an excuse, but Sandstrom, Gretzky, Millen, Blake, Loach, and Rychel are out," he said. "Which team in the NHL could have that happen and keep playing at the level we were playing at? This is a good club. You watch, we're going to get through this period, and we're going to look back and this will have been a key time in our season."

The team responded to Melrose's pep talk with a 4-0 New Year's Eve loss in Vancouver. Even Blake's return didn't help. "It's not like we're on the Titanic here," Melrose said. Nor were they on the Good Ship Lollipop. There were holes in the stern and bow, and the vessel was sinking in a sea of amateurish mistakes. The Kings were in third place now, eight points behind the Flames and five in arrears of the Canucks, who were on a 13-0-2 roll at the Pacific Coliseum.

Even Kurri, who played so well in the beginning, was in a funk. He hadn't scored an even-strength goal since the night Gilmour slashed Sandstrom, a 17-game stretch. He had taken only 20 shots in nine games and gotten one across the goal line in none of them. "I'm definitely not putting up numbers like I was before," he said. "Maybe our line is being checked a little more closely. Teams are putting a checking line on us, sometimes an extra defenseman. It's part of the game." Despite the slump, Kurri remained the team's leading scorer with 57 points in 38 games.

Gretzky was itching to play and targeted January 16, a home game with Winnipeg, as a return date. "We probably won't start before then and we definitely won't start on the road," he said. "It's been like a breath of fresh air being given a second chance to come back. I probably could play right now, but I need some skating time. I haven't had any hard skating at all since April and it would be foolish to jump in there now. The way I skate, I skate so bent over that my back naturally gets a workout. I feel fine. There's no pain."

Happy New Year? Progress for the Kings on January 2 was blowing a two-goal lead in the third period, getting another 5-5 tie against the Canadiens, and hanging on in the five-minute overtime period. What was it about overtime with the Canadiens, anyway? After Kings killer Vincent Damphousse put Montreal ahead with 3:17 remaining, Blake re-tied the game with just 47 seconds to play. Their winless streak reached eight games, but the losing streak was over at five.

Trade rumors were just beginning, however. One was so ridiculous that it didn't seem worth discussing. According to someone's vivid imagination, the Kings were considering sending Robitaille and Blake to the St. Louis Blues for high-scoring winger Brett Hull. Did somebody think George Maguire, whose reign of error helped produce some of the worst teams in Kings history, was still general manager? Why in the world would Nick Beverley go for this deal? Melrose wouldn't approve, that much was certain.

"There are very few players I would trade Mr. Robitaille for," Melrose said. "Brett Hull is a great, great player, but you can't give up two great young players to get him." Melrose said he was "a little mad" at Robitaille for taking three consecutive penalties in the second period against Montreal, "but it would take a lot to get that guy out of here."

Melrose also was miffed at two of his young defensemen, Brent Thompson and Alexei Zhitnik. Both were playing regularly, but neither even dressed for the Canadiens game. "They were taking it for granted that they'll be in the NHL until they die," said Melrose, who was critical of the pair after the loss in Vancouver. "It's about time they gain a little respect for this league."

Perhaps the Kings as a whole could begin to recapture some of the magic that had been missing for so many weeks.

Wayne Gretzky passed a rigorous physical examination on January 3, scrimmaged with the team, and appeared to be on the verge of making a near-miraculous return.

Six

The Great Comeback

The mood was somber, almost funereal, in September when reporters were asked to huddle in the Forum Club, a private gathering place just a few paces from the Forum's inner arena where fans gather for drinks and conversation after hockey and basketball games.

The Kings scheduled a news conference that day to announce that Wayne Gretzky, the NHL's all-time leading scorer, might never grace a 200-foot sheet of ice again because of a herniated thoracic disk. Outside of the doctors who were present, few in the crowded alcove knew how to spell "thoracic," much less define it. The word soon became all too familiar, one to be typed onto the keys of a word processor or spoken into a microphone countless times in the three-and-a-half months that followed.

The Forum Club was becoming a place reporters preferred to stay away from. It is where Lakers star Magic Johnson, in November 1991, revealed he was suffering from the virus that causes AIDS. Then came the Gretzky bombshell. That's why reporters began to think of the place in terms of bad news. Perhaps coincidentally, the Kings didn't make another announcement there for the rest of the year.

But they didn't stray too far, only a few paces from the Forum Club on January 4, when Gretzky said he would play in 48 hours against the visiting Tampa Bay Lightning after missing the first

39 games. Two months earlier, Gretzky suggested he would never play again, but back specialist Dr. Robert Watkins pronounced the 31-year-old center to be in "excellent" shape. The plan was for Gretzky to wear extra padding to protect his back and, assuming there were no ill-effects from his debut against the Lightning, to accompany the Kings on a four-game trip to Winnipeg, Chicago, Ottawa and New Jersey. The only stipulation was that he would skip the Blackhawks game and continue what Watkins described as a "rigid" therapeutic program for an indefinite period.

Watkins would have relished being able to guarantee Gretzky would remain healthy, but he couldn't possibly make such an assurance. "Sure, there's a risk," Watkins said. "What type of injury might that be? It's a little hard to say. Obviously, if some guy's got a bad back and he gets hit from behind and he didn't see it coming, it would be a potentially injurious type thing. But that's why they have rules against that."

Watkins' last statement drew howls from reporters. And from Gretzky, who smiled and asked, "They do (have rules)? I won't get into that." He had blamed the cumulative effect of being hit during a 14-year career for hurting his back in the first place. But Gretzky, who was going to center a line with Tony Granato and Mike Donnelly, said he wasn't worried about getting hurt again. "Other people are worrying more than me. You can't play (feeling) apprehensive, that's when you get hurt," Gretzky said. "When you love to play, you don't think about the risks."

The thought of not playing was more "frightening," he said. "I'm getting a second chance, and a lot of people don't. But I worked hard to get it and I'm really glad I did. I think the guys have been a little apprehensive about hitting me (in practice) and, believe me, I'll get hit (in the upcoming Tampa Bay game). But I'll be fine. I'm really not even curious about it. If I didn't feel like I could play hockey the way I want to, I wouldn't play. Besides, I'm sure Marty (McSorley) will be following me around."

The Kings were mired in an eight-game winless streak (0-6-2) and had crashed from first place in the Smythe Division to third, but Gretzky insisted the team's problems were not factors in his quick return. "Maybe I did push myself to come back, but it had nothing to do with our record or on how the team is playing," he said. "There has never been any pressure on me to come back. We were talking about doing it January 16, but the doctors felt the extra two weeks wouldn't matter.

"I know I'm in a no-win situation. If the team was doing well, people might say, 'Look, you messed it up.' If the team was doing bad, they'd say, 'Clean it up.' " Considering the state of the team, coach Barry Melrose might immediately have handed Gretzky a mop and a pail full of soap. On the other hand, the utensils required to complete this job couldn't possibly be carried by one person. Not even Gretzky.

"One of the reasons this job was so attractive to me was to have the chance to coach a player like Wayne Gretzky," Melrose said. "I remember, after watching a couple of good practices in training camp, I was rubbing my hands together in anticipation. Then—bang! We had a new baby in the fold, but not a centerman." Gretzky's injury was diagnosed shortly after he left camp to be present for the birth of his third child.

Now, everyone was doing well, dad included.

And yet there were some Gretzky bashers who tried to lay the blame for the team's problems on him. Whispers abounded, including the crazy notion that he was little more than a meddling interloper who was going to ruin club chemistry. It was pointed out that the Kings' slide into oblivion coincided with Gretzky's very first day on the ice; since December 7, when Gretzky skated in Culver City for 40 minutes, the Kings were 1-7-2.

"I told people two months ago, we could be 35-0 and we'd still welcome him back," Paul Coffey said. "To say that we are a better team without Wayne Gretzky is just plain stupid."

Coffey turned nostalgic, recounting a conversation he had with Gretzky when the two were just beginning their careers in Edmonton. "Guy Lafleur was having some problems in Montreal, and Wayne didn't think that was right. He said, 'I'm not ever going through that. I'm playing 10 years and I'm getting out.' I said, 'Wayne, you're crazy. We're having the time of our lives.' But he was adamant about it. He said he'd play until he was 30, then he'd get out. Now look at him. He's almost 32, he's been out three months, and he can't wait to start playing again. Wayne's got the fire.

"Guys like Bobby Orr and Larry Bird and Magic Johnson,

they were forced to retire," Coffey said. "That shouldn't have to happen to anybody. A great athlete should be able to hop on a white horse and ride out on his own terms."

In a show of unity, Luc Robitaille agreed to relinquish the captain's "C" he inherited from Gretzky on the eve of the regular-season opener. "In my mind, when he comes back, he's captain of this team. There's no doubt in my mind about that," Robitaille said a few days earlier. "There's never been any other thought in my mind. I know that's the way it is. Besides, it doesn't really matter who has a letter on their jersey. It's what you do on the ice. A guy can lead by example."

Sure, Robitaille would take a dumb penalty every once in a while. But the 26-year-old winger was having his best season yet with 30 goals and 56 points in 39 games, and he was playing with great enthusiasm. That wouldn't change, with the "C" or without it.

"At the start of the season, I honestly didn't believe Wayne Gretzky would ever play again," Melrose said. "I think Luc has done an unbelievable job. He's emerged as a leader on this team. I think the captainship has been very good for him. It's made him think of other things. Rather than just being a one-dimensional player, he became a very committed two-way player and he doesn't have many peers in the NHL. I think being captain has probably been the best thing to happen to Luc.

"But Wayne Gretzky is going to be captain of this team. As Luc said, he's always been the leader of this team. He's going to be the captain because it means a lot to him. He wants to be captain of this team, and he's made that very clear."

Robitaille and Gretzky were concerned the issue of the captainship was going to be made into a focal point by the media. "It's not a big deal," Robitaille said. He already had discussed the situation with Gretzky and promised a smooth transition. Gretzky said, "Lucky did a tremendous job and the last thing in the world I want to do is create controversy. The team doesn't need that. I just want to slip back in there and play and not make a big thing out of anything."

Try as he might, the most famous hockey player in the world wasn't going to just "slip back" anywhere. It certainly wasn't going to happen on January 6 inside the Forum, where the atmosphere was electric, a mood that had absolutely nothing to do with the presence of the Lightning. Sure, Los Angeles fans were pleased to know that Warren Rychel was going to play after missing 13 games with an ankle injury, but all eyes were going to be glued to No. 99 on this night.

Turned out, Gretzky was the only King worth watching. He played 17 minutes, 40 seconds and drew two second-period assists, but the rest of the Kings barely put in an appearance. Tampa Bay scored three power-play goals, blew out to a quick 4-0 lead and coasted to a 6-3 victory that stretched Los Angeles' winless streak to nine games. Poor goaltending by Kelly Hrudey and terrible performances from the penalty- killing units — the Lightning scored on all but two of its five power plays — were major contributing factors. Hrudey was in a personal 0-5-3 slide that included a bloated 5.27 goals-against average. "The puck looks like a pea to me," he said.

The Kings looked like something else. "If you can't get motivated to play well with Wayne Gretzky in your lineup, you must be a . . . 0-and-84 hockey team," Coffey said. Disgusted, Coffey stalked off. Gretzky was subdued. At least his back was fine, in much better condition than his psyche. "Almost all the big nights in my career have been wins. If you don't win, it's just not fun," he said.

The fans squealed with delight when Gretzky made his first appearance in his 1,000th career game, a 40-second shift that came 50 seconds into the match. Nothing much happened, but about four minutes later, during a power play, Gretzky slid to his customary place behind the net and feathered a sweet pass to Tony Granato for a shot that goalie J.C. Bergeron went down to cover. A few seconds later, while cradling the puck with his aluminum stick, Gretzky moved into the right faceoff circle and snapped off a low shot, one of three he would take in the game. The crowd moaned when Bergeron made the save.

"It's a miracle as far as I'm concerned, and awfully courageous on his part," Bruce McNall said of Gretzky. "Certainly he didn't come back because of the money or the records. It's just his personal love for the game that brought him back."

The Kings were down four goals by the time Gretzky picked up his first point, which came on Rob Blake's power-play goal at 5:30 of the second period. After Gretzky set up Blake for a blast from the point that Bergeron kicked out, Donnelly banged in the rebound at the 14:02 mark, drawing the Kings to within 4-3. This Gretzky guy was doing fine, but the Kings eventually caved in. Again.

"It took me at least a period to get used to the flow, to get comfortable, to get the shakes out," Gretzky said. "I got real nervous about 20 minutes before warmups. That's the time you really bear down and get ready. When I went on the ice for my first shift, I didn't want to make a mistake." Gretzky pronounced his back, which was protected by a light pad, to be fit after he was drilled a couple of times by 200-pound defenseman Peter Taglianetti. "No problem," Gretzky said.

If only the same could be said of the Kings. They were 20-15-5 but fading fast.

Seven

Down and Out

Life on the road can be dreary, especially in the dead of winter. This is particularly true in a place like Winnipeg, which seems to be forever frozen. It is a friendly city of 600,000 and the capital of Manitoba, a Canadian province whose wind-swept landscape frequently is buried under a foot of snow. Winters are long and harsh. In January, the average temperature in the southern portion, bordering Minnesota and North Dakota, where Winnipeg lies, is 0 degrees Fahrenheit. Automobile engines, not to mention faces, have been known to crack when the prairie gusts swirl and drive the wind-chill factor to depths no living creature should have to endure.

It was in this winter wonderland that the Kings would begin a four-game excursion that might determine if the floundering season could be saved. But Barry Melrose had more than ear muffs and a nine-game winless streak on his mind when the team's commercial flight touched down on the Manitoban tundra. This was Canada, where hockey and Wayne Gretzky are king. If Gretzky has a hangnail, Canadians want to know.

The Kings' awful play of the previous four weeks was enough to worry about, and now their first trip with Gretzky along as more than a cheerleader would likely turn into a media circus.

"Ought to be wild," Melrose said. "You know it's going to happen, especially in Canada, where they tend to go a little overboard. I'm ready for it, but it's going to be a lot harder on Wayne."

Gretzky's patience for reporters' questions and fans' autograph requests is nearly inexhaustible, a phenomenon that can be traced to his childhood days in Brantford, Ontario, when extraordinary accomplishments forced him to cope with both. Unlike some athletes whose egos inflate as their contracts do, Gretzky is gracious and treats people with respect.

Yet even Gretzky was wary of what lay ahead; an unscheduled 90-minute autograph session during the Kings' stopover in Calgary would serve as a warmup. "It'll be hard. It's not easy," he said. "There are so many more media people now than there were, say, 10 years ago. I've been a pro for 15 years and it seems like there's always a 'first time around.' It'll be nice to get this one out of the way."

The hectic atmosphere surrounding Gretzky figured to help David Goverde, whom Melrose planned to start in goal against Winnipeg. The fourth-place Jets were closing in on the Kings, cutting a once-sizable lead to an uncomfortable nine points, and Melrose didn't like the way Kelly Hrudey and Robb Stauber were playing. Enter Goverde, a 22-year-old who had a 14-11 record and 3.73 goals-against average for a Phoenix Roadrunners team that wasn't doing much in the International League.

"It's no secret our goaltenders are struggling, and this kid has been playing great," Melrose said. Hrudey was winless in eight decisions, with an 0-5-3 record and 5.27 average. Stauber was winless in three decisions, losing them all and permitting 5.45 goals in them.

"If David plays great up here, he stays. That's the way the system works," Melrose said. "Robb and Kelly are going through some tough times. What's killing them is shots from the rush, the kind NHL goalies have to stop. I was hoping they would play out of it. Now I have to try something different."

The Kings were strictly status quo January 8, wasting two Gretzky goals in a 6-3 loss that left them 0-8-2 in 10 games and trying to remember when the last victory had come. For the record, it was December 12, a 6-3 decision over St. Louis. "Is that right?" Rob Blake asked. "Oh, yeah." The Kings still had a formidable task ahead to match the franchise record for futility, an 0-13-4 stretch that took place in 1970, but they certainly seemed capable.

For the third time in as many visits to the Winnipeg Arena, the Kings failed to hang onto a lead, blowing a 3-2 advantage with play so uninspired that witnesses swore they spotted a frown on the face of Queen Elizabeth, whose giant portrait hangs above the ice. Melrose didn't smile as he assessed the damage and hoped Goverde would be able to sleep without counting all the absurd errors his teammates had made.

"Are we frustrated? Frustration has nothing to do with it," Melrose snapped. "Frustration is for garage mechanics who can't find the hole in the gas tank." If only the Kings weren't making it so easy for opponents to find the gaping holes in their defense. It took the Jets just 57 seconds to welcome Goverde to the Kings' version of the NHL. Rookie Teemu Selanne had a step on Paul Coffey when he accepted a goalmouth pass from Alexei Zhamnov and rammed the puck into the net. When Coffey said, "We're playing awful," no one disagreed.

The silver lining in the dark cloud that hovered above the team was the condition of Gretzky's back. Gretzky felt so well that he lobbied for and received permission from the doctors to play in the January 10 game at Chicago Stadium, his third game in five nights. The original plan was for Gretzky to skip it and take three full days off, then suit up in Ottawa. "But my back feels fine and I don't want people to think I'm bailing out on the guys," he said. So Gretzky was going to play.

Charlie Huddy and Jari Kurri were not. The 33-year-old Huddy was beginning to look his age on the ice and though Kurri continued to lead the team in scoring, he had failed to produce a goal in 12 consecutive games. So Melrose benched them and stuck Jeff Chychrun and Jim Hiller in the lineup. "Maybe it'll be a wakeup call," Melrose said.

Neither was pleased. Huddy said he hadn't been benched in "six or seven years." Kurri missed only one previous game, a one-shot deal in 1988-89, for reasons other than injury or illness in his entire career. "There's no question I wasn't playing my game, but we've been struggling as a team," Kurri said. "It hasn't been only me."

Maybe the Kings would have beaten the Blackhawks anyway. They seemed to play their best hockey against the Hawks, dominating them in two previous engagements. The Kings didn't overpower Chicago this time, but they were good enough in a 5-

4 win that snapped the fifth-longest winless streak in club history and put smiles on some faces for the first time in weeks.

Stauber played well enough that Goverde was shipped back to Phoenix and Tony Granato, who would challenge for the Art Ross Trophy as the NHL's leading scorer if he played all of his games against the Hawks, contributed two goals and an assist. He snapped a 4-4 tie with 7:59 remaining after Gretzky sent him in on a breakaway. "Big-time relief," Granato said of the streak-busting win. Gretzky had two more assists, giving him six points in three games.

And so the Kings reached the halfway point of the season with a record of 21-16-5 and 47 points, a six-point improvement through the same number of games the year before. All things considered — the major injuries to front-line players, the inconsistent goaltending and erratic play of the special teams, the horrid 10-game slump — the Kings were in reasonably good shape.

Talk about a cacophony of emotions. The Kings experienced them all January 12 in Ottawa, where they managed to avoid the ultimate embarrassment of losing to the sad-sack Senators by the hair of their chinny chin chins. More precisely, by the stainless steel blade of Warren Rychel's left skate. Rychel was facing the net when a puck shot by John McIntyre hit him and bounced between his legs, then behind goalie Daniel Berthiaume, at 2:35 of the third period. The lucky goal gave the Kings a 3-2 win while poor Ottawa, which held Gretzky off the scoresheet, slid to 4-37-3.

During the game, news filtered to the teams that Pittsburgh Penguins star Mario Lemieux had been diagnosed with Hodgkin's disease, a form of cancer that attacks the lymph nodes. The prognosis was good, but the players were stunned. "We're all praying for him," Gretzky said, a sentiment every player expressed. "The most important thing right now is his health. The hockey is secondary." Coffey and Chychrun, who played with Lemieux in Pittsburgh, took the news badly. "We heard about it on the bench. It's just awful," Coffey said.

A few hours before the game, Gretzky, Kurri, and Robitaille were named to the Campbell Conference team for the NHL All-Star Game to be played February 6 in Montreal. Coffey already was in; he was voted to a starting position in balloting by fans.

Gretzky, who missed the first 39 games with his herniated thoracic disk, was added to the team by league president Gil Stein. "I'm honored and thrilled that they asked me," Gretzky said. "I love playing in Montreal. I love playing in that building." Kurri's invitation was especially sweet because he was left off the ballot after his 60-point season, one he had already matched.

Aside from all of this, Melrose had to shoot down yet another strange trade rumor, saying the Kings were not going to deal Robitaille and Kelly Hrudey to the Canadiens for goalie Patrick Roy. Robitaille was livid and accused reporters of manufacturing stories to sell newspapers. Robitaille's name is mentioned so often in rumors that Rogie Vachon, when he was Kings general manager, once said, "If we ever do trade him and I call to tell him, he won't believe me."

On the credibility scale of 1 to 10, with 10 being best, the Kings were barely a 1 when they closed out the road trip with a 7-1 beating in New Jersey. Huddy and rookie Alexei Zhitnik were scratched because of flu symptoms, but it was hard to believe any so-called professional team could play so poorly. "We stunk," Gretzky said. Don Perry, a former Kings coach who is now an advance scout, saw the team play for the second time. The other was the 8-3 defeat to Boston in October. "I guess I better stop coming," Perry said.

It was difficult to believe that the Devils, who rattled Stauber and Hrudey for 46 shots, were struggling to score goals and had just acquired Bernie Nicholls from Edmonton in exchange for Kevin Todd and Zdeno Ciger. The Devils would be Nicholls' fourth team in three years. He began his career with the Kings and ranks third in club history for goals (327) and points (758). Once more, it appeared, the Oilers were unloading a big salary.

And, once more, the Kings were holding a team meeting. They should have had a parliamentarian by now. "How do you go into a place like Chicago and play so well and then come into a place like (the Meadowlands) and play like this?" Rychel wanted to know. "Right from the beginning we weren't ready to play. I think we were feeling sorry for ourselves. I mean, I don't care how much flying we do. We're getting paid. We're supposed to be professionals. We can't make excuses about the travel, say that we're tired. We've got to go out and play hard, and that hasn't been happening lately."

It still wasn't happening when the reeling Kings returned home to face Winnipeg, which scored five consecutive goals in a 5-2 victory to pull to within three points. It was January 16. Exactly one month before, the Kings were 22 points ahead of the Jets. Even the fifth-place Oilers, the Kings' next opponent, had cut the gap to 10 points.

"We've been talking to a lot of clubs," Melrose said. "I've said all along I want bigger and stronger players. I've put in my Christmas list and we'll see what happens. The problem is everybody wants you to give up your first-born son. Let's say we're in an advanced state of apprehension." The truth be known, Melrose was beginning to sound like he was going off the deep end. The worse the Kings played, the more quotable he became.

"I've got a guru coming in from Tibet, but he's on a goat train and he's just over China right now," Melrose said. "He'll make it if he doesn't hit a blizzard. Goats die when it's 40-below, and they'd have to hole up in their tents. The next step is to do some chanting. We've got to come up with 25 mantras."

General manager Nick Beverley sounded like he was getting ready to pull the trigger on a deal. "Nobody wants to panic, to make a move just for the sake of doing something, but you get to the point of wondering how long you can go without doing something," he said. "Certainly we're exploring various options and we're definitely not pleased with the way things are going at the present time. When the point differential starts eroding like it has . . . even Edmonton is starting to creep up on us."

Beverley was at a loss to explain the team's dramatic plunge in a month, from the 20-8-3 team that was pulverizing opponents to the 2-10-2 club that was being squashed on a regular basis. Injuries weren't a reasonable excuse because, except for Tomas Sandstrom and Corey Millen, the Kings were healthy. And Beverley refused to blame the goalies, who he said were "struggling" but had to be given some leeway because the play of most every other player had slipped so much.

Hrudey and Stauber were taking quite a bit of heat, some of it justified. Their work had been, for the most part, well under par. This was hockey, unfortunately, not golf. At the same time, the Kings' forwards and defensemen were hardly ever playing the body to prevent a puck-carrier from barreling into the defensive zone under a full head of steam.

"Where do you put your finger on the button to pull it all back together?" Beverley said. "The scorers are not scoring, the general team defense is poor and the goaltenders are struggling. The way I look at it, this is a team thing. It's a team game. If two guys let down, the whole team suffers. The problem is, we've had two guys let down one night and two other guys on another night. Some nights half the team is very mediocre. It keeps bouncing around from player to player, from group to group.

"I think we have a good enough mix of different elements and overall I think we have a real good team in terms of character. I don't get a sense that players are complacent. I think they care more than ever before. But when a slump goes this long . . ." Beverley paused. "You figure to run into some down times, but you should be able to build on your earlier success so that when you do hit a skid, it will be relatively brief."

Thank goodness for the Oilers, who were turning into most hospitable hosts. Was it possible they were attempting to make up for all those times they keelhauled the Kings in the playoffs? Not likely, but the Kings ran their regular-season record to 3-0-1 against them with a 5-4 win before 16,686 at Northlands Coliseum, which was only a halfway decent crowd considering Gretzky was back in his old stomping grounds.

Kurri, too. He broke out of his horrendous slump with two goals, including his first-ever strength goal in 23 games. "I lost 10 pounds," Kurri said of the burden he was carrying all these weeks. Melrose put Kurri, Robitaille, and Lonnie Loach on a line and the three accounted for four goals and five assists. Loach, playing in his second game after missing 11 with a broken thumb, picked up a goal and fed Robitaille for what proved to be the winner late in the third period.

Hrudey made 37 saves, withstood eight Edmonton power plays and was named the game's first star after posting his first win since December 3. He hadn't started since January 6. "Kelly's taken a lot of heat, but he never complains or blames anyone," Melrose said. "You have to feel good for him after a night like this."

A bigger test would come at the Forum when the Canucks visited in two days. The Kings had lost to them three straight times and gone 3-9-1 in 13 Smythe Division games since November 12. All of the wins, and the tie, came at Edmonton's expense.

Unlike Melrose, who downplayed regular-season games during training camp, Canucks general manager-coach Pat Quinn wasn't concerned about his team expending so much energy now that there would be little left for the playoffs. Vancouver was in a heated battle with Pittsburgh, Montreal and Chicago for the league's best record and he wasn't interested in letting up. "First is very important," Quinn said. "First is bragging rights. First is crowing rights. I just can't believe there's a coach or a player in the business who would cruise on purpose just so they could kick up their game in the playoffs."

No one could accuse the Kings of cruising. Foundering in heavy seas and attempting to avoid hidden mines, maybe, but not cruising. Sandstrom was ready to try his hand at working the rudder, not to mention his left arm, against Vancouver. Since having the arm broken by Doug Gilmour, he had missed all but two periods of the 24 games the Kings played. Those came December 22, when he fell on it in the second period and went on the shelf again. "I made a quick turn and I was going down when I stuck my arm out to brace my fall," Sandstrom recalled. According to the Kings, Sandstrom did not break the arm again, but he did experience considerable pain. The muscles atrophied during the previous layoff and were not strong enough to absorb such a blow, even with a hard plastic sleeve.

In the meantime, Corey Millen began a series of acupuncture treatments to relieve the pain from his groin strain. Millen hadn't played since December 19, the last time the Kings were in first place, and he still wasn't close to returning. "We're trying everything," Dr. Ron Kvitne said. Millen wasn't even skating anymore.

Playing for the first time in exactly two months, Sandstrom took five shots and deposited three of them into Canucks goalie Kirk McLean's bank, but the rest of the Kings cashed in just one of 41 shots and Vancouver strolled out of the Forum with a 5-4 victory. The Kings couldn't figure out how McLean was left off the Campbell Conference all-star team, considering his gaudy numbers: a 19-9-3 record and 3.04 goals-against average. Melrose wondered what had become of his Tibetan guru. "Must have got lost coming across the Cascades," he muttered.

There were no cute one-liners from Melrose the night of January 23 when the Rangers came to town and took the Kings apart, 8-3. "We quit," Melrose bellowed. "We just packed it in."

The Forum was half-empty by the time Mike Gartner shoved a rebound into a gaping net with 7:09 remaining to complete a five-goal, eight-shot flurry, but the fans who were left booed and cursed the Kings off the ice. The Rangers entered the game with an 0-6-1 record in their previous seven games on the road. The Kings departed 0-7-1 at home since December 12.

Robb Stauber went the distance in goal and looked bad after the Kings fought back from an early 3-0 deficit to tie the score. New York's Steven King added to Stauber's horrific evening when he put a 30-foot squib shot from a bad angle between his legs. The Kings' penalty-killing was brutal and gave up four goals on six chances, with two of those goals coming after Sandstrom was ejected in the second period for cutting Phil Bourque under the eye with a high stick.

Like the fans, Melrose was positively embarrassed and outraged by what he had just seen. "We've got to do some deals," he said. "We've got to get different players in here. Either that or get a different coach. It's got to be one or the other. I want some different people in here. It's a case of a team not having enough courage to play. We quit in the third period. We played for nine minutes in the second. We don't have enough guys who can play 60. Right now our best players are Dave Taylor, Pat Conacher, and Darryl Sydor — two 35-year-olds and a 20-year-old, so figure it out."

The Kings were about as visible in the dressing room as they were on the ice, but Paul Coffey went where few of his teammates dared to tread and faced a gantlet of notebooks, microphones and cameras. "I know we didn't quit," he said when told of Melrose's damning comments. "I don't think we quit. I hope we didn't quit. Barry's been more than fair, I can tell you that. I haven't seen him this upset in a long, long time, but he has a right to be upset. We're all embarrassed."

Melrose didn't say he was blaming Stauber and Hrudey for the staggering number of goals the Kings were giving up. How could he, considering the manner in which the rest of the team was making a mockery of the game? But neither did he give them a ringing endorsement. "We've got to play with whoever we have," he said. "I can sit here and wish upon a star ... I don't want to single out guys. There are a lot of people who shouldn't be proud of themselves."

The plain truth was, the Kings had been torched for 92 goals during the 3-12-2 slump and allowed five goals or more in all but five of the games. So, regardless of what was happening in front of them, Stauber and Hrudey simply had to stop more pucks if this slide into oblivion was going to end. The Kings were fourth in the Smythe Division now, 13 points behind first-place Vancouver.

Stauber emerged the next day and described his play in the Rangers' game as "brutal." The most important part of a goaltender's job, other than keeping frozen pieces of vulcanized rubber from littering the inside of the net, is to put his team in a position to win. If that means standing on one's head to thwart one offensive thrust after another, so be it. Stauber hadn't been able to do that against New York, and his 2-6 record and 5.50 goals-against average since December 15 showed he wasn't having much success accomplishing the task against anybody else.

"If you could crawl into a hole, you would," Stauber said. "But there's nowhere to hide. I felt a little insecure about my job. I'd be lying if I said otherwise because I'm not *that* good. It was a terrible feeling to play the way I did. You go behind the net to stop a puck and the fans let you have it. When you're playing poorly, you notice things like that because your focus isn't what it should be."

Even when traveling at speeds of 100 miles per hour, the puck is crystal clear to a goalie who is on his game. An extra sense kicks in and he floats effortlessly in his own little world, oblivious to virtually any distraction. But Hrudey and Stauber were struggling, and so the puck was a small, black blur.

Hrudey, under normal circumstances, is one of the most accommodating players on the Kings, a genuinely nice man who considers dealing with reporters as much a part of the job as putting on his bird-cage mask and pads. Some conversations were more pleasant than others, of course. Hrudey would much rather talk after a 4-2 victory than, say, a 6-4 defeat, but he never failed to appear in front of his locker for a post-game interview. Win, lose or draw. When the enigmatic Daniel Berthiaume was employed as his caddy, a tenure that lasted 17 months, Hrudey made every attempt to convince him that reporters aren't insensitive dolts. Most of them, anyway.

Hrudey, whose emotions drip through his sweater, was on edge the day after the Rangers shelled his partner. Hrudey's mood was perfectly understandable; he wasn't playing well, the team was in the sewer, and his wife, Donna, was due any day to give birth to their third child. Hrudey was in a hurry to leave the club's snazzy new dressing room at Iceoplex and get home. So there might have been a better time to ask if Melrose's vow to make changes was a concern.

Hrudey snapped. "I'll tell you one thing outright, I don't worry about being traded," he said, his voice rising. "I could care less and I say that honestly. If people think a goalie's going to be traded, good. It makes no difference to me. I know one thing, I've played 10 years and I've seen it in every city in the league. When times go bad, the goalies get the blame. That's just the way it is. I've never seen it different anywhere.

"I know back home in Canada, that's all they're writing. I'm getting traded every day. I know because my family has told me," said Hrudey, who returns to Edmonton in the off-season. "If you think it's a crisis in your life, well, let's just put it in reality. What's the worst thing that can happen if you get traded? You play somewhere else. You still get paid, don't you? At times it bothers you, but right now it's not. I have more important things to worry about than a trade. I have a baby coming."

Hrudey did not want to be traded. He has been a King since February 1989, six months into the Wayne Gretzky era, when he was acquired from the New York Islanders for Mark Fitzpatrick, Doug Crossman and Wayne McBean. But he plainly was annoyed with those who placed the blame for the team's problems in the crease.

"These people, they love you when you get good and they hate you when you get bad," Hrudey said. "They kick you when you're down and they want to trade you, and they take some joy in it. Well, big deal. Trading's a part of this business and if you can't handle it, quit. When I was with the Islanders, the fans hated Billy Smith and all he did was win four Stanley Cups. You can't override everything in your life because there are rumors. People who are pointing their fingers at you, maybe they don't know anything about the game."

Hrudey also was angry at himself because the strain of his seven-week struggle — he carried a 1-6-3 record and 4.98 goals-against average since December 8 — had spilled over to his family life. Puzzled by one bad game after another, he was staying up until the wee hours of the morning to study video-tapes and search for technical flaws.

"My game kept slipping and slipping and slipping away from me," he said. "Eventually, somewhere along the line, I lost all balance in my life. I went over the edge a little bit. I mean, there's your hockey life and then there's your regular life. I had always prided myself on my ability to separate the two, but I haven't been able to do it. There's more to life than just trying to stop pucks. I'm a husband and a dad. You have to forget about the hockey part and focus in on what's good in your life.

"Part of the problem," Hrudey said, "is that I haven't gotten away from the hockey. I've been sitting at home, scouring tapes like a fool. I've got to throw out that VCR. I mean, my wife's in bed and I'm sitting there going over tapes. I've been beating my head against the wall and I've got to stop. This is not my normal personality and I've got to get back to normal. I've been a big part of the problem and I've got to be a part of the solution."

Cap Raeder knew where Hrudey's head was at. Raeder tended goal at the University of New Hampshire and for two seasons in the World Hockey Association, long enough to under-stand the anguish and stress that goes with the position. "I don't think people understand what you go through," Raeder said. "As hard as you try not to, you can let your play affect your whole life. It's hard not to take the game home with you. But Kelly is so strong. You've got to love him for it. He'll pull through."

The Kings got healthy at San Jose's expense, cruising to a 7-1 win that extracted some measure of vengeance for the 6-0 and 7-2 drubbings the Sharks administered in the previous two meetings. Hrudey made 34 saves as the Kings snapped an 0-7-1 Forum winless streak and asked reporters if it would be all right for him to rush home. His wife still hadn't given birth. Wayne Gretzky celebrated his 32nd birthday with two assists but didn't score a goal for the eighth consecutive game. Tomas Sandstrom scored two goals and the Paul Coffey-Rob Blake defensive pair-ing contributed two goals and seven assists. Coffey had five of the assists, one shy of Bernie Nicholls' franchise record, despite blurred vision from a first-period hit.

Still, the Kings weren't out of the woods yet and players were almost expecting Nick Beverley to make a trade. Since his last deal, the one-sided Bob Kudelski swap, the Kings were 4-10-1. "You know it's reality, part of the game," Coffey said. "If you're not winning, more times than not, changes are made. It's not pleasant, but that's just the way it is." Melrose repeated his desire for change but he said, "It's easier for me to blast people in the papers and say what I would like than for Nick to do it. It can be hard to make moves because of salaries and such."

Trade discussions between the Kings and Detroit Red Wings heated up for the first time since October, when Beverley and Melrose chose to ride out Gretzky's back injury with Jari Kurri at center rather than deal for Jimmy Carson. If the Kings were still interested in Carson, a potential 40-goal scorer who was playing on the third line behind Steve Yzerman and Sergei Fedorov, they weren't telling. But Gretzky and Kurri were struggling and Corey Millen was about to miss his 16th game with a groin problem. And it wasn't as though the Kings were scoring a lot, barely over three goals per game since tumbling out of first place.

The Red Wings were interested in Coffey. Detroit needed a tough guy on defense and Coffey couldn't fill that role, but Murray absolutely percolated every time he thought of Coffey headmanning the puck to guys like Yzerman, Fedorov and Paul Ysebaert, and quarterbacking the power play. The Red Wings were a Stanley Cup contender, Coffey could help put them over the top, and they wouldn't have a problem absorbing his contract, worth $1.1 million now and $2.75 million over the next two years.

On the other hand, Coffey was tied with Quebec's Steve Duchesne for the NHL lead among defensemen with 57 points, everybody on the Kings liked him, and there was his close friendship with Gretzky to consider. Why cause a stir with the big guy?

Yet the Kings conceded their marquee defenseman was being mentioned in talks with other teams. "His name has been brought up. He's a very marketable player," Melrose told the *Los Angeles Daily News*. "He's played very hard for me and I don't want to move him, but his name has been mentioned." Melrose denied Coffey was being shopped, however, and he said NHL general managers also were inquiring about Robitaille, Blake and Marty McSorley, as if the Kings were going to unload any of them. "I'm sure you know which guys other teams want," Melrose went on. "There are no secrets."

One of the worst-kept secrets was that Melrose remained enamored with several players he had coached at Adirondack, including wingers Marc Potvin and Gary Shuchuk, neither of whom fit into Detroit's plans. Whatever the Kings did, apparently, wouldn't include Hrudey. Rumors flew that Rangers goalie Mike Richter was on the block, but Melrose said Hrudey's strong game against the Sharks "meant a lot. One game is not a season, but Kelly was really sharp." It was a good day all the way around for Hrudey, whose wife gave birth to 7-pound, 6-ounce Kaitlin Melissa in the morning.

Two more embarrassing skids came to an end at the Forum the next night, but, unfortunately for the Kings, it was the Calgary Flames who celebrated. Their 2-1, come-from-behind win snapped a Calgary record-tying 11-game winless streak and a seven-game road winless streak; despite the hellish droughts, the second-place Flames still led the Kings by eight points.

The game was noteworthy for other reasons: Coffey left the front of the net to check Theoren Fleury, freeing Gary Roberts to score the tie-breaking goal at 2:11 of the third period; video goal judge Jeff Raelson ruled that Kurri intentionally used his left arm to steer a deflected puck into the net with 4:50 to play and negated what would have been the tying goal; and Sandstrom left the game with a cut mouth and several broken teeth when he was inadvertantly struck in the face with a Coffey slap shot with 4:16 remaining.

Oh, and Kings owner Bruce McNall used the occasion to blast the team. "Here we are, losing and playing horribly. There are times when I want to put a paper sack on my head and be the anonymous owner," McNall said. "It's pretty dog-gone difficult not to be frustrated. I'm sitting there thinking, 'People are upset and they're paying $50 a seat. How do they think I feel? I've got a $50 million investment.'"

Once as visible as Gretzky, McNall no longer was traveling with the team that frequently, partly because his position as chairman of the league's Board of Governors was taking up so much of his time. But he made no apologies for that. "Look at all the road trips I went on for five years," he said. "I don't see any Stanley Cups around here."

But McNall was thrilled by the interest his team was generating, even if he couldn't fathom why fans had filled the Forum nine consecutive times to watch a team stumble around the ice. "I'm grateful," he said. "They keep coming, so they must be crazy about the sport. There are nights when I don't want to be here."

When dawn arrived January 29, Coffey was gone. To Detroit. In exchange for Coffey and Jim Hiller, whose season had gone south for the winter, and minor-leaguer Sylvain Couturier, the Kings received Carson, Potvin and Shuchuk. Most players expected something to happen, but they were shaken nonetheless. The reaction, mostly negative, registered somewhere in the vicinity of a 6.0 on the Richter scale; not a killer jolt, but most definitely a powerful one.

Not only that, the Coffey blast that struck Sandstrom the night before fractured his jaw in two places and smashed four teeth. Even Sandstrom, whose pain threshold was legendary, was going to feel discomfort for a while. He definitely would miss four weeks, the doctors said, and probably six. Other than that, it was a fairly ordinary day.

"I lost my two best friends," Warren Rychel, who shared a beach house with Coffey and Hiller, said in a quiet dressing room after practice. Gretzky left without commenting. McSorley, who usually will talk about anything, used hand signals to indicate he did not wish to speak. Blake, who idolized Coffey, was one of the first players the new Red Wing had telephoned. "I never thought they would trade Coff," he said, looking glum. Everywhere you went in the room, the responses were the same. "It's sad. I guess nobody is safe," Kurri said. "It's a tough thing to swallow any time you lose friends," Granato said. "It takes a little time to heal." Robitaille said, "We lost, so a good guy leaves."

Carson, 24, a first-round pick of the Kings in 1986, scored 92 goals for them in two years before he became a part of hockey history and was included in the package that brought Gretzky to Los Angeles. He had 25 goals and 51 points in 52 games as a third-line center in Detroit. "For a guy who hasn't played much, his numbers are fantastic," Melrose gushed. "Coffey is a great player and he played very hard for me, but we needed a shakeup. We gave up one guy who was playing regularly for three guys who will be regulars."

Well, maybe Shuchuk could play regularly, but Potvin's resume was suspect. A muscular 215-pounder who stands 6-feet-1, Potvin didn't remind anyone of his second cousin, former

Islanders great Denis Potvin, whose scoring records were all broken by Coffey. Marc, 26, didn't know the meaning of the word finesse. He fought 34 times in 51 games under Melrose at Adirondack the year before and had eight goals and 109 penalty minutes in 37 games there when the trade was made after missing 11 games with a bone chip in his thumb. Potvin did share one distinction with Gretzky: he also was a team captain.

Shuchuk, 25, showed more than glimpses of scoring potential in the minors — he was the AHL's leading scorer with 24 goals and 77 points in 47 games — and he was said to be a Granato clone, a pest with the ability to goad opponents into taking penalties. Shuchuk, who looks skinnier than the 190 pounds he is listed as carrying on his 5-foot-11 frame, centered a line with Granato at the University of Wisconsin and was expected to do the same with the Kings.

But Carson was the key, and management didn't give a hoot about his reputation for playing "soft." Carson is a goal-scorer and the Kings needed one. "Certainly it isn't easy any time you move a player of Coffey's caliber," Nick Beverley said. "He really did a great job for us and you've heard all of us saying a lot of nice things about him. But we don't say any of this with any apology for making the deal. Jimmy Carson is a great player in his own right."

Certainly Carson wasn't a stranger to the Los Angeles scene. He owned homes in Redondo Beach and Palm Springs when he previously played for the Kings as a wide-eyed, teen-aged rookie. Now he was 24 and married to a Southern California girl. He grew up in the Detroit area and idolized Marcel Dionne, then a Red Wings star who took Carson and Robitaille under his wing when they joined the Kings in 1986-87. Carson never was happy in Edmonton following the Gretzky blockbuster, went AWOL on the Oilers, and eventually was traded to the Red Wings.

"I certainly was happy in Detroit," Carson said. "My family is there, I was playing for a good team and I had kind of accepted my role. But L.A. would have been my first choice if I had to be traded. It's funny because I remember Bruce McNall told me, 'I'll get you back someday.' I never really took him seriously. The one thing I'm not looking forward to is the traffic."

Carson said he hadn't given much thought to being traded, in separate transactions, for two certain Hall of Famers. "Paul

Coffey is one of the best defensemen of all time and Wayne Gretzky is the best player of all time," he said. The two combined for 3,377 points heading into the season.

Coffey wasn't happy, but he seemed to handle the move a lot better than his former teammates did. When he answered the telephone at 7 that morning and heard Beverley's voice, Coffey knew he wasn't being invited to breakfast. "I don't know if it came as a shock. When a team isn't playing well, moves are inevitable," he said. "Five years ago, Wayne Gretzky was traded, so anybody can be. You try and look at the positive things, but I loved it in L.A. The hardest part is leaving Wayne, not only as a hockey player but as a friend. I broke in with Wayne and I was hoping to finish my career with him. From that standpoint, this is devastating."

The Gretzkys, Wayne and Janet, were crushed. Coffey called them when he and Hiller were through speaking with Beverley and related the following conversation: "Janet answered and she said, 'What's wrong?' I mean, it's 7 o'clock in the morning. She thought I was in a car accident or something. I told her I had been traded and she started crying. Then Wayne starts panicking. He sees Janet is crying, he knows she's talking to me, and now *he* thinks I've been in a car accident or something. Wayne didn't have a clue this was happening. He doesn't have anything to do with that."

Certainly the Roy Mlakar-Beverley-Melrose regime had erased the widely-held perception that Gretzky was a sort of skating general manager who wielded great influence with McNall in the area of player personnel. Gretzky was sensitive to the charge and always denied it, but he undoubtedly would have nixed this trade had he been consulted. He wasn't. Melrose's fingerprints, not Gretzky's, were all over the deal.

Melrose was convinced his young defense corps needed room to grow, and in that sense Coffey was an impediment. Coffey's departure and the acquisition of three reasonably young forwards would force Rob Blake to take on more responsibility and give him some depth up front, all in one fell swoop. "We're putting our future in the hands of the kids," Melrose said.

Melrose also put the "A" Coffey wore as assistant captain on McSorley's sweater. An olive branch? "He's playing hard and physical. He's being a leader," Melrose said of McSorley.

If only patching up Sandstrom's shattered jaw and teeth would be as simple. He was ordered to stay inactive for a week after he underwent four root canals and had the jaw wired shut. Because Sandstrom's nose had been previously broken, he was going to have some difficulty breathing. He'd be stuck with a liquid diet that likely would cause him to lose 15 pounds and he was required to carry a pair of wire cutters as a precaution against choking.

"You could put a motorcycle helmet on him and he'd still be vulnerable because of where the break is," Dr. Ron Kvitne said. "Actually, he's lucky. He could have been hurt a lot worse." Sandstrom had scored six goals in four games after he missed two months with his broken arm. Overall, he had 18 goals and 38 points in 26 games. "How can a guy have this kind of luck?" Blake said. "People say Tomas is soft, that he's injury-prone. But the other night, when they were putting needles and stitches in him, he just sat there. He is one tough guy."

The Kings tied the Blackhawks, 2-2, and slipped into fourth place, one point behind Winnipeg. Among the newcomers, only Potvin's name would appear in the newspaper summary the next morning. Under the heading "penalties." He fought Cam Russell on his very first shift, which came 2:22 into the game. Carson took a couple of shots — on goal — and Shuchuk took one, but it was Dave Taylor who nearly stole the show.

Taylor, playing in his 1,061st career game, took a pass from McSorley, broke into the Chicago zone and split between defensemen Chris Chelios and Steve Smith. He continued down the slot, deked goalie Ed Belfour, and rifled a shot inside the right post. Not bad for a 37-year-old, especially one who missed 18 games with a bruised brain stem. "The guy won't let me take him out of the lineup," Melrose said. "I haven't found anything yet to replace his heart." The goal gave the Kings a 2-1 lead at 4:20 of the third period, but it didn't hold up. Jeremy Roenick's attempt at a wraparound hit Darryl Sydor's right skate and ricocheted between Hrudey's legs with 5:27 left to tie the game.

Gretzky was held without a shot and stretched his goal-scoring slump to 10 games. Responding to the trade of Coffey, he said, "It's hard, it's tough, but you just play. Everything happens for a reason. Trades are tough on everybody. I'm sure Dave Taylor was upset when Marcel Dionne got traded. (Coffey) is my friend and I don't mind saying so. But I know the young guys are looking to me. I'm getting paid to help them as much as I can. We've still got to win a championship here. Any time you make a trade, it shakes everything up. When a team isn't winning, it's just a matter of time before something is done."

Beverley wasn't necessarily finished. He was hoping to pick up a veteran defenseman, one who knew his way around the defensive zone, provided he could acquire one reasonably cheap. But that could wait.

Gretzky was growing impatient with his less-than-sterling numbers as the Kings left town for a two-game trip to Quebec and Montreal, the last games they would play before the NHL All-Star break. Gretzky had 14 points in 12 games since returning from his back injury, decent statistics for most players. But Gretzky isn't just any old player. Besides, his goal-scoring slump was 10 games now; both of his goals came in the January 8 game in Winnipeg and he had since taken only 13 shots on goal.

"I've got to find myself," Gretzky said. "All in all, after 12 games, I think I've played all right. I don't think my play has been poor. I'm not playing the way I want to play, but it's tough after missing all that time. I've been okay, I guess. I can't expect the five- and six-point nights, but I feel like I can contribute my share. Right now, I'm trying to keep my game simple. Hopefully, I'll start to get some breaks around the net. No excuses, but I'm doing the best I can."

Gretzky would later reveal he discussed his troubles over dinner with Melrose and Raeder in Quebec. "I was out of answers and I turned to them to figure out what the future held," Gretzky said. "I didn't want to embarrass them, I didn't want to embarrass the organization, and I didn't want to embarrass myself."

Coincidentally, a year ago to the very day, Gretzky spoke about his hockey mortality and the circumstances under which he would seriously consider a premature retirement. By Gretzky's standards, he was enduring a mediocre season, in part because the hyperextended back he suffered in the 1991 Canada Cup tournament bothered him when the season began, but also because of the anguish he felt when his father, Walter, was stricken with a brain aneurysm.

Gretzky had 20 goals and 71 points in 46 games at the time, statistics that projected to 33 goals and 116 points for the year. He trailed league scoring leader Mario Lemieux, who was having back problems, by nine points. To Gretzky, the gap might as well have been 99 points.

"I don't compare myself to anybody else," he said then. "I compare myself to Wayne Gretzky, it's as simple as that. For me to score 100 points isn't enough. I would have to say that 100 points is very mediocre. There have been a lot of circumstances I've had to face, which is why I'm not going to put a lot of stock in these numbers. But if I have the same numbers next year, then I'd have to look at my future."

That future was now, and it wasn't pretty. Not that Gretzky or anyone else could have known that circumstances would again turn a season upside down. "We all felt down," Melrose said, "and Wayne is bigger than anybody else, so he takes it more personally. It was a tough time for all of us. We had a lot of guys hurt and we weren't winning. February is a tough part of the season anyway. So the three of us went out and had a nice supper. It was just three friends meeting for supper. It was good for us. Wayne was down and we weren't winning."

A 3-2 loss at le Colisee didn't lift anyone's spirits, and the Kings used the occasion to vent their frustration at referee Terry Gregson. With time winding down, Gretzky was forced to make an extra move — wasting a valuable second — to avoid a stick thrown by Quebec's Adam Foote before he took a shot from the right faceoff circle. Mike Donnelly stashed the rebound under goalie Ron Hextall's left arm, but time had expired. The Kings didn't have a gripe about the clock, but they wondered why Foote's stick-throwing exhibition didn't result in a penalty shot.

"It was definitely a penalty shot," Gretzky said. "I don't understand it. Either we have rules or we don't have rules." Quebec's Mats Sundin was awarded a penalty shot in the second period after Marty McSorley hooked him to the ice on a breakaway, but Hrudey squeezed his pads together and made the save to keep the Kings within 2-1.

Hrudey credited a one-hour session with Melrose's guru, Anthony Robbins, for the turnaround in his play. His record since the visit was 1-2-1, nothing to get excited about, but his goals-against average in that span was 1.97. In other words, the Kings' offense had dried up completely.

"He's an incredible human being, a powerful person," Hrudey said of Robbins. "He doesn't know the sport and he doesn't know me, but he knows people. The thing is, he didn't tell me anything I didn't already know, but he did tell me about things I had forgotten. It's hard to describe how I felt when I got out of there, but he has a way of getting things out that you have inside you. All of a sudden, the weight of the world wasn't on my shoulders. I felt like a million dollars."

The Kings played as if they were worth considerably less the next night in Montreal, where Hrudey and Robb Stauber actually performed admirably in a 7-2 drilling. Bad as it was, the margin of defeat would have been considerably larger had the goalies not stood on their heads and various other anatomical parts. Old friend Vincent Damphousse opened the scoring 33 seconds into the game and the Kings never caught up.

Robitaille drew the Kings to within 3-2 with his 36th goal early in the second period, then a comedy of errors enabled the Canadiens to regain their two-goal advantage and eventually pull away. First, Gary Shuchuk was checked off the puck, a mistake that forced Rob Blake to take a holding penalty. Then, during the ensuing Montreal power play, Darryl Sydor and Tony Granato lost their sticks, making it relatively easy for Denis Savard to score. "We've been horrible for a month," Warren Rychel said. "We've hit rock bottom. We've got to do something real fast."

For now, getting out of town as quickly as possible seemed to be the most agreeable option. The once-mighty Kings were in a downward spiral, 5-17-3 over the past two months and 24-23-6 overall with five off-days sandwiched around the NHL All-Star Game to contemplate their plight. "When we come back from this break, we've got to be a mean and ugly team," Hrudey said.

They already had one half of the equation solved.

Eight

All-Star Follies

An All-Star break is supposed to be an enjoyable respite from the daily grind that can eat an athlete alive. No coach, referee, or linesman is immune to the pressure, either; if left unchecked, it can turn unhealthy. So sticking an otherwise meaningless exhibition game right square in the middle of a National Hockey League season that nearly stretches into summer now can be compared to lifting a boiling pot of water off its burner before the contents can shoot out.

Naturally, there are drawbacks. The game itself has become a farce devoid of anything remotely resembling body contact or defensive maneuvers. The odds of a penalty being called during a pillow fight at a slumber party are greater than they are in an NHL All-Star Game, which some players view as an annoyance that denies them the chance to get away from the rink for a few days.

Also, the players who need the most rest, the ones who log the lion's share of ice time in the regular season, don't get it. Wayne Gretzky's idea is for the NHL to take a week or two off at midseason, which would give every player the opportunity to go on holiday and recharge his batteries. The overall product, he believes, would benefit. Still, the majority of the league's elite, Gretzky included, consider it an honor to participate in the game and skills competition, such as they are.

Besides, playing the 44th NHL All-Star Game at the hallowed Montreal Forum made it special. And bittersweet. The Canadiens are hoping to move into a new building by 1995-96, which means a wrecker's ball eventually will smash hockey's venerable shrine to the ground. "When I was a kid, to come to a game here was like a Christmas present or a birthday present," Luc Robitaille said. "When I jump on the ice here, I'm almost shy to look up at the banners."

So this likely would be the final All-Star Game ever played in the 69-year-old Forum, home to 23 Stanley Cup banners, so many Canadiens spirits, and probably the most famous dressing room in all of professional sports.

One wall is covered with pictures of former Montreal greats such as Maurice "Rocket" Richard, Guy Lafleur, Jean Beliveau, Henri Richard and Howie Morenz. Above the pictures are the lines "To you from failing hands we throw the torch. Be yours to hold it high." The words are from the poem "In Flanders Fields," written by Canadian physician John McCrae in tribute to soldiers who died in World War I. The opposite wall is covered with wooden plaques listing the rosters of every Canadiens team.

"This place is special," said Lafleur, who was going to play in the Heroes of Hockey game. "It won't be the same in another place, no matter how many flags they bring in."

Jari Kurri must have wondered if he had entered a time warp instead of the drab visitors' dressing room — no inspirational words or photographs here — to change into his black, orange and white All-Star uniform before practice. Within a half hour, Kurri was asked by three different reporters if he felt anxious about playing in his first All-Star Game. Each time he politely answered, "Actually, it's my seventh." A few reporters, Martians maybe, asked Kurri to identify himself. "What's with these people?" he said later, looking flustered.

The daffiness was just beginning. A hot rumor that Gretzky wanted the Kings to trade him to the Toronto Maple Leafs was making the rounds and spread so quickly that Bruce McNall was forced to call a news conference in order to refute it. According to the rumor, Gretzky was angry about the deal that sent Paul Coffey to Detroit and he was no longer speaking to McNall.

What was it about the Kings and All-Star Games? In January 1990, after a day filled with rumors and denials, star center Bernie Nicholls found out he had been traded to the New York Rangers in exchange for Tony Granato and Tomas Sandstrom. He got the news shortly after the skills competition ended, less than 24 hours before the game . . . in a darkened hallway deep inside Pittsburgh's Civic Arena.

Now Coffey, after sitting beside Gretzky to pose for the Campbell Conference team picture, was wondering if this rumor might actually have some merit. "I'm a firm believer, and Wayne is too, that sometimes where there's smoke, there's a little bit of a flame," he said. Maybe Coffey was on to something, or maybe his trade of the previous week had made him leery.

"Wayne was unhappy before the trade," Coffey said. "He's just down, period. A little of that might have to do with the trade, but he knows trades are a part of hockey. He's not blind to that. He just wants to win, to play 40 minutes a game and to be competitive. If he doesn't get the chance to do it, then he's disappointed. He's disappointed maybe in the people who aren't giving him a chance to do that. He's disappointed in himself.

"Things just aren't fun for him right now," Coffey went on. "Seriously, if you told Wayne Gretzky that he'd play three more years and he wasn't going to have any fun, he'd quit the game today. But he's a strong individual and things will work out."

Gretzky said the whispers were news to him. "I haven't heard anything. Maybe they want me to go up there and look after the Rocket," he joked. Former Notre Dame star Raghib "Rocket" Ismail, now with the Raiders, was playing for the Toronto Argonauts at the time. "I think somebody may be stirring up the pot. I won't be losing any sleep over it. I'm happy where I am and I don't want to be traded, but I don't have any say. It's up to the Los Angeles Kings."

McNall put an end to what turned out to be nothing more than an imaginative fairy tale. "It's absurd, a joke, irresponsible journalism at its height," McNall said with emotion. "It's total nonsense, absolutely insane."

Gretzky did not want to be traded, he was among the handful of players who accompanied McNall in his private jet for the flight from Quebec to Montreal earlier in the week, they *spoke* during dinner after the Canadiens game, and, besides, McNall wouldn't trade Gretzky under any circumstances. "If Wayne Gretzky ever got unhappy and wanted to be moved, I would release him and allow him to do whatever he wants," McNall said.

"Our relationship has never changed," he said of the alleged rift. "And he is not unhappy with the trade, he is unhappy that he lost a friend. The team is playing badly and Wayne blames himself for everything. Sure, he's down. He feels responsible for every loss. Sometimes you have to relax, and he can't do that. Remember, the guy had a serious injury and everybody else is in midseason form. He shouldn't be playing at all probably. But he has never used that as an excuse. He won't even use it as an excuse to himself."

And that, McNall said, was that.

Perhaps the Kings' contingent should have gone home then. Robitaille made a decent accounting of himself in the accurate-shooting portion of the skills competition when he hit targets placed in all four corners of the net, but Kurri hit posts with three of his shots and he shot too high on another, banging the puck off the glass. Gretzky, perhaps distracted by the media circus, skated in the puck-control relay and fell.

The All-Star Game was even worse than anyone could have expected. Mike Gartner of the Rangers scored three of his four goals in the first period, the Wales Conference bolted to a 9-0 lead before the second period was five minutes old, and the final score was 16-6. Can a nightmare take place during the day? The game was televised across the United States by NBC, but even the guys who played in it couldn't believe anyone would have watched for much longer than a period. If that.

The highlight of the afternoon took place before the game when all of the players were introduced. Pittsburgh's Mario Lemieux, who was undergoing radiation treatment for Hodgkin's disease, put on a Wales Conference sweater that was presented by Penguins coach Scotty Bowman. The sellout crowd of 17,137 gave Lemieux a standing ovation.

It was all downhill after the puck was dropped. Among the records set in the figure-skating display that passed for a game: Most combined goals (22), most goals by one team (16), most combined shots (90) and most assists in a period by one player (four, by Boston's Adam Oates). Fifty-four points were scored in all, but Kurri's assist with 2:57 remaining in the game was the only one delivered by a King.

"The game is boring when there isn't any checking," said Bowman, who handled the Wales team, "but the focal point shouldn't be on the competitive aspect. This just shows me what a great game (real) hockey is and that we can't change it too much."

Calgary Flames goaltender Mike Vernon gave up six goals on 15 uncontested shots in the second period and wondered if potential hockey fans who tuned in out of curiosity were ultimately turned off. "I think we're misleading a lot of people," he said. "I guess not too many expected a defensive battle, but this . . . I can tell you it wasn't much fun for me."

As Chicago Blackhawks goalie Ed Belfour was being strafed for six goals on 22 shots in the opening period — Belfour usually doesn't give up that many goals in three games — Vernon turned to the Campbell Conference's other goalie, Jon Casey of the Minnesota North Stars, and said, "Let's sneak out the back door."

With few exceptions, the players would like to see new NHL commissioner Gary Bettman tinker with the format, try anything to make the game more competitive without running the risk of injuries. Even a meaningless exhibition game, they said, should look a little bit like hockey.

"Maybe we need a change just to shake it up," Gretzky said. "It's definitely a Catch-22 situation. It's hard for you guys to see this every year and then say it's the worst thing you've ever seen, while the fans in the city where the game is played remember the whole weekend and maybe aren't as dismayed.

"I don't know how to rectify the problem. If you make it like a league game, people will be upset if someone gets hurt. I don't think the players would mind a competitive game, but I think ownership and management would be concerned."

For Gretzky, and the rest of the Kings, reality would rear its ugly head soon enough.

Nine

Weathering
the Storm

For Barry Melrose, the All-Star break was a misnomer. The Kings had won only four of their previous 22 games, they were in danger of slipping into fifth place in the Smythe Division, and there would only be 31 games left to straighten out problems when the season resumed. So Melrose spent most of the break poring over game tapes, wracking his brain for ideas and discussing a variety of possible solutions with Cap Raeder and Nick Beverley.

Melrose had already grabbed a number of psychological ploys from his bag of tricks, among them benchings and biting criticism as well as positive reinforcement. Instructional and/or motivational videotapes are important tools for Melrose, who uses them in every pregame meeting. "It's a video generation," he said. "These guys have all been brought up on MTV."

While the coaches prefer to emphasize positive clips, Melrose occasionally asks Raeder or the team's video coordinator, Bill Gurney, to include a play that will provide comic relief. "One time we showed Alex (Zhitnik) accidentally hitting a referee," he said. "We were showing a bunch of hits another time, then all of a sudden Luc (Robitaille) is getting clobbered by (Minnesota's) Mark Tinordi and his stick goes flying. The guys were whooping it up."

By all accounts, the players enjoyed watching the tapes and

they appreciated the fact that everyone eventually was given a starring role. "In the past, all the emphasis was on the people who got the points," Marty McSorley said. "The guys who do the so-called little things are getting rewarded now. These tapes help bring those things to light."

Based on the play of the Kings lately, Raeder and Gurney didn't have many positive plays to choose from. They would have been better off skipping the time-consuming routine and sticking a "Three Stooges" cassette into the VCR for all the help the usual practice was providing.

Finally, Melrose decided the best way for his team to start making an impact was for him to revamp his forward lines. He was going to do this by placing one big man on each one of them. "I want us to start attacking the net more, play more aggressively," Melrose said. "This is crunch time. The time for talking is over. Just show up and play."

When the Kings lined up against the Edmonton Oilers on February 9 to begin a four-game homestand, 202-pound Warren Rychel would skate on a line with Wayne Gretzky and Tony Granato; the 225-pound McSorley would move from defense to a unit with Jimmy Carson and Luc Robitaille; and 215-pound Marc Potvin would be with Pat Conacher and Dave Taylor. Melrose didn't have any more big forwards, so Jari Kurri would play with Gary Shuchuk and Mike Donnelly.

There were other moves. Two defensemen, Tim Watters and Rene Chapdelaine, were called up from the Phoenix Roadrunners. Another, Jeff Chychrun, was sent down. Chychrun's demotion seemed peculiar because (a) at 6-feet-4 and 215 pounds, he was one of the beefiest players on the team; and (b) since his November 5 acquisition from Pittsburgh, he had played in only 17 of 40 games, hardly much chance to show whether he belonged in the NHL or not.

Chychrun was stunned and visibly upset after he emerged from Melrose's office at Iceoplex. "I can't believe this," he said with emotion. Chychrun grabbed a sandwich from his locker and slammed it, plastic basket and all, into a trash bin. Then he stalked off. Later, he quietly wondered how he would break the news to his father, who was to arrive from Canada that day. Chychrun's mother passed away shortly before he was traded to the Penguins in the Paul Coffey transaction the previous year.

"We had Chick here a long time and the bottom line is we didn't . . . right now we need guys who can give us 10 minutes of quality time, 10 minutes of mistake-free time," Melrose said. "We didn't feel Jeff could give us that. Jeff has to play, and he hasn't been playing. He had some chances to jump in there and play. In Jeff's situation, he had to grab us and show us he should play more."

Oh, well that explained it.

Melrose said Rob Blake was going to play 25-30 minutes per game from now on, with Darryl Sydor and Zhitnik each getting 20-25 minutes and Charlie Huddy around 20. Watters and Chapdelaine would be given the odd shift. Brent Thompson? He was sidelined with an abdominal strain, an ailment that had gotten progressively worse because he hid it from the team for three weeks. "I just didn't want to miss any games," Thompson said. "It was a mistake."

Dave Taylor was having problems with dizzy spells again, so he wouldn't play in the Edmonton game, either. Taylor had played in 17 games after missing 18 with his bruised brain stem. Tomas Sandstrom wasn't close to returning, but he bragged through clenched teeth about his ability to eat spaghetti and hamburgers despite a fractured jaw that was wired shut. He used a blender to prepare his meals, concoctions that included a mixture of milk and meat sauce and spaghetti, as well as fast-food hamburgers. Sandstrom simply siphoned the stuff through a straw.

If only the Kings could find the right formula for a victory. Now they couldn't even fatten up on Edmonton. The Kings spent too much time in the penalty box and the Oilers took advantage, scoring two power-play goals in a 6-3 decision that moved them to within six points of fourth place and dropped the Kings to .500 for the first time since the second game of the season.

Blake didn't play anywhere near 25 minutes; he took a major high-sticking penalty early in the second period and spent the rest of the game in street clothes. Penalties to McSorley created two 5-on-3 skating advantages, one of which led to the winning goal. Then McSorley speared Craig Muni with two seconds to play. His third major stick foul of the year, all in the final two seconds of games, meant an automatic two-game suspension. "Somehow we've got to find a bright spot, though right now it's like being in a dark cave with a flashlight," Blake said.

Not that the Kings needed to look very far for trouble, but it was brewing in the form of Coffey and the Red Wings, who were about to enter the Forum under a head of steam. Detroit was on a 5-0-1 tear and getting a lot more production from Coffey and Jim Hiller — four goals and 10 points in three games — than the Kings were receiving from Jimmy Carson, Marc Potvin and Gary Shuchuk — two assists and 26 penalty minutes in four games.

Coffey liked playing in the Forum, but he wasn't looking forward to skating against his old friends. "Playing against Wayne again will be hard," he said. "I couldn't stand Tony Granato before I got there and he couldn't stand me, now we're good friends. And then there's Blakey. No, it won't be easy. But I'm sure the fans will be into it. People talk about L.A., say L.A. doesn't have any hockey fans. But they draw 16,000 every game and make as much noise as any place. They know what's going on. My sister and nephew came out for a game and they couldn't believe how loud it was."

Nick Beverley couldn't believe what he had just read in one of his morning newspapers, yet another Robitaille-for-Brett Hull fairy tale. Beverley was trying to figure out how someone could write a story of such magnitude without at least attempting to ask him about it first. Then he "guaranteed" Hull wasn't heading to Los Angeles, for Robitaille or for anybody else. "We just made a major deal and we're trying to get the team settled," he said. "Going out and making another major deal now just doesn't make any sense to me." But Beverley repeated his desire to pick up an experienced defenseman.

Coffey, nervous and tentative, was barely visible in the 6-6 tie between the Kings and the Red Wings. Robitaille had a big game with his 38th goal and four assists, and Carson finally delivered his first goal and added two assists. "It's kind of like starting the season over," Carson said. Robb Stauber struggled, though he made a sprawling save on Steve Yzerman's shorthanded breakaway in overtime to salvage the valuable point. "We gave up too many goals, but we played with a lot of emotion," Robitaille said.

The Kings would be playing without Taylor for a while. His neurologist told him to take off between two and four more weeks, or until the dizzy spells and vertigo disappeared. "He said I probably don't have a brain problem, but I probably have an inner-ear problem," Taylor said. Sandstrom, meanwhile, left for Sweden with his wife and 12-week-old son. He was going to be out for another month.

The next time David Goverde receives a telephone call from Los Angeles, he will be tempted to hang up. Displeased with Stauber's play in the Detroit game, management summoned Goverde from Phoenix and threw him in against the Washington Capitals. The youngster is still wondering where the rest of the Kings hid during his two periods of torture, which included seven second-period goals and an 8-3 deficit. Melrose showed more compassion than the Capitals or the fans did, pulling him as a "Hru-dey, Hru-dey" chant bounced around the Forum. Kelly Hrudey never knew he was so popular. Washington added two goals for a 10-3 rout that knocked the Kings a game under .500.

McSorley's suspension forced Melrose to use John McIntyre, who long ago had lost his job as fourth-line center to Pat Conacher. With McSorley out, Conacher was moved to wing. "John hasn't deserved to play," Melrose said. He thought McIntyre was lazy and too skinny to play the bang-and-crash game that was required for him to stay in the league. "He's told at the end of every season to come back in the fall at 185 or 190 pounds, and every fall he comes back at 170," Melrose complained. McIntyre insisted he tipped the scales at 190, but a reporter's suggestion for a weigh-off at center ice was rebuffed.

Another of the Kings' centers was "scared." Corey Millen's groin problem wasn't improving, he had missed 22 games, and he was playing out the option year of his contract. He tried every therapeutic procedure known to man, including acupuncture, and the injury didn't respond to any of them. "The pain is the same as it was a month ago," Millen said.

Still another center was "embarrassed." Gretzky hadn't scored a goal in 15 games now, the longest slump of his illustrious career. "I feel like I'm letting people down," he said. "I have an obligation to make a contribution and I haven't set the world on fire. It's frustrating because I'm not contributing the way I want to."

How the fortunes of a team can change so drastically from one game to the next will forever remain a mystery of sport. Everything came together February 15 in a 3-0 win over

Vancouver, a club that manhandled the Kings in the four previous meetings. Well, almost everything. Gretzky still couldn't buy a goal. But it never hurts when a goalie is sensational, and Hrudey outplayed Kirk McLean with a splendid 43-save performance that ranked as his best of the year. Kurri, Carson and Granato scored goals in a five-minute span of the third period as the Kings snapped a seven-game winless streak and moved back into third place.

"We don't want to talk about the last two months," Hrudey said. "We've been pelted by everybody with negative thoughts and we've also done it to ourselves. If you pelt yourself with negative thoughts, you're going to play bad."

An already weird year took another bizarre twist after the game when Beverley announced the Kings had signed Rick Knickle, a 32-year-old goalie and a veteran of 14 minor-league seasons, for the rest of the year. The move was hardly seen as a vote of confidence for Stauber. "Kelly showed today why he is our No. 1 goalie," Beverley said. "What goes on after that will be decided by the other guys." Goverde, sent back to Phoenix, wouldn't be one of them.

Knickle had put up some eye-popping numbers for the San Diego Gulls in the International League, a 33-4-4 record and a 2.17 goals-against average, but the Gulls were an independent team whose roster was generously sprinkled with older players, many with NHL experience. In return for Knickle, the Gulls would later receive defenseman Rene Chapdelaine on loan. Knickle would be paid $68,000 in salary, $500 for each win and $2,000 for a shutout. "This could be a Cinderella story, give you something to write about," Melrose said.

The Kings would spend the next 10 days on the road, visiting Minnesota, Chicago, Washington, Tampa Bay and St. Louis. Taylor was staying home, but he was relieved to find his inner ears were not the cause of his vertigo and dizziness. He and the doctors suspected a hit in the last Montreal game triggered the symptoms and that his brain stem needed more time to completely heal.

So now the Kings were off to Bloomington, Minnesota, perhaps for the final time. North Stars owner Norm Green wouldn't be moving the team to Anaheim, but he was fixing to transplant it in Dallas. For Minnesotans, the situation looked bleak. "Minnesota is hockey country and it's hard for me to imagine it without a team," said Stauber, who has a home in the Twin Cities area. "If the North Stars should go, it just wouldn't seem right to me."

Perhaps Gretzky sensed this would be his last Met Center appearance and felt obligated to put on a show for the crowd of 14,911. The Great One slipped back into Gretzky's uniform and proceeded to singlehandedly dismantle the North Stars, scoring his first goal in 17 games and adding four assists in the Kings' 10-5 win. Gretzky wore a big grin at 11:51 of the opening period when he redirected a Mike Donnelly pass between goalie Darcy Wakaluk's pads for his first goal since the two he collected January 8 in Winnipeg.

More impressive was the pass he made to Tony Granato at 8:57 of the second period. Gretzky was standing in the right corner and facing the boards when he took two strides, deked a defenseman, and slid the puck between several sticks and skates onto Granato's tape for a goal and a 5-2 lead. "If it's not on Wayne's stick, chances are it wouldn't have gotten to me," Granato said. He smiled and added, "But it was."

Gretzky had not produced more than two points in any of the 18 games he played since his return from his back injury. "I thought I played pretty well in the first seven or eight games, but maybe it was my emotion and excitement that carried me through," he said after the dam burst. "Maybe I wasn't in as good of physical condition as I thought. Maybe that caught up to me."

Norm Green, who was in Dallas while the Kings were tearing his team to shreds, received as much ink in the local newspapers the next morning as Gretzky. Wrote *St. Paul Pioneer Press* columnist Bob Sansevere: "The Greedy One spent the day in Dallas, hoping to weasel money out of that city and the folks who run Reunion Arena. The only hint of Green was his Rolls Royce, which was parked inside Met Center. The way folks around here feel about him, Green had better be extra careful when he turns his key in the ignition."

The Kings' first winning streak in over a month — two games — came crashing down in Chicago Stadium, where the Blackhawks finally defeated their West Coast tormentors and spoiled Knickle's NHL debut, 7-2. Knickle, who was still feeling the effects of a two-week-old bout with food poisoning, kept the

Kings in the game for two periods but finally wilted under Chicago's relentless pressure. The Hawks scored four goals in the third period and finished with 46 shots to the Kings' 27.

"The guy was stellar. If they had won the game, it would have been because of Knickle," said Chicago's Jeremy Roenick, who had two goals and two assists. The Kings didn't give Knickle, who was fighting dehydration, much support. They trailed 3-1 after 40 minutes despite a 33-15 disadvantage in shots. Knickle was more upset with his inability to shake his illness, which he blamed on a batch of bad chicken. "I tried to eat as much as I could in the afternoon and I had enough energy for two periods, then I ran out of gas," he said. "I could barely lift my stick on three of the goals."

Stauber was upset, but for different reasons. Now that the Kings were carrying three goalies, someone would have to sit in the press box. For now, he was the designated sitter. "Obviously, they're sending me a message," Stauber said. "It's definitely a message, but what it means for the duration of the season, I don't know. If Rick plays well, obviously there wouldn't be much time for me. I certainly hope I continue to get a chance. It's a bit confusing. I really can't try to read too much into anything."

Had the Kings been able to use all three goalies at the same time two days later at the Capital Centre, it's possible Washington would not have rolled to a 7-3 decision. The Caps scored on four consecutive shots in a 2 1-2 minute flurry near the end of the second period to expand their advantage to 6-0 and chase Hrudey. At least Stauber got to play, if only because Knickle was ill. "The guys panicked a little," Melrose said. "Thank goodness they didn't fall completely apart.

"I feel worse now because it's starting to sink in," Hrudey said. "At the time they're scoring, you don't think about it. You just try to keep your composure and stop the next one. You've got to try and stay calm when you're getting belted around."

The Kings had an inkling it was going to be a bad day when the bus that was supposed to take them to the game arrived at the wrong hotel. Several players used the hotel van and others grabbed taxis. Bruce McNall drove five players in his rental car.

More bad news: Gary Shuchuk's bruised right forearm wasn't bruised, the elbow was hyperextended and had a chip fracture. While the rest of the team prepared for its first regular-season trip to Florida, Shuchuk flew back to Los Angeles. He would miss the next four games.

Knickle earned a $500 bonus along with being named first star of the game by turning aside 43 Tampa Bay shots in a 5-2 win. His effort overshadowed a one-goal, three-assist night for Gretzky, coming as it did before an Expo Hall sellout crowd of 10,425 that included Knickle's parents, George and Janet. Knickle handed the puck commemorating his first NHL win to his father, and the two embraced.

"I'm so happy for myself and especially for him," Knickle said. "He's been so supportive of my career. He coached me when I was nine and 10 and taught me all the things you need to know at a young age. I looked over there and saw my mom and dad, and my father was doing cartwheels after the game. After all the years in the minor leagues, playing in every little town you can think of and all those bus rides, it was all worth it."

Melrose was right, Knickle's was a Cinderella story. Or Cinder*fella*. He spent more time in places like Muskegon, Erie, Flint, Saginaw, Peoria, and Albany than a Greyhound bus. He claimed his contract was sold from a team in Flint to one in Albany for $1 in 1990; four months later, pressed for cash, the Albany franchise folded. His first pro contract, in 1980, was worth $8,000. He went to Edmonton's training camp on a tryout basis in 1987 and was cut after a week. Knickle retired, but he couldn't resist the urge to head to Peoria five months later when the St. Louis Blues called.

"I really felt my game was ready for this level," he said. "Every day I feel more and more like I belong, that I can hold my own. But it's weird. I've always watched SportsCenter on ESPN, now I'm on it. But I'm not a savior. I didn't come here to step on anybody's toes."

The Kings jumped from the sand into the snow in St. Louis, where a raging blizzard dropped a foot of the white stuff and snarled traffic. Unfortunately for the Kings, roads leading to the St. Louis Arena were cleared in time for the game, a 3-0 win for the Blues. Knickle kept the Kings within striking distance, but they didn't force the masked man at the other end, Curtis Joseph, to make many difficult saves. The loss gave the Kings a split of the four-game trip, but sunk them a game under .500 again.

Make that two games under .500. An unflattering 5-2 Forum

loss to Toronto left the Kings 2-11-3 in their past 16 games at home and dropped their overall record to 27-29-7, the first time since January 22, 1992 they had slipped that far under .500. The only highlight was a first-period goal by Luc Robitaille, who reached the 40-goal plateau for the seventh consecutive year. Presumably, the goal wasn't mentioned during the 25-minute meeting that followed the game. "We just played bad, use whatever word you want," Gretzky said.

It wasn't necessary for Melrose to say anything at practice the next day, other than to inform his tattered troops that they wouldn't need to bring any sticks onto the ice. Nor would there be any pucks, a sure sign he was more than a bit perturbed. Skate, skate, skate. Take five, then skate some more. Seventy-minutes worth of wind sprints later, class was dismissed.

"We've got 21 games to find out how much work is going to be necessary to get the kind of team we want," Melrose said later. Nick Beverley already was on the prowl for a defenseman, now Melrose was adding a forward to the wish list, preferably a big one. Tomas Sandstrom had missed 37 of the past 41 games, and Corey Millen's non-playing streak was about to hit 30 games. Tony Granato was playing his heart out, as were a few others, but Melrose needed depth, and he couldn't expect to get much help from Phoenix; the cupboard there was bare.

"We've got to build a team that can win in the playoffs," he said. "I think our young defensemen have played very well. We've got guys there who are going to be around for the next 10 years. But we want some more guys who are 6-1, 6-2, big men who are good skaters. I knew all along we needed to get bigger, stronger, and more physical players for us to play the way I want over a full season. Our small guys give what they have, but even a hard-working guy like Granato can't be expected to check a big guy all night. Vancouver never puts Pavel Bure in a situation where he has to check a big man. I want smaller guys sprinkled in with big men, not the other way around."

All of the Kings men played big in a 6-2 wipeout of Calgary to open the month of March. It was possible the teams would meet in the playoffs, and the Kings had lost to the Flames in three of the previous four meetings. "It's time to send some messages," Melrose said. Knickle turned aside 33 shots in his Forum debut, Robitaille checked in with a hat trick, and Gretzky scored on two of his game-high eight shots.

There was little satisfaction gained in an 8-6 nail-biter over Ottawa that handed the sorrowful Senators their 33rd consecutive road loss, but nobody asked the Kings to give back the two points, and they weren't volunteering. Knickle didn't play well at all; three of Ottawa's goals handcuffed Knickle to the short side.

The most disappointed person in the Forum had to be Bob Kudelski, whose December 20 trade to Ottawa was about as one-sided as a deal can get. He had a goal and two assists against the Kings, giving him 19 goals and 28 points in 33 games as a Senator. The way Kudelski was playing, the locals might consider overlooking his U.S. citizenship and elect him to Parliament. "It's tough around here," Kudelski said. "It's hard knowing your chances of winning aren't that good. At least now we're in most of the games. We were getting blown out before."

Third place and riding a three-game winning streak, that summed up the situation after the Kings shelled Bill Ranford with 52 shots and pounded Edmonton, 6-1, a victory that increased their lead over the fifth-place Oilers to 13 points and moved them three points ahead of Winnipeg. Gretzky and Kurri, whose places in Edmonton history are secure, poked holes in the Oilers' postseason hopes by combining for two goals and three assists. Knickle was more than adequate and registered his third win in a row.

"Hopefully," Tony Granato said, "they're behind us for good." The Kings, whose lives were made miserable by last year's first-round playoff exit, were 4-1-1 against the Oilers, who were in danger of missing postseason play for the first time in their storied history. "They're not out of it, but no question this was a huge win," Kurri said. "They made it hard for us last year. It always feels good to beat them."

Lonnie Loach was in a pretty good mood, too. He had just been recalled from Phoenix, where he played in a 7-2 win over Salt Lake City. Loach spent four years in the minors before the Kings rescued him from the Ottawa organization and he had absolutely no desire to go back. According to Loach, Beverley told him, "You're going to Phoenix and there's a return flight Thursday. If you don't play well, you won't be on it." Loach promptly delivered a goal and two assists.

The Kings were hitting the road again, only this time it would be in style. When Bruce McNall decided it was time to take his luxury plane out of mothballs and permit the team to use it for the stretch run, Melrose didn't object. The Kings were going to play nine of the next 12 games on the road, including four on an East Coast swing through New York, Pittsburgh, Philadelphia and Buffalo. "I think the guys realize now that it's a luxury and not a right," Melrose said.

Lucky Kings. Brian Leetch, who arguably is the league's best defenseman, returned a week early after missing 34 games with a stretched nerve in his neck and shoulder. All Leetch did was give the Madison Square Garden crowd of 18,200 reason to be more rowdy than usual and spark the Rangers to a 4-3, come-from-behind win. After referee Ron Hoggarth gave Carson a questionable tripping penalty with 6 1/2 minutes to play in a 3-3 game, Leetch played quarterback on the power play and set up Mike Gartner's winning goal. The Kings expended a lot of energy complaining about Hoggarth's call, but he wasn't responsible for their blowing a 2-0 lead.

The Kings paid a price for taking another bad penalty March 11 in a bitter 4-3 overtime loss in Pittsburgh, where Mario Lemieux, his cancer in remission, played his fourth game since completing radiation treatments. Super Mario stuck his nose into every Penguins' scoring play, contributing a goal and three assists to the cause. The outcome was decided at 3:18 of the extra period on Jaromir Jagr's goal after Tony Granato went to the penalty box for slashing Ulf Samuelsson in front of the Pittsburgh net.

"This is two games in a row we've played hard, played good enough to come out with two points or at least one and we haven't come out with any," said Gretzky, whose goal and assist stretched his point-scoring streak to five games. Stauber, playing in place of the flu-ridden Hrudey, made 16 of his 31 saves in the first period when Pittsburgh threatened to blow the Kings away, but his first start in a month was wasted.

The Kings were happy for Lemieux, though. Two months earlier, the 27-year-old megastar was diagnosed as having Hodgkin's disease. Now, despite 22 radiation treatments that should have sapped his strength, Lemieux looked as strong and frightening as ever. "You realize there are a lot of other things in life besides hockey, things that are more important," Luc Robitaille said. "I can only imagine what he was thinking when they told him he had cancer, but I do know that he appreciates playing more than he did before."

Edgar Allan Poe could not have dreamed up a more cruel fate than the one that befell the Kings in Philadelphia. Dave Schultz and Moose Dupont never wreaked as much havoc as the mighty blizzard that battered the East Coast, created snowdrifts six feet deep, and disrupted life in and out of the sports world. The Kings' March 13 game with the Flyers at the Spectrum fell victim to the storm when powerful winds blew out a large window on the concourse level during the first period, spraying glass onto the lower seating area in a corner of the building and forcing ushers to direct fans to other seats.

"I heard a big bang," said Charlie Huddy, who was sitting on the bench when the window went. "I turned around and I saw people scrambling. You could hear glass hitting the (outside of the) boards. It was pretty scary."

About 2,000 fans braved treacherous travel conditions to get to the Spectrum, which was barely visible from the parking lot, and only one person was reported to have been injured by the shards of glass; a woman working at a concession stand suffered a cut hand while attempting to protect her face. The period ended in a 1-1 tie as workmen stood in an elevated bucket and tried to patch the empty window frame with wood, but they gave up when the bucket began to sway in the howling wind. Building officials, concerned more windows could go, postponed the game.

Fans responded to the news by hurling cups of beer, hot chocolate and soft drinks onto the ice. They were in a festive mood earlier, when a "Jingle Bells" tape blared over the public-address system.

"If this happened in the minors," Warren Rychel joked, "they'd fix the hole with cardboard and duct tape and finish the game." Goalie Rick Knickle said, "This'll be chapter 14 in my book." Melrose said he'd seen some bizarre scenes in the minors, "but never anything like this."

The broken window wasn't the only problem. Water was dripping from a hole in the roof onto the ice, creating a soft spot near one of the blue lines. Workmen sprayed chemicals on the ice before and after the period, and the entire ice surface eventually was covered. "We were shocked when they told us the game was off," Wayne Gretzky said. "This is pretty wild."

The bus ride back to the hotel would have required an "E" ticket at Disneyland in the old days, but even more horror was in store the next morning after the Kings were informed they were to fly to balmy Buffalo and play that night, league and team officials having deemed it ludicrous to attempt to play in the afternoon as scheduled.

Problem was, after hitching a ride on a bus chartered by the Denver Nuggets, whose basketball game was postponed, and picking up referee Don Koharski, who was going to work the Buffalo game, the Kings' plane couldn't get off the ground. More specifically, pilot Winston Trantor was waiting for snowplow operators to clear a path from a private terminal to the main runway at Philadelphia International Airport. The wait lasted five hours.

Annoyance turned to anger at 12:35 p.m., five minutes after Air McNall was boarded, when players and staff were informed that the Buffalo game was going to be played the following day, a Monday, at 5:30 p.m. Weren't the folks who were making these decisions aware that the Kings were scheduled to play division rival Winnipeg at the Forum on Tuesday? The Kings put the distance between Buffalo and Los Angeles at, oh, roughly 2,200 miles. Nice trip. All they'd have to do to regain third place in the Smythe Division, assuming a snowplow would appear before the spring thaw, was defeat the Sabres and then, within 24 hours, fly clear across the country and take down the Jets.

This disturbing piece of news was relayed by Nick Beverley, who had been on a scouting trip and gotten to Buffalo before the worst storm in decades unleashed its full fury. Buffalo Memorial Auditorium workers, it seemed, had been told to stay off the potentially-slick roads and therefore would not be setting up the hockey rink until Monday. Unless the Kings and Sabres were willing to decide matters on the indoor lacrosse field that was covering the building's floor, they would have to wait until Monday. The Flyers game, Beverley informed the team, would be replayed in its entirety April 1, turning a five-game trip into a six-game marathon.

Melrose was clearly annoyed. "If we didn't have our own

jet," he sniffed, "we wouldn't be doing this." The players were outraged, but none was more outspoken than captain Wayne Gretzky, who usually does anything and everything to avoid controversy.

"This is crazy, we're getting shafted. This is absolutely asinine," Gretzky said as the film "Goodfellas" began to play on the aircraft's TV monitors. "This is yet another situation where the players have no say." Then Gretzky proceeded to rip the Kings organization. "We never take a stand. We're always the nice guys. We're always the ones in the end who bend over backward to help out the league," he said. "This organization is always too accommodating. We're too nice and we get pushed around. We've got the hardest schedule and the league should be catering to us. Instead, we give in on everything."

Workers began to de-ice the plane's wings at 3:20, but there wasn't a snowplow in sight. After 25 minutes passed, Cap Raeder took a poll. "Do you want to watch 'Saturday Night Live' or 'Silence of the Lambs?' " he asked his captive audience, many of whom were fast asleep. Several card games had broken out. The movie won. Rick Minch, the team's director of media relations, considered asking Gretzky to autograph a stick to be used as a bribe for a snowplow operator but decided against it.

Finally, around 5:15, the snow was cleared and the wings de-iced again. Air McNall was actually airborne by 5:40 for the 50-minute flight to western New York, and the bus transporting the team from Buffalo's airport to downtown pulled into the hotel at 7:10. The 7-hour, 25-minute ordeal was over.

Not unexpectedly, Beverley was not pleased to hear about all of the grumbling that took place on the plane. And he was particularly miffed about Gretzky's charge that the organization caved in to league demands rather than looked after its own best interests. "I don't think having that attitude is putting any kind of positive light on the situation. Just go and do the job," Beverley said. "He can say what he wants, but the league did everything possible to find the best solution. We could refuse to do this and the league could mandate us to play, but it didn't happen that way. Everyone cooperated."

Beverley said he conferred with NHL president Gil Stein, Buffalo general manager Gerry Meehan, Kings president Roy Mlakar and the league's scheduling coordinator, Phil Scheuer.

Beverley pointed out that several other teams were affected by the storm, and that Toronto's April 1 game with Philadelphia was moved to another date to allow the Kings and Flyers to make up their game that night.

"We were looking at alternatives, but there were just so many conflicts," Beverley said. "The importance of (the Winnipeg game) was not lost on anyone, but sometimes you have to do things you don't want to do. I will make certain that all of the players are apprised completely because we certainly wouldn't want to offend any of their sensitivities."

The sarcastic nature of that last remark was not in keeping with Beverley's usual manner of communicating with the press. Beverley is a pleasant enough fellow, downright engaging at times, but he chooses his words carefully and rarely lets his guard down. Beverley would never comment as he did unless he was especially peeved.

When the Kings are involved, expect the unexpected. They played a near-perfect game, captured a 4-2 decision from the Sabres, and then hurried to a waiting bus to be whisked to the airport for the five-hour flight home. The Kings were expected to get there around midnight, Pacific time. "We talked about the situation before the game," Gretzky said. "Everyone was expecting us to lose both of these games and we want to do the opposite. Mentally, maybe we were the toughest we've been all year. We just didn't want to lose."

Gretzky wouldn't let them. He set up Luc Robitaille and Rob Blake for goals and a 3-0 lead in the second period and put Buffalo away with a shorthanded, empty-net goal in the last minute. Robb Stauber was exceptional in goal, with 11 of his 30 saves coming against Buffalo gunners Pat LaFontaine and Alexander Mogilny. "It's us against everyone else," Melrose said. "When everyone else is trying to shaft you, you've got to channel your aggressions into performance on the ice."

Robitaille's goal was his 11th in seven games and 50th of the season, just three shy of his career high. "It was a stupid trip that didn't make any sense," he said. "We still don't think that it was right that we had to play tonight, but there's no more anger. Barry told us before the game to put it behind us." Funny guy, this Melrose.

The only people feeling the effects of jet leg the next night at the Forum were Winnipeggers. Or so it seemed. Robitaille supplied two more goals, Gretzky a goal and two assists, and Tony Granato chipped in a key shorthanded goal to pump life into weary bones in the Kings' surprisingly easy 8-4 win that expanded their hold on third place to three points. Maybe the Kings ought to spend more time in cramped quarters. "Don't give 'em any ideas," Gretzky said.

Darryl Sydor couldn't play because of a sore shoulder and Rick Knickle had to leave after two periods when he came down with stomach cramps — save to Kelly Hrudey — but the emotional win, coupled with Dave Taylor's first appearance in 17 games, made for an uplifting evening. Then it was off to dreamland.

"Now I'm thinking of using buses, keeping these guys grounded for as long as possible," McNall said with a smirk. He shrugged when asked to comment on Gretzky's inflammatory remarks in Philadelphia. "Well, he's the captain and he has to stick up for the players. But if he had been a part of all the phone calls that were made, he would have seen that everything that could have been done was done. Wayne's always had the feeling that the Kings are low men on the totem pole, sort of the forgotten stepchild in the backyard."

The Kings didn't play nearly as well when they beat the Islanders, 7-4, for their third consecutive victory and sixth in eight games. They were outshot, 46-21, and needed third-period goals by Alexei Zhitnik, Gretzky and Robitaille to snap a 4-4 tie. Jimmy Carson scored twice and Charlie Huddy tied a career high for points in a game with a goal and three assists. Marty McSorley picked up 12 minutes in penalties, hiking his 68-game total to 364 to break Dave "Tiger" Williams' club record of 358 penalty minutes in 1986-87.

Strangely, Kelly Hrudey was gone before reporters arrived in the dressing room after the game. It wasn't unusual for the room to be deserted—especially after a loss—but Hrudey never bailed out on the writers; if anything, it annoyed him when other players did it. He had played extremely well and probably won the game for the Kings. In fact, it was his first win since February 17, his first start since February 27.

The next day, three days before the March 22 trading deadline, Hrudey sat at his locker after practice and said he would no longer be granting interviews. "I've been doing this for 10 years and I just think it's time to give it a rest," he said. "I just want to get away from it. I'm not trying to make your job harder, I just need some time. Do me a favor and tell the other writers."

When asked if he was worried about the trading deadline, Hrudey responded, "Wouldn't you be?" Maybe. But after Hrudey left, Melrose said he was happy with all three goalies and planned to keep them for the rest of the year, playoffs included. "They've all put a claim to (the No. 1 position) and it's made it tough for us to pick one guy and go with him, but that's better than having them all be bad," he said.

When Tomas Sandstrom is in the lineup, the odds that the Kings will win increase immeasurably. Naturally, the chances that he will break a body part — or, in the case of Doug Gilmour, have one broken for him — also rise, but the Kings were willing to take the risk. Their three-year record with Sandstrom on the ice improved to 82-42-17 after he returned and scored a goal in a 3-2 win over St. Louis.

Sandstrom now had 19 goals and 39 points in 27 games, a 59-goal, 121-point pace over a full season, which is something he likely will never see. He already had missed 45 games, 21 with the fractured jaw, and he hadn't played in two consecutive games since November. Still, getting Sandstrom back enabled the Kings to improve themselves without having to pull the trigger on a major deal. "It's a bonus," Gretzky said. Sandstrom's wires were removed a week earlier, and he spent three hours in the dentist's chair to undergo four root canals the day before. "I felt strong. I just wanted to get back as soon as possible," he said.

John McIntyre wanted to get out of town as quickly as possible on March 22 after Nick Beverley dispatched him to the New York Rangers in exchange for Mark Hardy, who defined experience in a defenseman. Hardy, 34, was a second-round draft pick of the Kings in 1979 who spent parts of nine seasons in Los Angeles before he was traded to New York for Ron Duguay in 1988. Duguay's flowing locks, which he refused to hide under a helmet, were the most famous in hockey. But Hardy wasn't called "Harpo" for nothing earlier in his career, though even he had to admit the nickname was hardly appropriate now.

McIntyre had been in Melrose's doghouse for weeks. Only 23, he lost his job to a man 10 years his elder, Pat Conacher, and was deemed even more expendable when the Kings announced

Coach Barry Melrose showed he could get his players' attention and keep it.

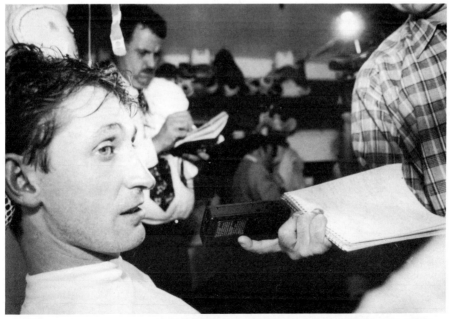

Captain Wayne Gretzky had to spend as much time with the media as he did on the ice.

Art Foxell/Bernstein Assoc. Inc.

Feisty Tony Granato scored 37 goals and registered a career-high 82 points.

Dave Taylor remained a valuable asset in his 16th season with the Kings.

Art Foxell/Bernstein Assoc. Inc.

Defenseman Alexei Zhitnik led all Kings rookies in goals (12), assists (36) and points (48).

Kings goaltender Kelly Hrudey, who started the last 17 playoff games, made a big save on Toronto's Wendel Clark in the Campbell Conference final.

Jari Kurri, an effective two-way forward, drew double coverage against the Maple Leafs.

Luc Robitaille's uncanny shooting touch around the net resulted in 63 goals, an NHL record for left wingers.

For the first time in franchise history, Los Angeles hockey fans had reason to celebrate.

It was a banner year for the Kings and their long-suffering fans.

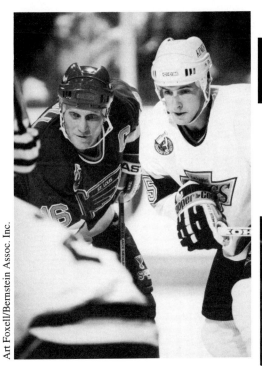

Rookie defenseman Darryl Sydor kept stars like St. Louis' Brett Hull covered all year.

Tony Granato doesn't mind sticking his slight frame in the slot, daring wide-bodied defensemen to drive him out.

When he is healthy, Tomas Sandstrom is one of the NHL's very best power forwards.

Defenseman Rob Blake was at his best in the playoffs, protecting the front of the net for goaltender Kelly Hrudey.

Defenders have to keep close tabs on Luc Robitaille, who has been a perennial NHL All-Star since he joined the league in 1986-87.

Stanley Cup playoff fever was contagious at the Forum.

Captain Wayne Gretzky and the Clarence Campbell bowl were the centers of attention after the Kings advanced to the Stanley Cup finals. That's team owner Bruce McNall on the right.

Kings players and staff members exult in their dressing room following the presentation of the Clarence Campbell bowl.

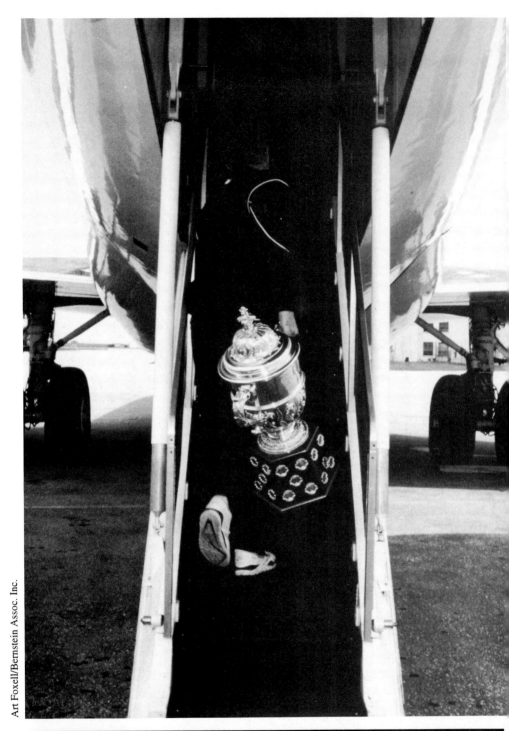

Fragile, handle with care. The Clarence Campbell bowl is hauled onto the Kings' private plane in Toronto for the flight to Montreal and the Stanley Cup finals.

that Corey Millen was ready to play, giving them five centers. "I kept going further and further down the totem pole," McIntyre said, "but I'm not the type to get upset and storm into someone's office. I want to play, but you can go crazy trying to figure out why you aren't."

Beverley wasn't about to criticize McIntyre, other than to say his play remained "static" from the previous year and "we were looking for improvement." Beverley said a deal to acquire a forward fell through, but he didn't sound overly concerned about it.

Hardy was so ecstatic about the deal that he didn't even mind the prospect of selling the home he had just built in a New York City suburb. "But I was hoping the Rangers would trade for a guy who might want to buy it," he said. Hardy, who wore Nos. 20, 25 and 5 during his purple-and-gold days with the Kings, planned to wear No. 24 in his second stint. "All my other numbers are taken, and I figured I'd better get this one before they retire it," he said with a laugh. Jay Wells, Hardy's one-time defensive partner with the Kings, wore those digits while accumulating 34 goals and 1,446 penalty minutes in 604 games.

Hardy wouldn't be in Vancouver when the Kings opened their marathon six-game trip. He was given permission to take care of personal business and join the team in Edmonton. Air McNall wouldn't be around at all, not until the playoffs, because of engine problems. But Millen, who was beginning to make Sandstrom seem like a cover-boy candidate for a health magazine, said he would play after missing 38 games with his groin strain. Heck, Gretzky only missed 39 games with a herniated thoracic disk.

"It's still a little sore, but I'm at the point where I've got to try it, see how it reacts in a game situation," Millen said, sounding nervous. "I need these last 12 games to get ready for the playoffs," he said. "Either I get going again or I've got to call it a year." Things had changed since Millen last played. The Kings were on a four-game winning streak, their longest since November, but they were 14-21-3 without Millen and fell from first place in the Smythe Division to third.

Except for horrific goaltending by Rick Knickle and inept play by the special teams, the Kings looked absolutely brilliant in an embarrassing 6-2 defeat to the Canucks, who lost their previous four games and needed a confidence boost. Vancouver scored four goals on its first 10 shots and knocked out Knickle at 13:47 of the opening period. Two of the Canucks' goals came on power plays and they killed all seven of the Kings' man advantages. Even Robitaille, who had a 10-game goal-scoring streak, couldn't put a puck past Kirk McLean.

The game, a rough one from the very beginning, got out of hand in the third period. Vancouver enforcer Gino Odjick slashed Tim Watters and was handed a major penalty and game misconduct with 19 seconds to go. "They must be from L.A. because they know how to act," Odjick said. "Those guys were dropping like dead fish all night, any time a stick went near their heads." Maybe somebody ought to remind Odjick that sticks aren't supposed to be carried anywhere near a player's head.

The evening wasn't completely wasted. Millen drew an assist and showed no ill-effects of his injury or layoff, Sandstrom was still in one piece, and Kelly Hrudey looked a lot better while relieving Knickle than he did the next morning.

Hrudey was ill as he boarded the team's commercial flight to Edmonton, where a Kings victory could clinch a playoff berth and eliminate the Oilers. Hrudey's stomach was killing him. "Looks green. I know how he's feeling because I've been there," Knickle said. Suspecting food poisoning, the Kings checked Hrudey into University Hospital when they arrived in Edmonton. He was found to have an intestinal virus and felt fairly comfortable once fluids were administered, but Stauber would have to start in his place against the Oilers.

Vengeance was sweet at the Northlands Coliseum, where 11 months earlier a 3-0 loss in Game 6 of the Smythe Division final put the Kings out of the playoffs and ultimately landed coach Tom Webster on the unemployment line. Sandstrom scored two goals, Stauber made 34 saves, and the Kings pocketed a 4-1 win before a silent sellout crowd of 17,503. The Kings were in and the Oilers were out.

"We're the team that was supposed to be out and now we've put them out. It's nice," Barry Melrose said. "It's nice not to have to deal with them anymore." Former Oilers like Wayne Gretzky and Marty McSorley rejoiced inside as they considered the lucrative playoff payoff Edmonton owner Peter Pocklington wasn't going to bank, but neither gloated on the outside. "I gave up those feelings long ago," McSorley said. "This is my fifth year in L.A., and I refuse to get all caught up in that stuff." Gretzky said, "They've given us fits. I'm glad we won't have to face them, that's all."

Some players expended more energy belittling memos that were recently sent by Nick Beverley, who praised the team for playing well, but expressed displeasure over its reaction to the schedule revisions that were made following the East Coast blizzard. At least one player, as delighted teammates watched, deposited his copy of the memo into a trash can without even reading it.

Hrudey's self-imposed gag order remained in effect, but he didn't mind discussing his health on the flight to Winnipeg. "I think the virus is probably what I had in Pittsburgh," he said. "I just don't think I ever got completely rid of it. But I feel a lot better now." Regardless, Stauber would start against the Jets and Knickle would be the backup.

Stauber's "mental" makeup impressed Melrose, a positive sign considering the goalie didn't start for a month until Hrudey became ill in Pittsburgh. He'd won three games in a row since then and allowed only five goals. "He's handled his situation very well," Melrose said. "Certainly his on-ice skills have never been questioned."

Melrose strongly suggested he had doubts about Luc Robitaille's commitment to the team after the Kings blew yet another two-goal lead in Winnipeg, turning a 3-1 game with nine minutes to play into a 3-3 tie. It was the Kings' final visit to Manitoba, and, considering what the Jets did to them there all season, they were eternally grateful to be getting out for good. Unless, God forbid, the clubs met in the playoffs.

Barely five seconds after Melrose addressed the team behind closed doors, he walked past reporters standing in a hallway and stormed into the room that passed for his office. His face was red, his hands clenched and his head bowed. Robitaille, still wearing skates, followed right behind. The door was slammed shut, but Melrose and Robitaille huffed, puffed and nearly blew it down during an obscenity-filled argument that lasted perhaps 20 seconds. "You're selfish!" Melrose bellowed. "Am not!" Robitaille screeched. "Yes, you are!" Melrose bellowed. "No, I'm not!" Robitaille screeched. The exchange reminded no one of the Lincoln-Douglas debate.

Melrose was angry that the Kings permitted Jets rookie sensation Teemu Selanne to break loose in the third period. Selanne scored two goals and picked up an assist when Alexei Zhamnov tied the game with five seconds remaining. Melrose was upset at Robitaille for failing to pick up a line change and getting caught up ice when Zhamnov scored. The way Melrose saw it, Robitaille was more interested in trying to score an empty-net goal—Winnipeg's Bob Essensa was lifted for an extra skater—than doing what it took to preserve the 3-2 lead.

Not that Melrose was going to admit to any of this, mind you. "The press is big on blaming people, but I'm not a big blamer," he said. "We were talking about a fishing spot up in northern Quebec. We were talking about whether it's best to use 10-pound test line or 15-pound test line, that's all. This is not a big deal."

Robitaille wouldn't discuss the incident. He sat in the trainer's room with an ice pack on his shoulder for a while, then he dressed away from his cubicle and hurried out. Apparently, none of the other players were aware Melrose and Robitaille had argued. "Barry went around and shook everybody's hand, like he always does after a win or a tie," Rob Blake said. "That's all I saw."

Melrose and Robitaille can be stubborn, but they were smart enough not to allow the situation to fester, and patched up their differences at the morning skate the next day in Detroit. "Unfortunately, you (reporters) were listening (to the argument)," Melrose said. "We're both fiery individuals. When two things that are alike meet, there's a reaction. Lucky's fiery, I have no problem with that. I'm fiery, too. I challenge my players, I don't have robots. But after it's done, it's all forgotten. It's not a personal thing."

Robitaille explained to Melrose that he erred in judging how much time remained after Gretzky dumped the puck into the Winnipeg zone and headed for the bench on a line change. "I went to force the play and when I looked back, I was alone on the ice," Robitaille said. "I didn't think there was enough time for them to bring the puck back into our zone. But when I looked up at the clock, there were still 29 seconds left and I was stuck. Everything's cool. I know what I did and we had a good talk."

The Kings did more than talk after entering Joe Louis Arena, where the usual standing room-only crowd of 19,875 came to see the beloved Red Wings run their winning streak to six games and take over first place in the Norris Division. But Gretzky and Jimmy Carson each delivered a pair of goals and the Kings buried Detroit, 9-3. They chased goalie Tim Cheveldae after one period and converted six of 12 shots against Vincent Riendeau in the third period, which was more than enough to offset Rick Knickle's so-so performance in the crease.

"The Winnipeg game was a tough one to take because we played so well and let a point slip away," said Gretzky, whose four points boosted his season total to 59 in 37 games. "We're happy with the way we're playing. It's all coming together at the right time. Teams that play well heading into the playoffs usually do well in the playoffs."

And maybe, just maybe, Carson was about to go on an offensive tear that would carry into those playoffs. His goals in Detroit were only his 10th and 11th in the 26 games the Kings had played since his acquisition. He had not scored a goal in 18 of them. "Of course I want to score, that's why they got me," he said. "But I'm not going to start cheating (defensively) looking for goals. The team is winning and you can't sacrifice other parts of your game trying to score goals."

Whatever happened after this soap opera of a season ended, the Kings knew for certain that beginning in 1993-94 they never again could be called Smythe Division failures. The Smythe Division, as well as the Norris, Patrick, and Adams, were going to be kaput in 1993-94. On April Fool's Day, after the Kings arrived in Toronto, NHL commissioner Gary Bettman announced that the Board of Governors unanimously approved the league's first major realignment in 12 years.

Geographical names would be used for the conferences and divisions, and the Stanley Cup playoff system would be based on conference play. The Smythe Division would become the Pacific and include the Kings, Mighty Ducks of Anaheim, Calgary, Edmonton, San Jose and Vancouver. Winnipeg would move to the Central Division (nee Norris) with Chicago, Dallas (farewell Minnesota), Detroit, St. Louis, and Toronto. The top eight teams in the conference, whose name would be changed from Campbell to Western, would qualify for the playoffs, with each division champion guaranteed a No. 1 or a No. 2 seed.

The Eastern Conference (nee Wales) would include the Atlantic and Northeast Divisions, replacing the Patrick and Adams.

Florida, New Jersey, the New York Islanders and Rangers, Philadelphia, Tampa Bay and Washington would play in the Atlantic. Pittsburgh would join Boston, Buffalo, Hartford, Montreal, Ottawa and Quebec in the Northeast.

"It will be easier for casual fans to follow, and it will create more interest for more teams," Bettman said. The Kings had no problems with the name changes and weren't about to plead that Winnipeg be retained in their division. "Yeah," Melrose said, "but we're still going to have to play them four times." But only twice in Winnipeg.

As if four games with the Maple Leafs and Doug Gilmour weren't too many? The Kings had lost two prior meetings heading into Maple Leaf Gardens, and lost Sandstrom to a broken arm in the only engagement they managed to win. So even a 5-5 tie on a muggy night in which Toronto's Nikolai Borschevsky scored in the last 5 1-2 minutes was acceptable to the Kings. They were dead tired, 2-1-2 on the trip with just one game remaining, and on a 6-1-2 roll that was reminiscent of the good old days of October and November.

Even better, the Kings had seen the last of the Leafs. Good riddance.

It was downright balmy, not a single snowflake in sight, when the Kings' charter arrived in Philadelphia. Rain and fog had delayed their Toronto departure for an hour, but to the Kings this was a minor annoyance compared to what they'd been through recently. But couldn't the hotel rooms have been ready?

In the end, none of these things mattered because the Kings were quite ready when the puck was dropped inside the nicely-repaired Spectrum. They spotted the Flyers a 1-0 lead on Mark Recchi's 50th goal of the season and roared back for a convincing 3-1 victory. Robitaille, Blake, and Darryl Sydor responded with goals for the Kings, Gretzky added two assists and Hrudey, playing for the first time since he took ill, made 27 saves.

"All in all, I think we're satisfied," said Pat Conacher, whose magic act consisted of making Eric Lindros invisible and helping to kill off all six of the Flyers' power plays. "A lot of people were counting us out, especially after we got smoked in Vancouver. But we muscled up, played hard, and made a good trip out of it."

Better than good. The Kings went 3-1-2 despite playing six games in nine nights, crossing the U.S.-Canadian border four times and flying 6,130 miles. They had closed to within three points of second-place Calgary and would play four of their remaining six games at the Forum.

"In all my years in the NHL, this was the hardest trip I've ever been on," Gretzky said. "We went from one coast to the other and played in some tough buildings each night. We played with a lot of heart."

If nothing else, the Kings would be primed for the playoff grind.

Splat! So much for catching Calgary. A dreadful 3-0 loss to Minnesota, coupled with the Flames' overtime win over San Jose, widened the deficit to five points. The important thing now was to hang onto their two-point lead over fourth-place Winnipeg and avoid a first-round playoff encounter with Vancouver.

The Kings could have skated on molasses for all the excitement they generated against a North Stars team that had gone 0-8-1 since owner Norm Green announced he was going to desert Minnesota for Texas. Green didn't have long to enjoy the rare win; a disgruntled fan poured a beer on him after the game.

As a concession to tacking the Flyers makeup game onto the end of their just-completed trip, the Kings met Minnesota at night instead of in the afternoon, but the extra rest was worthless. The weary Kings were a step behind from the start, took 10 penalties that resulted in North Stars power plays and could only kill eight of them off. "There comes a time when you can't get any more out of a team. We didn't have anything left to give," Melrose said. "It's like having four mules stuck in the mud. You can whip them forever, but you still can't get them out of the mud."

Losing the game was bad enough. Blake hurt his lower back in the first period when he rammed into a goal post after being hooked to the ice by Brad Berry and couldn't return. Robitaille took the penalty shot referee Ron Hoggarth awarded Blake, but Jon Casey made the save. Casey also was sharp in the third period when the Kings showed some spark and outshot Minnesota, 14-2.

"We worked our tails off to get this close, but we didn't play too smart," Tony Granato said. "Obviously we would like to finish as high in the standings as possible, but we want to make sure we're playing our best hockey going into the playoffs. We still have some momentum and we want to keep it."

Some more of that momentum was chipped away by the Flames, who left the Forum with a 3-3 tie and virtually ensured the Kings would finish no higher than third. The gap was seven points now, and only four games remained. The Kings made the mistake of sitting on a 2-1 lead in the second period, forgetting that three periods of hockey were still required. They needed a goal by Robitaille, his second of the game, with 88 seconds to go in regulation to avoid another come-from-ahead defeat.

Robitaille was having a truly remarkable season, threatening to become the highest scoring left winger in NHL history. His 59 goals were one short of the record set by Montreal's Steve Shutt in 1976-77 and his 115 points were eight shy of the record Pittsburgh's Kevin Stevens set in 1991-92. Sure, the expanded schedule meant Robitaille would play in four more games than the 80 Shutt and Stevens dressed for during their record seasons, but he didn't care. "If I get the records," he said, "I'm still going to enjoy them."

Blake's sore back prevented him from playing April 8 when the Sharks visited town and the Kings were toying with the idea of keeping him on the sidelines until the playoffs. Blake was having a career year with 16 goals and 59 points, and he was punishing people with bruising body checks, but it didn't make much sense to risk a more serious injury with the real season fast approaching.

Arturs Irbe, as had become his custom, made life miserable for the Kings once the game started, but neither they nor Robitaille were going to be denied. Forty-four shots and two Robitaille goals later, the Kings had a 2-1 win that kept their three-point lead over Winnipeg intact and Robitaille had himself an NHL record.

Both goals came in the third period, giving the Kings their second win in 32 attempts when trailing after 40 minutes. Robitaille tied Shutt and the game 6:57 in after San Jose's David Williams was given a major penalty for cutting Granato with a high stick. Irbe went down to stop Alexei Zhitnik's point shot and Granato's stab at the rebound, but Robitaille drove to the net and lifted the puck over the goalie's left arm for his 60th goal. Number 61 came with 4:21 left when Robitaille corraled the rebound of a Gretzky shot and shoved it into the net as he was being dragged to the ice.

"It means a lot to me," Robitaille said. The win and the record. Robitaille's favorite Canadiens player had been Yvan Cournoyer, but he also took a shining to Shutt, a Toronto native who stuck out like a Maple Leaf on a eucalyptus tree during the Montreal days of the Flying Frenchmen. "My dad didn't like him, but I was always there to defend him," Robitaille said. "He was a pure sniper, he had such a quick release. But every time his name came up, my dad and I would have these big arguments.

"Personally, I always followed the centers. Maybe because it's the glamour position. When I came into the league, the only high scoring left winger was Michel Goulet. A lot of guys with lefthanded shots switch to center, but it seems like there are a few more of us now. I played center until I was 16, then the coach moved me. He said it was my only chance to make the team. I played on the fourth line."

The Irbe show continued at the Cow Palace two nights later, but again he cracked late and the Kings escaped with a 3-2 overtime win. Gretzky purposely banked the puck off the side of the net to Sandstrom, who danced through the goalmouth and scored on a backhanded shot at 3:22 of the extra period. Stauber, making a bid to start the playoff opener, made 29 saves.

Sandstrom's first goal in seven games came on the Kings' 49th shot and will live in history as the final regular-season goal ever produced at the 58-year-old building. Many in the sellout crowd of 11,089 wore souvenir T-shirts depicting crying cows bidding farewell to the Sharks, who in 1993-94 moved from the Daly City rink near San Francisco to a brand-new building in San Jose.

Finally, the Kings' playoff fate was decided on April 13, in the 83rd game of an 84-game season. The Kings were in Vancouver, down by a goal early in the first period, when it was announced to the Pacific Coliseum crowd that Winnipeg had lost to Tampa Bay. The Kings had clinched third place and would open the postseason against Calgary in five days. Perhaps it was coincidence, but the Kings immediately gave up four goals in an 89-second span en route to a 7-4 loss that so stunned Kelly Hrudey he might have started talking. If he had remembered how to talk.

"We were horrendous for 10 minutes," Melrose said. "At this stage of the game, the outcome doesn't mean much, but I've already taken three aspirin because I've got a massive headache." It might have turned into a migraine if the Kings had to play the

Canucks instead of the Flames. The Kings were 0-4 in Vancouver and 2-6 against the Canucks with one meeting remaining; the record against the Flames was 3-3-1 overall, 1-2 at the Olympic Saddledome.

"Nobody really talked about it, but we all sort of thought we'd be playing Calgary," Robitaille said. "They're a big team and it'll definitely be a physical series." Game 1 of the best-of-seven series would be played a day early, on a Sunday afternoon, to accommodate ABC-TV. Then the Kings would spend two days practicing in the Canadian Rockies resort of Banff, Alberta, despite Melrose's claim that he is "a gulag guy, not a resort guy." The Kings stayed in Banff, a 75-minute drive from Calgary when the roads are clear, when they upset the Flames in the opening round in 1990.

Kings owner Bruce McNall presented Robitaille with the Bill Libby Memorial Award as the team's most valuable player during ceremonies before the April 15 season finale with Vancouver. Robitaille responded by scoring his 63rd goal in the first period and he added three assists to finish the year with 125 points, breaking Stevens' record for points by a left winger. Gretzky scored his 16th goal and contributed two assists and finished with 65 points in 45 games.

But the Kings still lost, 8-6, and Stauber probably let his final chance to start the playoff opener in Calgary slip between his legs, just as pucks did on consecutive shots 11 seconds apart in the third period, when the Canucks scored five times to erase a 5-3 deficit. Stauber had gone 4-1-2 with a 2.49 goals-against average in his seven previous starts, but he never looked comfortable against Vancouver, which left five regulars back home in British Columbia, and was replaced by Hrudey with 8:33 to go.

"Robb was struggling and he looked unsure of himself," Melrose said. "I'm sure he would have liked to get a few of those back, but that's neither here nor there. It was disappointing. I was hoping Robb would come up with a big effort here. But I haven't decided who's going to start in the playoffs. I have a little more thinking to do."

The Kings finished with a 39-35-10 record and 88 points, which ranked them 11th among the 16 playoff participants. More discouraging was the sloppy defensive coverage and poor goaltending that led to the 15 goals the Kings allowed in the season-ending, back-to-back defeats. They would have to play a lot better than this to avoid another first-round exit.

"It's a disappointing way to finish the season, but it's over now and the most important thing is to put it behind us and get ready for Calgary," Tony Granato said.

Ten

Snuffing Out the Flames

Barry Melrose sure was acting odd on the eve of the Smythe Division semifinal series opener with the Calgary Flames. His lips were sealed. The mouth that roared was shut tight. For days Melrose insisted he couldn't decide on a No. 1 goaltender, couldn't choose between Kelly Hrudey, Robb Stauber, or even Rick Knickle. Would he stick with one goalie throughout the Stanley Cup playoffs? Defy tradition and try a rotation? Melrose insisted he didn't know.

Now that Melrose knew, he wasn't telling. "It's become such a big deal, I just don't want the guy who is going to play to have to answer a bunch of questions about it right now," he said. "He just doesn't need that type of question right now."

Hrudey's cone of silence was still in operation when the Los Angeles beat writers were around, so it wouldn't really have mattered if he was Melrose's guy. Hrudey wasn't going to be answering questions from anyone he suspected had been out in the sunshine for more than five minutes in the past four weeks.

But the smart money was on Hrudey, whose playoff experience had to count for something. He had 58 games worth of postseason experience while Stauber had none. Melrose kept saying the experience factor was meaningless, but no one believed him. Knickle, who last played March 29, was deemed out of the picture entirely.

"If I get a start, or a couple of starts, that would be fine," Stauber said earlier in the week. "I'm trying to make their decision hard. The thing is, I want to be a part of the team, to contribute. But no matter what happens, I'm not going to second-guess anyone's decisions."

There was little to choose between Hrudey and Stauber on a purely statistical basis. Hrudey had an 18-21-6 record and a 3.86 goals-against average overall; he went 3-2-1, 3.14 in his final eight appearances, three in relief, and was 2-2-1, 2.91 against Calgary. Stauber finished 15-8-4 with a 3.84 average overall; he was 4-1-2, 3.31 in his last eight appearances and 0-1, 4.00 against the Flames.

But just as Hrudey's huge edge in experience had to be factored into the equation, so did Stauber's poor showing in the regular-season finale. When it came right down to it, maybe Melrose just didn't feel like talking about the obvious.

There was no such controversy swirling around the Flames, who in Calgary — and probably a few other places — were expected to take out the Kings in five or six games. Mike Vernon wasn't the greatest goalie in the world, but he was reliable. And durable. His 64 regular-season appearances were the sixth-highest total in the NHL and his 29 wins were the fifth highest. Vernon was going to play, no question about it.

Unfortunately for the Kings, Rob Blake was not. His bruised lower back prevented him from playing in the final five regular-season games and it was still sore. Blake was easily the team's best defenseman and his absence would hurt. "I can't bend over to my left or forward, and I can't shoot pucks," he said, sounding depressed. "All the muscles are still contracted." Thirty-three-year-old Tim Watters, who didn't dress for nine of the last 11 games, would play instead.

And yet the Kings sounded confident they could spring an upset. The Flames were good, but they weren't *that* good. Calgary's 43-30-11 record came out to 97 points, nine more than the Kings had, but the Flames didn't dominate at the Olympic Saddledome anymore. Winning a game in Calgary was once a chore for the Kings, but those days were over.

Besides, the pressure was clearly on the Flames. They held home-ice advantage and would have to win the first two games to keep it. The Kings, on the other hand, had won just seven of 25 previous playoff series and been knocked out in the first round

11 times. "It's time for us to turn this thing around," Luc Robitaille said. "The regular season doesn't mean anything, it's what you do in the playoffs that counts. We've all been disappointed before. I mean, look at the fans. They've deserved a lot better than what they've gotten."

Game 1 was a wipeout . . . for the Kings. Rookie Darryl Sydor scored 16 seconds in, Calgary was held without a shot on goalie Kelly Hrudey for the first 9 minutes, 45 seconds, and Jimmy Carson scored twice in a 6-3 win that was marred only by an injury to Wayne Gretzky. His back was okay, but he spent the final 28 minutes of the game in the dressing room with what the Kings were calling a charley horse.

So what else was new? Sore ribs, a lacerated ear, and a hyperextended back the previous three years made life miserable for Gretzky in the playoffs, now this. Gretzky said he was hit on the right thigh late in the first period. Gretzky said he didn't know who nailed him, he just knew that his leg hurt more than a little bit. The good news was he would have two days instead of one to work on the pain before Game 2.

"This is just a little leg injury," Gretzky said. "I'll try it even if it's a little sore. But it's frustrating because I felt like I have been playing as well as ever." It was Gretzky who set up Sydor in the left faceoff circle for a quick shot that skimmed between Mike Vernon's legs. "I was so excited," Sydor said, "I didn't know what to do."

The biggest goal was provided by Carson at 3:13 of the second period. With Brent Ashton serving a delay-of-game penalty assessed to Vernon for clearing the puck over the glass, Jari Kurri gave the puck away and Gary Suter scored a shorthanded goal to tie the game. Carson's goal came on the same power play, just 25 seconds later, and it wasn't long before the Kings held a commanding 4-1 lead. "We responded quickly," Carson said. "Then all of a sudden we got a couple more and we had control of the game."

Hrudey was feeling fairly self-satisfied. He shattered his silence after the game with a blistering, scattergun attack that apparently was meant to mow down anyone, family excluded, he had come in contact with since September. He called the season "the most difficult" of his career, claimed he was "pelted" with unfair criticism when the team slumped, and said it was ludicrous that anyone doubted his ability to beat out Stauber and Knickle in the end.

"I was expecting the ball to come back to me," Hrudey said. "Contrary to what the goofs and dummies want to say or write or believe, I can still play this game. And I don't care if I offend people with my comments because I'm just telling you exactly what I think. In a general sense, everyone is so phony and fickle anyway. If you expect anything out of the game other than what is there — a temporary occupation — then you are wrong. But I never pouted and I never moped. I wasn't a distraction to the team. I just did my job, worked hard in practice and waited for my chance again."

But the goaltending controversy didn't end there. Melrose fueled it by benching Stauber and using Knickle as the backup for Game 1, a scenario that wouldn't change for Game 2. Stauber was outraged. He accepted Melrose's choice of Hrudey as the No. 1 goalie, but Knickle was rusty, hadn't played in almost a month. Stauber believed he'd had a real chance to be No. 1 and now he was No. 3. "What happened to No. 2?" he asked. "Not that I'd be happy with No. 2, but I feel I should at least be a part of this team in the playoffs. I think I've worked hard enough for that."

Melrose disagreed and went so far as to question Stauber's character, saying the rookie wilted under pressure each time he was asked to win a big game. There had been four such occasions over the course of the year, Melrose said, most recently the 8-6 loss to Vancouver in the regular-season finale.

"An elite goaltender has to carry the ball when you give it to him," Melrose said. "The mark of a great goalie is that he isn't satisfied to be the backup. I'm not blaming Robb for the losses, but if you're going to be No. 1, you've got to be able to walk your talk. You've got to be able to play when everything is on the line. Robb Stauber has a great deal of ability, but maybe I expect more from him than he does. I think maybe he needs to watch a couple of games from the stands."

The criticism stung Stauber to the core. "I expect more from myself than anybody, including Barry Melrose," he responded. "What I've been through the last four years — two knee operations, a herniated disk in my back, shoulder surgery — what more can I go through? I obviously do expect a lot from myself, otherwise I wouldn't be here."

Blake was cleared to return to the lineup, though he'd need to wear a pad to protect his back, and Gretzky said the two off-days had done wonders for his charley horse. "He's got a muscle strain," Dr. Ron Kvitne said. "The muscle fibers get stretched and spasm, but we're talking about a guy who came back from a career-threatening injury in only a few months."

The Kings were bucking history heading into Game 2. They had never won the first two games of a playoff series on the road and owned an unimpressive 2-7 record in second games after opening with a win. "This is a critical game, extremely impor-tant," Gretzky warned. "Teams that win the first game, before you know it, they're down 2-1 in the series. There's a big differ-ence between 2-0 and 1-1. Calgary's a good road team, they've won in L.A. So we won't be satisfied with a split."

A sweep didn't appear out of the question 71 seconds into Game 2 when Carson, suddenly a scoring machine, stole the puck from Greg Paslawski and ripped a shot behind Vernon for his third goal in four periods and yet another quick lead. But by the time Carson scored the Kings' next goal — it came 5 1/2 minutes into the third period — they were well on the way to a resounding 9-4 defeat.

The Flames scored five unanswered goals in the second period and Kings defenseman Marty McSorley was on the ice for four of them. His misery continued in the third period when Robert Reichel lined up a shot that hit McSorley's left skate and bounced into the net for Calgary's sixth goal.

After Game 1, Melrose bragged about the Kings' "secret defense." Apparently, the secret was out. Reichel and Joel Otto, the latter of whom held the hobbled Gretzky to one shot on goal, each scored twice for the Flames, while Al MacInnis and Gary Roberts each contributed three assists. The Flames also domi-nated the special teams with three power-play goals and a shorthanded goal, a complete turnaround from the first game.

"The weakest point of that team is the defense," Calgary's Ron Stern said of the Kings. "I'm not saying they're bad, I'm just saying that with three good offensive lines, scoring is L.A.'s strength. We've got to keep banging them, wearing them down." The Kings were so inattentive in front of Hrudey that Otto had time to pick up the stick he dropped and take a pass from Roberts before he scored his first goal, which tied the game early in the second period.

"My team shocked me," Melrose said. "We got outworked, that's the bottom line. They did to us what we did to them the other day." Blake came back to give the Kings all six of their regular defensemen for the first time in three weeks, then Charlie Huddy suffered a groin strain and missed the last 30 minutes. "It's pretty sore," Huddy said.

All the Kings were pained by the 5-2 drubbing Calgary inflicted in Game 3 at the Forum. Flames backup Jeff Reese, playing because Vernon pulled ligaments in his ankle, looked like the second coming of Ken Dryden whenever he faced the Kings. This night was no different. Reese made spectacular saves on Carson and Gary Shuchuk in the first six minutes, and then Calgary's swarming defense took over. The Flames used an explosive offense to blow the Kings away in Game 2, but on the road they were willing to play it conservative, force errors, and pounce on them.

To Melrose's utter dismay, the Kings cooperated to the fullest extent. Otto, a 220-pound moose of a man from Elk River, Minnesota, continued to nullify the 170-pound Gretzky and he scored another goal. Theoren Fleury, the 5-foot-7 pest whom the Kings despised, put the game on ice with his second goal of the night; it came while the Flames were shorthanded and expanded their lead to 4-1 two minutes into the third period.

The Kings' troubles were compounded by mental blunders that resulted in a never-ending parade to the penalty box. Luc Robitaille let his emotions get the best of him and he took three bad penalties when it was still possible for the Kings to mount comebacks. The most glaring took place with a little over four minutes to play in the second period while the Kings trailed 3-1. Robitaille drove Otto to the ice deep in the Calgary zone, which was bad enough. But then he cross-checked Otto behind the head and forced the Kings to spend the rest of the period shorthanded.

"I was stupid," Robitaille said. Part of his frustration stemmed from the checking job the Flames were administering to him and his linemates, Gretzky and Tomas Sandstrom. The unit had seven assists in the series — Robitaille had one of them — but it had yet to score a goal.

"Your best players have to be your best players," Melrose said. "Those guys have to score." If Gretzky's leg was bothering him, he wasn't saying. "I don't even want to discuss it," Gretzky said. Melrose changed his lines before the game, but the experiment didn't work and he went back to the old ones in the second period. "We've been playing pretty disciplined defensively," Calgary's Joe Nieuwendyk pointed out. "We learned some lessons in the first game. You can't ever give those guys chances."

Considering the condition of their offense, it was imperative for the Kings to play better in their own end and refrain from taking so many dumb penalties. "Even if (Calgary) doesn't score, we're tiring our own guys out killing penalties, guys you need to get some offense going," Gretzky said. "A good, logical, legitimate penalty is okay, but a penalty that takes place 200 feet from our own net is not a good penalty."

And another thing: The Kings' power play was in shambles. They had only three goals in 22 power-play opportunities, and two of those were scored during five-on-three situations. Calgary, on the other hand, had four power-play goals and three shorthanded goals. Winning the battle of the special teams could go a long way in determining the outcome of the series.

Melrose contemplated all of these things after practice on the off-day between games and said he probably would consider taking his thoughts to the beach later that afternoon. "It's relaxing to watch the waves crash. I spent a lot of time there in December and January," Melrose said. Thinking of ways to end the Kings' worst skid of the year, no doubt. "Thinking of jumping off the pier," he said.

It was likely Robb Stauber, who replaced Rick Knickle as Kelly Hrudey's backup in Game 3, would be given the critical Game 4 start. If Melrose's stinging comments earlier in the series hadn't stoked Stauber's competitive fire, nothing would. "When the team is struggling, you've got to try everything," Melrose said.

Rob Blake vowed to play with more smarts than he showed on two Game 3 plays that led to Calgary goals. He left Otto open in the slot to check Brent Ashton behind the net in the first period and he wasn't paying attention when Greg Paslawski snuck behind him to score in the second period. "I don't know what I was thinking," Blake said. "It's done, but it's certainly not forgotten. The way I played was a joke. The game was lost because of my two mistakes. If we win the series, I'll forget about them. If we lose, they'll stick in my mind the whole summer."

With royalty sitting among the 16,005 fans who ventured into the Forum for Game 4, how could the Kings lose? Ronald and Nancy Reagan, who were surrounded by Secret Service agents, watched from ice-level seats as the Kings posted an impressive 3-1 victory that tied the series at two games apiece.

Reagan was becoming quite the good-luck charm for the Kings. Back in 1989, after the Kings lost three of the first four games of their playoff series with the Edmonton Oilers, Reagan wrote a letter that asked the Kings to "win one for the Gipper." Robbie Ftorek, who was coach at the time, read the letter to the team before Game 5 and it responded with a 4-2 win. The Kings won the final three games to take the series.

This time, the Reagans' presence would have to do. Though if either could skate, Melrose might have fiddled with the idea of putting them on a line with Gretzky. Or with Robitaille, Sandstrom, and Granato. The series was four games deep and still the Kings' biggest guns weren't firing. "If you told me we'd be tied after four games without getting a goal from any of those guys, I'd have said you were crazy," Melrose said.

The Kings relied on a punishing hitting game led by Blake, superior goaltending from Stauber, a power play that actually produced a goal (rookie defenseman Alexei Zhitnik got it), and goals by unsung forwards Warren Rychel and Pat Conacher, who spent most of the year mucking it up on the checking line. Melrose juggled all of his lines, but the move that stood out most was Rychel's shift to the left side with Gretzky.

"The checking is tighter in the playoffs and the guys who are willing to take an extra whack going to the net are going to get their chances," said Rychel, whose NHL-leading 30 major penalties and 314 penalty minutes were evidence he was prepared to accept some abuse on behalf of the team. He knocked down Calgary's Trent Yawney on his way to the net and banged a loose puck in to snap a 1-1 tie at 4:48 of the third period after Reese made a big save on Sandstrom. The outcome was in doubt until seven seconds remained when Conacher scored into an empty net.

"Barry had me on the checking line in the regular season and my job wasn't to score goals," said Rychel, who had six in 70 games. "It was clear what I was supposed to do, be a checker and a grinder. Yeah, you can get typecast, but look at the left wingers we've got on our team—Robitaille, (Mike) Donnelly, Sandstrom. It's unbelievable. So I'm a checker and a grinder and a scrapper. I do what I have to do to stay in the league."

If that meant sticking a fistful of knuckles into a guy's face on occasion, so be it. But Rychel, who bounced around the minors for five years, always considered himself more than a mindless slugger. Sure, he exchanged pleasantries with San Jose's Lyndon Byers two seconds into a regular-season game, he said, because "there was this electrical thing between us," but when given the chance Rychel could mix a bit of skill in with the toughness. Two years earlier, when he was toiling for Indianapolis in the International League, Rychel had 33 goals to go along with 338 penalty minutes, enabling him to join Al Secord and Rick Tocchet as the only members of professional hockey's 30-300 club.

"I was pretty proud of that. It's a pretty good stat. It shows you can play hockey," Rychel said. "I scrapped for Barry this year and played hard. Now I'm in a situation where I'm getting a little more rope and I'm getting rewarded for it. It was the same thing in the minors. At first I was doing a lot of fighting and then I became a player. I didn't have a lot of points this year, but I was around the net a lot. Hey, I think I can score 30 goals in this league."

On a day made for bold statements, Stauber stopped 28 Calgary shots and showed Melrose he was quite capable of being a big-game goalie. "I think Barry knows what I can do," he said. "I imagine part of what he did was motivational. I got things off my mind and he got things off his mind. But you can't play this position mad. It's a delicate position and you can't play frustrated. I wanted to prove to myself, not to anybody else, that I belonged. I was a little nervous, but I started smiling during the national anthem. I told myself, 'This is going to be great.' "

Even Hrudey, who served as Stauber's backup after back-to-back setbacks, was in good spirits. His 7-year-old daughter, Jessica, gave him a huge emotional lift by drawing a picture of him and captioning it "Best goalie in the world." Hrudey said, "If that doesn't brighten your day and make you see the big picture of the world, then you are missing a lot."

If only the Not-So-Fab-Four could get untracked. Gretzky, Robitaille, Sandstrom, and Granato, even though they missed a total of 87 games, combined for 141 goals in the regular season.

But they were barely visible against Calgary, totaling precisely zero goals. Zilch. Zippo. *Nada*. Gretzky had three assists and nine shots, Robitaille one assist and eight shots, Sandstrom four assists and nine shots, Granato two assists and six shots.

When asked if his leg hurt, Gretzky forced a smile and said, "Our egos hurt." Los Angeles had 15 goals in the series, eight from Carson, Rychel and Zhitnik, who scored just 30 between them as Kings in 182 regular-season games. It was hard to fathom the Kings advancing to the Smythe Division final if they had to continue to depend on these guys so heavily.

"When you get to the playoffs, the focus is to win," Gretzky said. "If you're worried about your own individual statistics as far as scoring goals, you're in the wrong situation. We need goals out of people, no question, but it can't be a focal point. If you said to me, 'We're going to win 14 more games and you're not going to score another goal,' I'd be the happiest guy around because that would mean we'd win the Stanley Cup. Points don't mean anything at this time of the year. Winning means everything."

No argument there. But the Kings probably weren't going to win two more games and survive the series, let alone 14 more and a Stanley Cup, if blanks kept coming out of Gretzky's stick. Ditto the rest of the Gang That Couldn't Shoot Straight. "All four of us are maybe thinking too much, but one little thing will happen and — bang — it will all turn around," Robitaille predicted.

Those who witnessed the 9-4 pounding of Calgary that gave the Kings a 3-2 series lead heading back to Inglewood wondered where Robitaille had purchased his crystal ball. Or where Jeff Reese's reflexes went. The Kings bombed him for the game's first five goals, two of which were supplied by Robitaille and one by Sandstrom. Gretzky and Granato joined the act in the third period, when Mike Vernon was strafed for four more goals.

By the time the ice chips cleared, the Kings' big shots had delivered five goals and 11 points, five more goals and one more point than they mustered in the first four games combined. "Now we can save the foursome for June when we're playing golf instead of being known as the foursome that didn't score any goals," Granato said.

The joy ride began at 2:52 of the first period. Carson hit Sandstrom with a cross-ice pass on a two-on-one rush into the Flames zone, then Sandstrom stepped around the sliding Reese and flipped the puck into the unguarded net. Robitaille's turn came at 6:53 of the second period. Gretzky dumped the puck off the boards, it squirted into the left circle, and Robitaille pounded it between Reese's legs. Robitaille also scored on his next shot, converting Gretzky's pass at 10:59 on another two-on-one rush to give the Kings a 5-0 cushion.

"On the first one, the puck was rolling and I kind of missed it," Robitaille said. "It was probably just as well, because I've been taking solid shots and nothing's been going in. Barry told me to relax, to shoot and not hesitate. I guess I might have been pressing a little bit. I knew I had to play better, but everybody raised their game."

Gretzky already had three assists by the time he hit the back of the net at 7:33 of the third period. First, he had to bang a shot off the left post. "I just threw it at the net," he said. The puck bounced up and off Calgary defenseman Kevin Dahl's nose — ouch — and then it struck Vernon and ricocheted across the goal line. In 20 years, maybe less, Gretzky could describe the strange play as a coast-to-coast rush and no one would know the difference.

Granato's slump-buster was scored in more conventional fashion, off a Corey Millen pass with 3:06 remaining in the game. Counting the regular season, it was his first goal in 12 games. No wonder Granato felt as if a mill stone had been lifted from his neck. "These guys have been taking a lot of heat," Melrose said. "I've been saying all along, if they get their chances, they're going to score."

The Kings had come to expect goals from Rychel, and he didn't disappoint. Frankly, his fourth of the series was the most important goal to be scored in Game 5. He stemmed a three-goal Calgary rally by lifting a Gretzky pass over Vernon's shoulder at 4:38 of the third period after the Flames had crept to within 5-3. Imagine if the Kings had blown this one.

Nearly overshadowed was another solid game from Stauber. Despite the lopsided outcome, the Kings went nine minutes without a shot on goal in the first period, when Stauber made 17 saves. The Kings were outshot 44-35 for the game. "Robb saved us a number of times," Melrose said.

It was pretty obvious that Stauber would get the call in Game 6 when the Kings attempted to wrap up the best-of-seven series so they could begin preparing for, ugh, the Vancouver Canucks in the division final. Hrudey had made 21 consecutive playoff starts for the Kings and played in 39 of their 40 postseason games since his 1989 arrival before Melrose pulled the plug in Game 4. But Stauber was playing well and Hrudey knew the rookie deserved to keep his pads on.

"I don't think it's a bad decision at all," Hrudey said. "Certainly Robb warrants the ice time he's getting. It's well deserved. Hey, I think you should use everyone on your roster. Robb and I have a great relationship. I'm a big supporter of his. He's somebody who I think can do a lot in the NHL. Besides, I don't think I've had my last play."

If it was possible, Flames coach Dave King would have rented Hrudey on April 29. Or maybe even propped a cardboard cutout of a goalie in front of the Calgary net in Game 6, anything to avoid having to use Reese again. But Mike Vernon, his ankle still bothering him, could barely walk. So there was Reese, getting swamped again on a night when a mediocre performance might have been enough to extend the Flames' season.

The Kings snuffed it out, 9-6, thanks to an embarrassing show by Reese. During one stretch, he relinquished six goals on seven shots. Finally, after the Kings scored on all but one of their four shots in the second period to take a 6-5 lead at the intermission, Vernon was given a pain-numbing injection. Unfortunately for Calgary, it took half the third period for the medication to have an effect. Reese could be forgiven for failing to appreciate the warm ovation he received from the Forum sellout crowd when King brought out his hook with 10:04 remaining and the Kings in front, 8-6.

"(Vernon's) ankle was swollen and sore," King said. "We froze it during the intermission, but we decided he wouldn't go in if Jeff was looking good." The way Reese was playing, it was hard to tell if he was looking at all. At the puck. The Kings needed only 18 shots to pump eight goals by him. Stauber wasn't much better, but he did face 42 shots and managed to make a number of difficult saves.

"I played with one of the greatest goalies of all time, Grant Fuhr," Gretzky said. "He used to say that it doesn't matter how many goals you let in. If you go up by one and you make the big save, then you've won the game for us. Robbie sure did that for us tonight."

Jari Kurri led the Kings attack with a goal and three assists. Sandstrom scored two goals, and Gretzky had a goal and two assists. Gretzky's leg surely didn't bother him when he set up Rob Blake for a shorthanded goal and a 5-4 lead at the 15-minute mark of the second period. While the Kings were killing Robitaille's holding penalty, Gretzky spun around Trent Yawney and Al MacInnis in the neutral zone, then he spotted Blake in the clear and hit him with a perfect pass.

"Unreal," Blake said. "You know he's going to reward you if you go to the net. So you try to reward him with a goal. But that's the kind of play that only Gretz can make."

Four times the Kings built two-goal leads and still they had problems extinguishing the Flames, but they had won the series, four games to two, so why complain? The 33 goals they produced in the series were a club record, four more than were scored in a first-round victory over Calgary in 1990.

For the first time in franchise history, the Kings would be strapping on skates in May instead of golf shoes. Their bitter playoff experience of the previous spring was a distant memory. This was a time to look ahead, to the Vancouver Canucks in the Smythe Division final.

"My whole team is going to give me a heart attack, but a win is a win. I don't care if it's 1-0 or 100-99," Melrose said. "And I'll tell you something, one series means nothing to us. That's been the whole mindset in L.A., just get out of the first round. Well, it's not good enough anymore."

Eleven

Breaking
New Ice

How in heavens were the Kings going to handle the Vancouver Canucks, one of the finest teams in the NHL? Unlike Calgary, the Canucks were a legitimate Stanley Cup contender. They finished the regular season with a 46-29-9 record and in first place in the Smythe Division for the second year in a row.

Pat Quinn, Vancouver's president, general manager and head coach, had done a remarkable job of turning the fortunes of the franchise around since he left the Kings under a dark cloud in January 1987. Quinn, a 50-year-old cigar-chompin' Irishman, was expelled from the NHL by league president John Ziegler when it was revealed he had signed a lucrative contract and accepted a signing bonus to join the Canucks the following season. Quinn, who holds a degree in law, acknowledged he was contractually bound to the Kings at the time, but maintained he acted honorably.

Quinn's expulsion was lifted and his penalty changed to a temporary coaching ban before the 1987-88 season, enabling him to begin the monumental chore of rebuilding a team whose last winning record had come 12 years earlier. Progress was slow, but Quinn used high draft picks and shrewd trades to acquire winning players such as goaltender Kirk McLean, forwards Pavel Bure, Trevor Linden, Cliff Ronning and Geoff Courtnall, and defensemen Jyrki Lumme and Adrien Plavsic.

Quinn, a successful coach with the Philadelphia Flyers a decade earlier, eventually moved behind the bench and guided the Canucks to a club-record 96-point season in 1991-92, a 31-point improvement that earned him the Jack Adams Trophy as Coach of the Year.

The Canucks were even better now, loaded on both sides of the red line. Once small, slow and timid, Vancouver boasted size, speed and muscle, though its defense was still a bit on the plodding side. Led by Bure, an electrifying winger from the former Soviet Union who had 60 goals in the regular season, the Canucks scored 346 goals, the fourth-highest total in the league. McLean and his backup, Kay Whitmore, permitted only 278 goals — 62 fewer goals than the Kings allowed and fifth best in the NHL.

"We have three scoring lines, so certainly it's harder to shut us down than when I first got here," Quinn said. "Because we're big, some people say we're slow, but team speed is relative to how fast you move the puck. The kind of team I want to watch should be willing to make defensive and skill sacrifices in order to make the transition to offense. We're not the kind of team that just wants to sit back."

The Canucks dominated the Kings in the regular season, winning seven of nine meetings by the combined score of 46-31, the last three by scores of 21-12. Even more significant, the Canucks won all four meetings at the Pacific Coliseum, and the Kings would need to win at least one playoff game there in order to advance beyond the second round for the first time. Seven previous trips resulted in eight victories and 28 defeats.

Barry Melrose was undaunted. The Kings had ripped Calgary to shreds, hadn't they? Statistically, the Flames' defense was every bit as good as the Canucks'. Melrose didn't even care that the Kings would be facing much better goaltending than they did in the semifinals. McLean held the Winnipeg Jets to 17 goals in Vancouver's six-game series, one less goal than the Kings scored against Calgary in the last two games alone.

Didn't matter, Melrose said. "Calgary broke down," he said. "Break down against us and we'll put the puck in the net." Melrose promised to keep using the kind of run-and-gun tactics that make playoff traditionalists cringe and snicker almost at the same time.

"I'm not a purist like some older people," he said. "I guess 2-1 games were nice in the forties and fifties, but hockey is more exciting now. The way we want to play, we want to play fast and attack. If we have to grind we will, but we're a lot better team when we play a wide-open style. I can guarantee you the people in L.A. had a lot more fun watching our 9-6 game with Calgary than they would have if it had been 2-1. It's the kind of game we like to play and it's the kind of game we're going to play."

Melrose also scoffed at the experts who predicted the high-powered yet disciplined Canucks would score at will against sacrificial lambs Robb Stauber, who would start Game 1, and Kelly Hrudey. "Calgary said goaltending was our Achilles' heel and we beat them, four games to two," Melrose said. "If that's an Achilles' heel, I hope it stays."

The Kings expected a tough series with Vancouver, but not one to include the high sticks, slashes and cross-checks that were so prevalent in the Calgary series. Defenseman Charlie Huddy needed eight stitches to close a gash near his right eye after Ron Stern nailed him with a high stick in Game 6 and the subsequent swelling affected his vision, but he was going to play.

Wayne Gretzky's health was an obvious factor, and his charley horse was getting better every day. Gretzky had two goals and five assists in the last two games with the Flames and led all Kings scorers with 10 points after a slow start. "I don't want to dwell on it, but, yes, I really started getting healthier in Games 5 and 6," he said. "Wow, the way this year started, I didn't think I'd be playing at all. To end up like this, where I feel like I've played some of my best hockey the last few games, it feels good."

Not much good happened in the Kings' first-ever foray into May. Perhaps the noon start dictated by ABC-TV was responsible for the sluggish manner in which the Kings went about their business. It wouldn't have been a bad excuse if the Canucks had slept in, too. Only 15,016 fans, more than a thousand under capacity, watched Vancouver dominate, 5-2, and hand the Kings their 17th loss in the past 20 second-round games. When Dave Babych, the third Canucks defenseman to collect a goal in Game 1, closed out the scoring midway through the third period, the Kings had been outshot 40-18.

Vancouver received precious little production from its top three playoff scorers—Bure, Linden and Petr Nedved—and still owned a huge territorial edge. From the Kings' standpoint, that was distressing. The Kings were limited to five shots in the first period and they had only one shot during a 16-minute stretch that began in the opening period and carried into the second. Gretzky scored a goal in the second period, his third in as many games, but Luc Robitaille and Tomas Sandstrom didn't even register a single shot on goal.

Stauber wasn't bad, but he wasn't good enough on a day when near-perfection would have been necessary. He kept the Kings in the game for a while, until defenseman Gerald Diduck beat him to the short side with a soft wrist shot at 12:50 of the second period, a bad goal that expanded Vancouver's lead to 4-2. "Robb played well, but he should have had that one," Melrose said.

Charlie Huddy was in a foul mood. As poorly as the Kings were playing, they trailed by only a goal late in the first period when referee Kerry Fraser sent him to the penalty box for holding Bure's stick. With three seconds left on the penalty, and 16 seconds remaining in the period, Courtnall deflected Lumme's blast from the point behind Stauber for a 3-1 Vancouver advantage and a great emotional letdown for the Kings.

"If he's going to call chintzy stuff like that, call it the same for the whole game," Huddy said. "I told Kerry that, too. Fine, I don't mind taking a penalty, but be consistent about it." Late in the second period, with the Kings down 4-2, Fraser penalized Huddy for high-sticking Ronning. The Canucks didn't score, but the Kings could have used the penalty-killing time to attack. "It was ridiculous," Huddy complained. "(Darryl) Sydor got cut on the lip in the first period and there wasn't a call. A lot worse went on than what I did. They've got to call this stuff the same on both sides."

But the Kings knew they couldn't pin the blame for this loss on Fraser, who in reality gave them one more power play than he did Vancouver. Emotion or fire, whatever you want to call the character trait that fueled the Kings in the Calgary series, they would have to get it back for the next game.

"We have to lay the body on them or they will kill us," Mike Donnelly said. Rob Blake, the usual leader in the body-flattening department, hardly laid a finger on anyone and was on the ice for three of Vancouver's goals. Marty McSorley also played too passively.

"Without question we played a lot harder against Calgary," Gretzky said. "Vancouver is just as physical, just as big as Calgary, and we have to play them the same way. And I'm not talking run and gun, but we have to be more aggressive, forecheck and attack. We weren't physical at all and we've got to play them nose to nose. We took it a little bit easy on them as far as hitting goes. We really didn't bump anybody."

Make no mistake, this series was going to be decided on the ice, not in the newspapers. But even Melrose couldn't have come up with a more stirring motivational tool than the one Vancouver writers provided in their accounts of Game 1. The Canucks were a fine team and deserved to be called championship material, but the Kings thought it was a little premature for the reporters to start making travel plans for the Stanley Cup final.

"You get the distinct impression everything is breaking Vancouver's way," wrote Mike Beamish, a columnist for the *Vancouver Sun*. Jim Jamieson, in the second paragraph of his *Vancouver Province* game story, said the Canucks' road to the Stanley Cup final was "easier" now because they were the highest-seeded Campbell Conference team left and would have home-ice advantage in the next round.

In the next round? Sure, the Canucks were a very good team and had to be considered the favorites in this series. But the last time the Kings checked, it was a best-of-seven series, not a one-shot deal like the Super Bowl. Besides, it wasn't as if dozens of championship banners were hanging inside the Pacific Coliseum; the Canucks didn't exactly make a habit of putting teams away in the playoffs.

Melrose didn't have to be hit over the head with a morning newspaper to recognize the stories were extraordinary bulletin-board material, and it didn't matter that not a single derogatory comment had come from the Canucks coaches or players. Melrose spent breakfast contemplating how much per diem he was willing to spend on stick pins.

"Yeah, I'll mention it," Melrose said. As if he ever considered keeping the articles to himself. "Everything you can use has value," Melrose said. "It strikes a chord with people. You can use it when people take you for granted. It happened in Calgary, too.

'This is just a formality, so why are we here?' People wrote us off in Calgary, but I think we won four out of six games against them. When you can show people they're wrong, it's the greatest thing in the world."

Quinn reacted to the stories with a growl. "I hope to hell none of the (Canucks) players saw that crap," he snapped. But the negative press was made to order for Melrose's "us against the world" approach to game preparation. "If they think it's over, that's fine, let them think that," Warren Rychel said. "But we've got some great players over here and we don't think it's over." Not yet, anyway, not after one game. "What matters is what we think," Robitaille said. "I think their players respect us. They always come out hard against us. If people are counting us out, you can always turn it the right way."

The direction of the series could change, but not without some serious alterations. First, the Kings would have to show they were interested in winning the series and play with some enthusiasm. And a decent start might help; the Canucks combined for 15 first-period goals in the Kings' previous four games at the Pacific Coliseum, forcing them to take dangerous chances while playing catch-up. Los Angeles also would have to negate Vancouver's quickness with body checks, even if tattooing a guy like Bure against the boards is more difficult than swatting a fly with a straw. Last, when the Kings were on the attack, they had to make McLean work for his saves.

"He's a pretty good goalie," Rychel said, "so we've got to get second and third whacks at the puck, get in his face, crash the net and get screen shots from the points. We have to get some pressure in their end, hound the puck, hit guys."

Blake insisted his back was fine and promised to lean his 215 pounds into onrushing forwards whenever possible to prove it. "I thought I was average in the first game, and I don't think average is acceptable," he said. "I have a lot to do to pick up my game. But I think we all have to pick it up. We're going to be more intense and we're going to have to hit some people. My back is 100 percent, there's no problem there. I can hit guys."

One other thing: Kelly Hrudey was the starter again. Stauber won three consecutive games before the Game 1 defeat, but he'd given up 11 goals in the last two games. "I'm not surprised," Stauber said. How come? "Because we lost. But I'm not going to worry about it. I'm not going to put extra pressure on myself to win. I don't think Barry is unhappy with me. It's just his decision and he's made a lot of good decisions this year."

Melrose said his move back to Hrudey was based on a "hunch." Not that upsetting the apple cart ever bothered him, but Melrose felt comfortable about changing goalies because Hrudey and Stauber had such a good working relationship. (Rick Knickle was being shunned by Hrudey and Stauber. Neither would relinquish a net at practice sessions, forcing him to work on his angles and take imaginary shots near the center-ice boards until the designated sitters on the team, dubbed the "Black Aces," sprang into action after the regulars left. Except to say he "might act differently" than Hrudey and Stauber, Knickle elected not to talk about his status as an outcast; the three eventually settled their differences.)

Hrudey lost six of eight games to the Canucks in the regular season, but he shut them out in February and was 20-11-4 against them in his career. "The time away makes you really want to play," Hrudey said. He hadn't played since Game 3 of the Calgary series. "I'm ready. I'm always ready to play," he said. "All I can do is be ready and make the best of it, just like Robb did."

Wayne Gretzky did his part to ensure the Kings would be prepared for Game 2 by addressing the team in the dressing room before the national anthems were played. Gretzky made another statement on the ice, scoring a goal and adding two assists, but the one he delivered following the Kings' 6-3 series-tying victory was the loudest of them all.

In an interview with ESPN hockey analyst John Davidson, Gretzky revealed that he had suffered a cracked rib, not a charley horse, on his final first-period shift in the opening game of the Calgary series. Gretzky was being injected with pain-killers before games, he said, and he wore a flak jacket in two of the games with the Flames. If the charley horse cover-up hadn't been created, Gretzky said, he would not have been able to play for fear of risking further damage to the rib.

Incredulously, 12 hours after the truth made its way into the newspapers, Melrose continued to play his role as the master of misinformation. "No, there's no truth in that," said Melrose, whose nose did not begin to grow like Pinocchio's. "He hurt his leg against Calgary and in the next game he strained a rib muscle, but there's no cracked rib," he said. "He did strain his ribs and we never told anyone, but there's no truth to (a cracked rib) at all."

Well, the rib likely was pretty much healed now. It wouldn't make sense for Gretzky to come clean otherwise. He surely didn't appear to be playing in pain, not with four goals and seven assists in the most recent four games, three of which the Kings won.

"We freeze it before games," Gretzky said the next day. "I feel good out there. It's not going to affect me if I get hit there. I mean, I got hit by (Gerald) Diduck in the first game and I didn't feel it at all. It's not a big thing. I cracked it, and now I'm at a point where it's pretty much healed. The last thing I want is people talking about my injuries, which are a part of the playoffs. People should be talking about the players and how they are playing, pitching in and helping us win.

"The last four games it felt really good, no problem. Physically I feel real good, but more important, mentally my emotional level is real high. I'm real excited about our team. I don't feel fatigue at all. I feel I can skate forever right now and that's a nice feeling. The games I missed this year may have been a blessing because I feel stronger now and I've gotten stronger in each of the last four games."

Dr. Ron Kvitne, the team doctor, said he didn't know if the rib was actually cracked or not. X-rays were never taken, he said, because "if Gretzky was taken to the hospital, that would have increased the chances of the news leaking out." Kvitne preferred to describe the problem as a "significant injury to the left side" and said whether the rib was cracked or broken was inconsequential in terms of the treatment Gretzky received.

"All we can tell you is it hurts," Kvitne said. "I have to check him after each (pregame warmup) to see if I have to give him more medicine." Kvitne maintained that Gretzky also suffered a charley horse but admitted it was the rib injury that forced him to miss the second half of the Calgary game. "We were trying to protect the doctor-patient relationship, to protect him and to allow him to play," Kvitne said. "But I can't tell you if it's cracked or broken or a contusion or a muscle bruise, and Wayne can't tell you because I have not gotten X-rays."

At this point, it didn't matter. Gretzky was virtually healthy and so were the Kings. The Canucks were not invincible after all.

It was not impossible to beat them on the road. The series was tied, 1-1, and the Kings were going home. "I guess we get to play one extra game now," Tony Granato said, a sarcastic reference to the attitude that prevailed among Vancouver's media.

Except for the play of their special teams, the Kings were as solid in every area in Game 2 as they'd been weak in Game 1. Vancouver scored two more power-play goals and the Kings didn't get any, but Gretzky set up Jari Kurri for a shorthanded goal to put them ahead for good, 2-1, seven minutes into the first period. A little over three minutes later, Gretzky led a four-on-two rush into the Canucks zone and left the puck for Rychel, who blasted a 40-foot slap shot between McLean's pads. The Kings had to figure it was going to be a good night when Mark Hardy scored 19 seconds into the game off a faceoff. "We were sick of getting behind in this building," Rychel said.

After the game, Kings owner Bruce McNall borrowed a notebook and pen from a reporter as media members surrounded Melrose outside the dressing room. "Coach, you earned your salary tonight, eh?" McNall yelled from in back of the pack. For once, Melrose was speechless.

Hrudey earned his pay by making 26 saves, and Granato put in overtime. He scored what proved to be the decisive goal off a Vancouver giveaway and aggravated Canucks winger Sergio Momesso into taking two stupid penalties. Momesso pulled Granato down late in the second period, then spit at him, earning a double-minor and a 10-minute gross misconduct from referee Mark Faucette. The Kings didn't score, but the Canucks were shorthanded for four minutes and they lost Momesso for 14.

Granato definitely has a way of crawling under an opponent's skin. He had 37 goals and a career-high 82 points in the regular season, along with 171 penalty minutes, the third-highest total on the team behind McSorley and Rychel. "He definitely is the guy who stirs our drink," Melrose said. "Tony plays with so much emotion and fire. He gets everybody mad at him and that fires all of us up."

The January 1990 trade that brought Granato and another feisty winger, Tomas Sandstrom, to the Kings in exchange for center Bernie Nicholls was one of the best deals then-general manager Rogie Vachon ever made. Granato has talent — he has scored 30 or more goals in four of his five NHL seasons — but he also is fearless when it comes to sticking his 185-pound body into situations where he could, and sometimes does, get hurt.

"Tony has an instigator-type nature," McSorley said. "He'll do stuff in the scrums, after the whistle when someone isn't looking. But he also takes a tremendous amount of abuse. For every shot he gives, he gets one back. I chased him around Madison Square Garden one night. I wanted to kill him. When he got traded here, I remember his wife asking me, 'Are you going to beat him up?' From my point of view, as a big guy, it gives me a lot of pleasure to see Tony stick his nose in there, stick up for himself and for the team."

Granato was toning down his act in the playoffs, he said, because "I don't want to get into a situation where I get a penalty in a close game. I don't want to put us in a shorthanded situation. But at the same time, I've got to play a certain way in order for me to be effective. I have to go to the net hard, try and draw some penalties, hopefully attract some attention in some way. If a guy is trying to take a run at me, that might open up some space for one of my teammates. If people don't like it, I don't care. If you're making friends on the other team and people like to play against you, I would think something is wrong."

Not much was going right for the Kings late in the second period of Game 3 at the Forum until Melrose realized his idea of taking Rychel off Gretzky's line was just plain dumb. So he put them back together and the result was a key goal. Rychel chugged past Anatoli Semenov and banged Gretzky's deflected pass behind McLean with 51 seconds remaining in the period to tie the game, 2-2.

"I'm flip-flopping lines, everybody's playing with everybody," Melrose said. "The way Gretzky is playing, anybody can play with him. But I put (Rychel) out there because it was late in the second period, we were running around a lot, and I didn't want us to go down 3-1. Besides, he goes to the net and the way he's playing, he deserves the ice time."

The Kings proceeded to score five goals on eight shots in the third period for a 7-4 win and a 2-1 lead in the series. Gretzky, who was given a pain-killing injection before the game, scored two goals, the 100th and 101st of his playoff career, the second one finding Vancouver's empty net with one second to play. Robitaille, whose only other playoff goals came in Game 4 of the

Calgary series, put in a rebound early in the third period and Jari Kurri beat McLean high to the glove side two minutes later after blowing by defenseman Gerald Diduck.

Kurri was 33, an old man by hockey standards, but he looked 23 on that particular goal, his fourth of the postseason. Kurri finished second to Robitaille in regular-season scoring with 87 points, a spectacular 27-point improvement over his dismal freshman year in Los Angeles. But 17 of his 27 goals and 40 of his 60 assists came in the first 35 games, after he was shifted from the wing to center.

Kurri continued to excel as a relentless backchecker and penalty killer who warranted consideration for the Selke Trophy, which annually is awarded to the league's top defensive forward. But how come his offense dried up? "He stopped scoring because when Gretzky came back and we got Jimmy (Carson), they were with our so-called offensive players more than he was," Melrose said. "But I'm not making excuses for Jari's points. A guy who gets his points and is a plus-19 has had a pretty good year.

"I never knew he was this good defensively," Melrose said. "He's unbelievable down low in our end, that's what attracted us to him as a center. He takes away the angles and passing lanes when he checks and he's a work of art killing off five-on-threes. He's intelligent and experienced. He's always on the defensive side of the puck, between the puck and the net. He doesn't cheat."

The local media voted Kurri the Kings' best defensive player, but he began the season as though a scoring title was possible. Kurri scored 71 goals one year in Edmonton and people wouldn't let him forget.

"I know I should score a lot of goals, but I feel my game is a lot more than scoring points," he said. "I like to work both ends of the ice. I like to work hard that way, but it seems people like to look at stats. They'll say, 'No goals, no assists, bad game.' That hurts me a lot. You can play so well and not get points and help the team in other ways. Those players never get as much credit as a guy who scores a goal and is a minus-three. I had some tough games, but it's a long season."

And getting longer, by the looks of things. If the Kings could take care of business in Game 4, they would grab a commanding 3-1 series lead and not have to fret so much about returning to the

Pacific Coliseum. They wouldn't have to win another game there and the Canucks would need to beat them three straight times.

When video replay judge John Pemberton ruled that McLean gloved Robitaille's shot inside the net and awarded him a goal 27 seconds into the second period, the Kings had the upper hand in the form of a 2-1 lead. They weren't very happy about referee Dan Marouelli, however. Pemberton took another look, but only after Gretzky's animated plea for Marouelli to request a replay was denied. The Kings also were upset midway through the first period when Marouelli blew his whistle a split-second before Dave Taylor jammed a rebound into the net, wiping out an apparent goal.

"Quick mouth," Melrose said of Marouelli. "He's got good hand-eye coordination. He can get the whistle to his mouth real quick." Melrose had problems with Marouelli once before, only it was *his* quick mouth that resulted in a gross misconduct penalty and $100 fine at the end of an overtime loss to Pittsburgh in March.

Marouelli should have been permitted to hand out gross misconducts to every Kings player who saw action in the subsequent 7-2 loss that was highlighted by six consecutive Vancouver goals. Melrose might have seriously considered depositing NHL rule books at each player's locker and defied anyone to locate a regulation that banned finishing a body check or protecting the area directly in front of the crease.

Funny, Marouelli also managed to infuriate Canucks coach Pat Quinn, who charged the Kings were allowed to manhandle Pavel Bure even as Gretzky was being "protected." No question Bure, whose blazing speed earned him the nickname "Russian Rocket," was being pounded, and it was just as evident he didn't particularly care for contact. A former comrade, Kings defenseman Alexei Zhitnik, was given the task of covering Bure, and he was doing a better job than Melrose could possibly have hoped. With only one goal and four second assists in the series, Bure was a non-factor.

According to Quinn, Zhitnik and virtually every other King who attempted to dissuade Bure from handling the puck was guilty of breaking the rules. "One (tactic) is punching him when he goes by," Quinn said. "The kid got cut the other night in full view of the referee and no penalty was called. If you're going to protect people, the rules have got to be the same for both teams.

"It's interesting to watch," Quinn said, "the protection that was provided for Gretzky. Of course, he milks it. He dives, he catches them all. Yet that same protection wasn't extended to Bure or to (Cliff) Ronning. If the rules are supposed to protect our most skilled players, what's happening here?"

Bure wasn't nearly as upset as his coach. "Cheap stuff, that's hockey," he said. "You have to take it. It's rough for everybody, not just for me." Melrose simply chalked up Quinn's comments as an attempt to gain an edge with the referees. It was a common playoff maneuver, no big deal.

Melrose's immediate concern was ensuring Kelly Hrudey's safety. Too often in Game 4 Hrudey was left to fend for himself, like the time Petr Nedved, who hadn't scored a goal in any of Vancouver's previous nine playoff games, snuck behind Tomas Sandstrom to tap in a rebound and tie the game 2-2 under three minutes after Robitaille's goal. Geoff Courtnall took the original shot as he was being shoved through the slot by Marty McSorley.

Murray Craven put the Canucks in front for good halfway through the period when he fended off McSorley's check and redirected Dixon Ward's centering pass behind Hrudey. Of course, if Tim Watters had cleaned out Ward, there would not have been a pass or a goal. The Kings didn't know it at the time, but a disturbing trend was set in motion in the first period when Vancouver's Dana Murzyn scored as Zhitnik made contact.

"We didn't play 100 percent and that bothers me," Melrose said. "On three of their goals we had men right there. We had guys checking, but we didn't finish our checks. It's a question of not doing the job. The difference between winning and losing is winning the physical battles and they won most of them."

The Canucks used their superior size to rattle the Kings, bang them around for really the first time in the series. "We wanted to take the body, that's an advantage for our team," Quinn said. "We got in some good hits and we got the puck into the right spots." For whatever it was worth, the Canucks had regained home-ice advantage. It was a best-of-three series now and two of the games, if the series went the distance, would be played in Canada.

Melrose decided, if the Kings weren't going to go the distance, they would not go down meekly. Changes were needed and he was going to make them. To his utter disgust, Corey

Millen peered into his locker before the morning skate and discovered he would not be playing in Game 5 that night. A gray practice sweater was hanging inside, and gray practice sweaters were worn by "extras," players who didn't get to play in the games. Millen was a "Black Ace," been conscripted, and he wasn't happy about it.

"I know I'm not setting the world on fire, but there are more variables in the playoffs, like ice time, and it's pretty hard to judge a performance by point production alone," said Millen, who had two goals and five points in the Calgary series but not a single point in this one. "I judge myself by the way I'm skating, how my legs feel, and this is the best I've felt physically since I came back from my injury. I have more quickness, more jump, in this series than I did against Calgary."

Melrose didn't agree, and so Millen was out. Ditto defenseman Mark Hardy. "Corey's been average and you don't win with average players," Melrose said. "Mark hasn't been playing well and Tim Watters is, so it's a case of Mark being the odd man out." Wingers Gary Shuchuk and Marc Potvin would dress instead. Shuchuk played an abrasive style similar to Tony Granato, though without as much skill. Potvin, a 215-pound slugger, had played just twice since mid-March.

No one could have foreseen the consequences, that Shuchuk would play such a pivotal role in the most important — and longest — game in Los Angeles hockey history. For 86 minutes, 31 seconds the Kings and Canucks banged away at each other with a fury not previously seen in the series. The action was feverish, endless end-to-end forays, spectacular goaltending by Kelly Hrudey at one end, Kirk McLean at the other.

A goal had not been scored since Vancouver's Trevor Linden, during a two-man advantage, bulled his way to the net and put in his own rebound at 13:40 of the second period to tie the game, 3-3. Granato was in the penalty box for tripping Linden when Zhitnik was called for high-sticking Bure. Hmm, were Quinn's Game 4 remarks having an effect?

It was sudden-death overtime now, which meant no more time constraints and no more penalties, unless decapitation occurred. This game would be decided at even-strength, referee Andy van Hellemond would see to that. The night dragged on through a scoreless third period, then a scoreless first overtime.

The tension mounted. The crowd roared and players gasped. How much longer could this go on?

And then, finally, it ended. Shuchuk, standing at the left side of the crease, took a pass from Robitaille and chipped the puck under McLean's right arm at 6:31 of the second overtime. It was the only shot Shuchuk took the entire game. The red light flickered and the exhausted Kings celebrated a 4-3 win. One more and the series — the Canucks, too — would be history.

"I don't know if I saw the red light go on, but I did see the puck cross the goal line," Shuchuk said. "But I'm not a hero yet. We still have another game to finish." Shuchuk nearly couldn't finish Game 5. Gerald Diduck flattened him with a monster hit halfway through the third period and it took a while for him to come to his senses. "I got my bell rung," he said. "He got me right on the jaw. But I didn't want to go to the room. They made me."

Melrose, who coached Shuchuk in the minors, would have been surprised if he hadn't returned. "He's a courageous little Ukranian," Melrose said. "I've seen him get hit in the face with a puck, with his upper lip split in half so you could see right into the back of his nose. You could see his nose cavity. And he kept playing. They got it stitched up and put a mask on him."

Melrose looked like a genius for going with Shuchuk, though he managed to use 22 line combinations without once calling on Potvin, who watched the entire game from the bench. Melrose and especially general manager Nick Beverley were still being criticized for parting with Paul Coffey in the January deal with Detroit that brought Jimmy Carson, Shuchuk and Potvin to Los Angeles. Carson contributed five goals in the first-round series win over Calgary while Coffey's Red Wings were being eliminated by Toronto, but the heat was still on. Carson's ice time was barely a trickle now and Shuchuk hadn't even been dressing.

"Barry stuck his neck out and gave me a chance to play," Shuchuk said. "It was tough for me to watch, but I'm a role player and role players have to take a back seat to the big names." Shuchuk made an impression on his first shift when he drilled Cliff Ronning into the boards, but he also was in the penalty box when Murray Craven scored a power-play goal to give Vancouver an early 1-0 lead. Gretzky got it back 32 seconds later with his seventh postseason goal.

"I'm really happy for him because he's such a great kid," Gretzky said of Shuchuk. "You don't win without these kinds of guys. When they don't dress, they have to have an attitude that is extremely positive. Gary hadn't played in a long time, but he stayed upbeat."

The Kings could not have won such a game without the kind of goaltending Hrudey gave them. He made 36 saves to McLean's 40 and every one of them seemed difficult. Hrudey had been there before and then some, stopping 73 shots for the New York Islanders in a 3-2 quadruple-overtime victory over Washington on April 18, 1987. The 128-minute, 47-second game remains the fifth-longest in NHL history. Van Hellemond was the referee in that game, too.

"I remember my toes were cramping and all my equipment was completely soaked," Hrudey said. "It was just a terrible, hideous feeling . . . until we won. Then it was great. This game was a far cry from that one. I still felt great at the end. I wasn't the least bit nervous and my pads felt light. But we still have a very difficult task ahead. Vancouver has finished first two years in a row. They have a tremendous team and we expect them to play their best game of the series."

Hrudey found out he wasn't much of a prophet early in Game 6 when the Kings came out firing in the first period, outshot Vancouver 21-8 and grabbed a 1-0 lead on a goal by Rob Blake. If this was the best the Canucks had to offer, they should have stayed home and saved the considerable air fare.

Vancouver managed to get its game together in the second period with Diduck and Jim Sandlak scoring in a three-minute span to sink the Kings into a 2-1 hole. Beads of sweat formed on the foreheads of the Forum's 16,005 patrons who couldn't help but recall bitter memories of past playoff collapses. Even owner Bruce McNall, while sitting in his private box in the upper reaches of the arena, was overcome with a feeling of impending doom. "So many things have gone wrong in the past," he would say later.

Disaster was averted when Shuchuk skated in on his white horse again, delivering an ordinary body check that nonetheless scrambled Dana Murzyn's common sense. Inexplicably, the Canucks defenseman retaliated to the clean hit by smashing Shuchuk into the boards. Still enraged even as referee Paul Stewart raised his arm to signify a penalty, Murzyn whacked Mike Donnelly across the back with his stick, knocking the winger down with a cross-check. Dumb, dumb, dumb, Dana.

The Canucks managed to kill off Murzyn's boarding penalty, but they botched a line change two seconds into his cross-checking penalty and were caught with too many men on the ice. Kelly Hrudey had noticed the Canucks were attempting to change and he sent a long, clearing pass to Alexei Zhitnik, who led a rush into the Vancouver zone. "Both of their defensemen wanted to change," Hrudey would explain, "but one guy turned around, saw Alex, and stayed on."

The Kings had scored only four goals in 32 previous power-play attempts in the series, but now they had a two-man advantage and used it to tie the game. Jari Kurri ripped a shot from the left faceoff circle that sailed past Kirk McLean's stick at 15:48 of the second period. Because the goal came so quickly, 39 seconds into the five-on-three, the Kings still had an additional 1:21 of power play time to go. They required only 17 seconds of it to take a 3-2 lead. McLean made a save on Darryl Sydor's point shot, but Tomas Sandstrom banged in the rebound at 16:05. Warren Rychel finished the three-goal flurry at 17:44 and the Kings took a 4-2 lead into the intermission.

"I really thought the power-play goals were the turning point in the game," Hrudey said. "I'm not a huge believer in momentum, but I think those goals really pumped us up, probably to a level we hadn't achieved all year long."

When Wayne Gretzky sent a screaming slap shot by McLean's glove at 8:54 of the third period, increasing the lead to 5-2, the noise in the Forum reached a new decibel level. Fans poured into the aisles to dance and a miniature Stanley Cup, an aluminum foil model, was tossed onto the ice. Gretzky raised his stick and skated, unconsciously apparently, close to the boards near the ice-level seat occupied by his wife, Janet. In a flash, he spun away and embraced longtime King Dave Taylor. "She always gets mad when I don't acknowledge her at hockey games. But I don't acknowledge anyone at hockey games," Gretzky said. "I'm just into the *game*."

The game, along with the Canucks' season, was over soon enough. The final score was 5-3. The Kings had outshot Vancouver, 50-28, had shot a defense called almost impenetrable full of holes. Hrudey had outplayed McLean again and Vancouver's best player, Pavel Bure, was rendered invisible. Zhitnik held Bure without a point in the last two games and to only one goal in the entire series; the "Russian Rocket" barely got off the launching pad.

And the Kings were Smythe Division champions.

"The way guys were hustling, really playing hard, there was no way we were going to blow it. There was no way we were letting them back in the game," Taylor said as he pulled on a black and silver championship T-shirt in a dressing room gone mad.

"After Gretz scored, the way the place was rocking . . . it was great," Taylor said. "The whistle would blow and people would be dancing. They were having a lot of fun and so were we. We sort of liked it whenever play would stop because then you could look around and soak it in. The way the game was going, you could sit there and savor it a little bit."

Bruce McNall was as giddy as ever. The paper bag he threatened to put on his head during the dog days of winter had long been discarded, and he finally was being paid a dividend after spending sacks full of money to build a championship caliber team.

"It's pretty emotional now," McNall said. "We've taken a lot of heat over the years and I'm pretty stunned. This T-shirt I'm wearing, it's like a symbol almost. I put this on and I was thinking that maybe I did make a contribution. I put it on for the million fans who have been begging and hoping we'd finally win something."

Not only had the Kings never advanced beyond the second round before, they had won only three games in their previous four second-round engagements combined. Now they were celebrating a four games to two victory over a heavily-favored Canucks team that crushed them in the regular season.

"The overtime game was the turning point," Melrose said. "It would have been very difficult to come home and play if we had lost a double-overtime game. But my job as coach is to not get too high right now. I mean, my mom just called and she was crying. This is definitely nice and all, a great feeling. But we haven't won nothin' yet as far as I'm concerned. Ask me how I feel when we win the Stanley Cup. There's an old saying, 'If you don't ask for much, be careful, you might get it.' "

A second-round victory hadn't seemed much to ask for in the past, yet the Kings could never deliver one. Now that the Kings had, it was the Canucks' turn to sit in stunned silence on an airplane and fly into an offseason of discontent, their second consecutive regular-season championship rendered meaningless. Pat Quinn wasn't even certain he wanted to coach again, though he was sure to remain as team president and general manager.

"It isn't unfair to say we were a team that was capable of winning if we executed well, worked hard and were disciplined," Quinn said. "(But) we were going into new territory (as favorites), we had to deliver under high expectations, and we didn't do it. We expected to be a club that advanced, but Los Angeles had something to say about that. They just did a better job than we did."

The Canucks' inability to control Gretzky was a major factor in their demise. He picked up at least one point in every game and finished with six goals and seven assists in the series. "Gretzky may have lost a step or two, but he's strong intellectually," Quinn said. Gretzky, who did not request a pain-killing injection before Game 6, had a club-record 23 playoff points in 12 games, breaking by one the mark he set in 1989. "I think Wayne is possessed," McNall said. "He's just so determined to win. You can see it in his eyes."

The Kings would meet either the Toronto Maple Leafs, and their old pal Doug Gilmour, or the St. Louis Blues in the Campbell Conference final. Despite all their problems with the Maple Leafs, a lot of the Kings preferred to play Toronto because so many of them were from Ontario and still had family there. The Kings would have to contend with Brett Hull and star goalie Curtis Joseph if they played St. Louis, but they would have the advantage of beginning a series with the Blues at home.

"No matter who we play, it'll be the responsibility of the guys who have won Stanley Cups to show the young guys that we better be ready to keep playing," Gretzky said. "We better be ready to come to practice and work even harder because we're only halfway home. It gets even tougher now."

Twelve

Hooray for Hockeywood

For 16 seasons Dave Taylor toiled in relative obscurity. He put up numbers that some day may get him into the Hockey Hall of Fame, but the need to wear dark sunglasses or a fake mustache in order to fool the paparazzi was never a problem for him.

Taylor liked it that way, preferring to carry himself with dignity while living quietly in a Los Angeles suburb with his wife, Beth, and their two daughters, Jamie and Katie. So that is where he elected to celebrate on the evening when the albatross of so many playoff failures had finally been lifted.

"But it's sure been a long time coming," he said the next morning. "Sixteen years and this is the only chance I've had. I had a beer in the locker room, I hugged (trainer) Pete Demers and (administrator) John Wolf, then I went home. It feels good. I didn't think I'd be nervous before the game, but I couldn't even take a nap in the afternoon like I usually do. I was sweating bullets all day."

The Kings still didn't know if they would be playing Toronto or St. Louis — those teams were bracing for a Game 7 in the Norris Division final — and Taylor didn't care. He spent the rare day off relaxing with his family and fielding congratulatory phone calls, including one from a dear friend, Marcel Dionne. "He said to keep it going," Taylor said. Dionne scored 550 goals in 12 seasons as a King, but he never came close to having his name engraved on a Stanley Cup; he felt good for the old timers like Taylor, Demers, Wolf, and broadcaster Bob Miller.

"Whatever happens now, I won't feel like I've been cheated out of anything," Taylor said. "This could be my last year, it could be my last chance at a Stanley Cup, but I'm always optimistic. I think we've got a shot."

The team's long-suffering fans — and apparently many who had no intention of actually attending any of the games — shared Taylor's confidence. It took the Kings more than two weeks to sell all of their tickets for the first two rounds of the playoffs, but tickets to every possible Campbell Conference and Stanley Cup final game at the Forum were gone 55 minutes after they were put on sale.

Not that every ticket wound up in the hands of the common fans. Many who were shut out accused ticket agencies of hoarding tickets to resell at higher than face value. The practice, called legalized scalping by some, is legitimate in California if the sale doesn't take place at the site of the event. Brokers were already charging $325 for a $95 ticket to a Stanley Cup final game, a price that was certain to rise if the Kings made it that far.

Wayne Gretzky felt it was imperative that they did. Both of the city's pro basketball teams, the Lakers and Clippers, were first-round victims in the NBA playoffs and neither of the baseball teams, the Dodgers or Angels, was expected to contend for a pennant. The opportunity for hockey to take center stage in a fickle place like Los Angeles was never better.

"We've been on this block a long time," Gretzky said, "and we haven't exactly set the world on fire. It's important that we take advantage of it while we have the chance. There aren't words to describe how big this is. It could be so huge for the organization."

As huge as the Kings' upset of Vancouver was, however, it paled in comparison to the Pittsburgh Penguins' stunning removal in the Patrick Division series. The New York Islanders, behind former Kings goaltender Glenn Healy, knocked off the two-time defending champions in seven games. If the Kings could somehow get to the Stanley Cup final, they would not have to contend with Mario Lemieux.

"I have to admit that one shocked me," coach Barry Melrose said. "You have to really, really respect what the Islanders did.

Hey, it's wild right now, really exciting. For the first time in a long time, no one knows who is going to win the Stanley Cup."

The Kings planned to spend the evening of May 15 glued to their television sets to watch the Maple Leafs and Blues slug it out, but it was a short night. They started packing for Toronto in the first period when it became apparent St. Louis was not going to put up much resistance. The Leafs romped, 6-0, and would open the Campbell Conference championship series at home in two days.

Toronto was expected to improve under its new management team of general manager Cliff Fletcher, who built strong teams in Calgary before moving on, and head coach Pat Burns, who spent the previous four years in Montreal. But no one could have predicted a 44-29-11 record in the regular season that gave the Leafs a club-record 99 points — a 32-point improvement for a team that missed the playoffs entirely the year before. "Our main goal was just to make the playoffs," captain Wendel Clark said. A second cousin to Melrose, Clark was a first-round draft pick in 1985 whose career had been plagued by injuries.

The team's loyal fans were as frustrated as those who followed the Kings, but they were gaining confidence a Stanley Cup banner could be added to the collection of 11 that hangs at historic Maple Leaf Gardens for the first time since 1967. Visions of an all-Canadian final matching the Leafs and Canadiens danced in their heads.

Why not? Eight months earlier, when NHL training camps opened, who would have predicted a Los Angeles-Toronto series in the conference final? "I think we're all surprised," Leafs winger Mike Krushelnyski said. "We all would have been shaking our heads if somebody had said these teams would still be playing now."

It figured to be an emotional, hard-fought series, and probably one devoid of many goals. Toronto outscored the Kings, 16-15, in winning the season series 2-1-1, and the Blues could scrape only 11 goals against Leafs rookie goaltender Felix Potvin, whose splendid play in the regular season allowed Fletcher the luxury of dealing Grant Fuhr to Buffalo for a first-round draft pick and 6-foot-3 power-play specialist Dave Andreychuk, a 54-goal man. The Leafs boasted a strong defense corps that featured Dave Ellett, Todd Gill and Jamie Macoun, but their not-so-secret weapon, Doug Gilmour, was the player the Kings would have to watch the most.

Stolen from Calgary the year before in a 10-player trade that was making Flames general manager Doug Risebrough look ridiculous, Gilmour was coming off a 32-goal, 127-point season, the best of his career, and he had a chance to win the Hart Trophy as the league's MVP. Gilmour was an extraordinary two-way player who likely would win the Selke Trophy as the NHL's top defensive forward, and Toronto was hardly the only place where he was regarded as the best all-around player in hockey. Unless the Kings kept the damage Gilmour inflicted to a minimum, they would not win the series and advance to the Stanley Cup final.

The Kings did not intend to make Gilmour pay for the destruction he caused in their 6-4 victory over the Leafs back in November. The two-handed slash that broke Tomas Sandstrom's arm, they claimed, was forgotten. "It doesn't matter anymore," Sandstrom said. "I wasn't happy when it happened, but it's in the past. I'm just going to go out and play. I don't think about it anymore. The only thing that matters now is winning the games."

There would be enough distractions without worrying about Gilmour. Nine Kings players, including Gretzky, were born in the Canadian province of Ontario. Putting aside childhood dreams of wearing the blue Maple Leaf wouldn't be a problem; those days were long gone. But attempts at accommodating the requests of family members and friends for tickets and time would be hard to ignore. And with only four teams left to cover in the playoffs, the number of media attending the series would swell.

"There are going to be a lot of people who want to get a photograph or an autograph," Gretzky said. "Personally, I've always felt you make it harder by pushing people away and telling them no rather than saying hello and being obliging. But my family certainly realizes and understands that it's going to be my responsibility to be working, not to be having lunch and dinner with them. I won't even see my family except for on the off-days or during the off-hours. Look, I've been through this before and I understand that all the guys on the team need to stick together."

Gretzky was one of six Kings with Final Four experience. The others were Charlie Huddy, Jari Kurri, Marty McSorley, Pat Conacher, and Sandstrom. They had played in 43 conference and

Stanley Cup final rounds between them and won a combined 17 championships.

"I think there are some things we can pass on to the other guys, but it is a little bit different here," said Huddy, who played on five Cup-winning teams with the Edmonton Oilers. "We were expected to get this far in Edmonton. Here, we weren't supposed to beat Calgary and we definitely weren't supposed to beat Vancouver. Most people didn't give us any kind of chance to get this far. It gets tougher now, obviously. The further you go, the tougher it gets. There are only four teams left and all of them are on a bit of a roll, fired up and all excited."

This was going to be an emotion-charged series, all right. After Toronto broke open Game 1 with three consecutive goals in the third period, the 225-pound McSorley aroused passions throughout the city by skating at the 170-pound Gilmour and smashing him to the ice with a tremendous hit to the jaw, one that resulted in a major penalty for elbowing and bedlam inside Maple Leaf Gardens.

Two minutes, 34 seconds remained in a game the Leafs would win 4-1 when the incident, seen by many as payback for the slash that fractured Sandstrom's arm and an earlier hit on Alexei Zhitnik, took place. Gilmour, the star of the game with two goals and an assist, was decked a moment after he delivered a pass during a Toronto power play. As Gilmour lay on the ice, Clark charged at McSorley and hit him with several punches. Then Dave Taylor and Todd Gill fought.

The scene was both ugly and extremely bizarre. Fans littered the ice with so much debris — a wooden crutch was among the items thrown — that Kings goalie Kelly Hrudey dove inside his net for protection. Gilmour, momentarily stunned, rose to his feet and skated to the Los Angeles bench, where he hung onto Darryl Sydor's stick and exchanged words with several players. Burns, in the meantime, moved from behind the Toronto bench to an area of seats that separated the teams. Burns screamed at Melrose, flailed his arms, and became more enraged when Melrose puffed out his cheeks to mock Burns' generous girth. Earlier, Burns poked fun at Melrose's unique hairstyle — "the Billy Ray Cyrus cut," Burns called it — by tugging on strands at the back of his own neck.

Despite the mature conduct of the coaches, order was restored. Referee Dan Marouelli handed game misconducts to

McSorley, Taylor, Clark and Gill. But the inflammatory nature of the postgame remarks, especially those emanating from the Toronto side, didn't bode well for a peaceful Game 2.

"I thought it was a real cheap shot," Fletcher said of McSorley's hit. "He used his elbow and his knee. The intent was there to put (Gilmour) out. Fortunately, he didn't." Fletcher vowed it wouldn't happen again. When asked how the Leafs could possibly guarantee Gilmour's protection, Fletcher grumbled, "Ever play in the NHL? Go ask someone who has." Gilmour likely would be assigned a bodyguard, probably Ken Baumgartner, a scarcely-used enforcer who once played for the Kings.

Burns was still steamed after the game, which is when he suggested Melrose ordered McSorley to take out Gilmour, who earlier in the third period sent Zhitnik head over heels with a crushing check the Kings saw as late and illegal. "If Baumgartner did that to Gretzky, he would have been hung on Parliament Hill," Burns said of McSorley's elbow. "Who else is going to run (Gilmour) except McSorley? I lost a lot of respect for that team. That wouldn't happen coming off our bench."

For reasons known only to Burns, he even took on Wayne Gretzky, who was on the ice for three of Toronto's four goals and outplayed by Gilmour. "I think Wayne plays maybe not the full 200 feet of the ice, plays the neutral zone a lot and waits for that opportunity to go," he said. "Dougie goes back to pick up his checks and finishes them at the other end."

Gretzky, perhaps figuring he couldn't win no matter what he said in rebuttal, merely shrugged. Melrose snapped. "Pat Burns is making a lot of money because of what Wayne has done for this game," he said. "Anyone in hockey who would criticize Wayne isn't very smart. Wayne is the greatest player who ever played and has done more for the game than anyone else. It's ludicrous to criticize Wayne Gretzky."

Gilmour was only a little more talkative than Gretzky after the game and a lot less loquacious than he was while visiting the Kings bench. "I don't want to comment. I had a couple of words to say, that's all," he said. According to Darryl Sydor, Gilmour warned the Kings it would be a "long" series. Did that mean they wouldn't be swept?

But the war of words was just beginning. The Kings hadn't forgotten about the "crybaby" taunts Burns hurled at them following the Gilmour-Sandstrom incident in November. "Part of the game," Burns called the slash that broke Sandstrom's arm. "That's hockey," he said. "Guys get whacked all the time. Guys get broken arms. The Kings are always crying about something ... you can't touch them without getting suspended."

Now that the skate was on the other foot, so to speak, the Kings were fairly amused by Burns' reaction. "Weren't we the biggest whiners in hockey? I think we've been surpassed," Melrose said. He vehemently denied McSorley's attempt to extract a pound of Gilmour's flesh was motivated by revenge, and he accused Gilmour and Bob Berg of using leg whips and hits to the knees to bring down Zhitnik and Tony Granato.

"When you stand up and hit guys high, that's fine," Melrose said. "That's the way the game is played. But a knee is a vulnerable area. A hit at the knee is intent to injure, and injure for a long time. It's like a crackback block in football. When you do that, it's only for one purpose, to injure."

Melrose said he had no idea what prompted Burns' tirade — "I thought he was ordering a hot dog. I think it's funny when people lose control" — and he made it clear he was fed up with Marouelli, a referee he flogged for the second time in a week and for the third time in two months. Now he was upset because the hit on Zhitnik did not result in a penalty; Zhitnik only missed one shift after staggering back to the bench, but he couldn't practice the following day due to a swollen knee.

"There's two sets of rules," claimed Melrose, who was beginning to sound like Pat Quinn. "Gilmour just about rips Alex's knee apart and he gets nothing. Marty hits (Gilmour) and maybe it should be a two-minute penalty and he gets five. They were running our smaller guys, it was a joke. The good news is we only get (Marouelli) once because this series is too intense for him." Melrose paused. "Oh, he's a great referee. I think he should go to the Hall of Fame with Gil Stein."

(Stein, the league's president at the time, was said to have orchestrated his own election to the Hockey Hall of Fame. He withdrew after the season ended.)

Melrose also blasted the Maple Leaf Gardens security staff, saying it was slow to respond when the Kings bench was pelted with garbage during the melee near the end of the period. "We're in the Stanley Cup semifinals and they've got two World War I vets with pea shooters," he huffed.

The fans' reaction reminded Hrudey of some visits to Madison Square Garden when he was playing for the Islanders. "But I can't comprehend somebody being a big enough idiot to throw a crutch on the ice," he said. "I know it's playoff time and everybody's excited, but there are a lot of mean tempers out there. I've never liked that feeling. I've never understood why fans litter the ice. They forget it's a game."

McSorley took his sweet time before emerging from the trainer's room, but one glance at his face was proof the extra minutes were needed for repairs. He wore a purple welt the size of a golf ball, several stitches beneath his right eye, and a few more stitches near the outside corner of the eye, all of the damage coming in the fight with Clark.

"What incident?" McSorley said at first. "I hit (Gilmour) at the blue line and two seconds later he was standing up and yelling at our bench, so how bad could it have been? They can call me a cheap-shot artist if they want, but I'm going to play just as hard in the next game. I was looking to hit him, not take his head off. Hey, I'll be out there if they want. They'll know where I am."

Several telephone messages were waiting for McSorley when he returned to his hotel room, none of them complimentary. The next day, when two large bouquets of balloons were delivered to the Kings dressing room after practice, Luc Robitaille yelled, "One's from Doug and the other's from Wendel!" Not likely. For all the commotion his hit was causing in Toronto, McSorley's picture was probably placed in every post office in town. "A McSorry Incident!" screamed the banner headline in the *Toronto Star*, which published a large color photograph of McSorley's battered face. McSorley was the talk of the town, none of it good.

Even Nick Beverley, who usually is a man of few words, felt compelled to defend McSorley after reading the local papers. "I think the word that was used with reckless abandon is 'vicious.' How anyone could call that a vicious shot is beyond me," Beverley said.

"I wish I was talented enough to go out and pick and choose who I'm going to hit," McSorley said. "My standpoint is I have to be physical. I made a check and they took exception to it. (Gilmour) cut across my path and I'm going to hit him every chance I get. We're just going to play hard-nosed hockey, that's all. We're certainly not targeting anybody or looking to take a run at anybody."

Burns was considerably calmer on the off-day between games. He joked about his considerable paunch, warning Melrose that "his stomach will go out some, too" when he hits 40. But Burns couldn't resist taking a dig at Melrose, boasting he could have been general manager as well as coach of the Kings a month before Melrose was hired as coach. "But what's the big deal? I love it in Toronto and I'm glad I didn't go to L.A.," he said.

The Kings denied ever offering any position to Burns. Rogie Vachon, who was general manager at the time, said he asked the Canadiens for permission to talk to Burns but did not pursue him because Burns was close to completing a deal with the Maple Leafs. Kings president Roy Mlakar said Burns' agent, Don Meehan, called to say Burns was leaving Montreal and was interested in the Los Angeles job. Mlakar said Melrose, Rick Dudley and Tom McVie were the only candidates the Kings interviewed.

With all the barbs being tossed in so many directions, it was hard to believe the teams had played only one game. Come to think of it, it was hard to believe they had played a game at all.

Which was perfectly fine with the Kings, whose performance in the third period was one they could learn to forget real fast. Giving up three goals in a 5 1-2 minute span was bad enough, but getting outshot 22-1 was downright pathetic. For the record, the shot was taken by Jimmy Carson. No one recalled if Felix Potvin needed to make a tough save.

Kelly Hrudey played so well in front of the net, when he wasn't diving inside it to avoid crutches and other falling objects, that he was named second star behind Gilmour. Defense was supposed to be the Leafs' strength, yet they outshot the Kings 47-28. "Do I look shaken?" Hrudey wondered. "If anyone knows anything about me, they know it takes a lot more than that to get my confidence down."

Nonetheless, the Kings' self-esteem rose several notches in Game 2, a 3-2 come-from-behind victory that was decided, in a deliciously ironic twist, on a goal by Sandstrom at 12:20 of the third period. Sandstrom took one stride into the left faceoff circle after accepting a Wayne Gretzky pass and powered a perfect shot over Potvin's glove to tie the series 1-1.

The bloodbath anticipated by many never materialized, but McSorley and Gilmour resumed their love affair late in the first period and created yet another controversy. The Kings were killing off a penalty when McSorley punched Gilmour in the face, a foul that referee Don Koharski missed. Gilmour eventually retaliated with a shove, McSorley pushed back, then Gilmour appeared to head butt McSorley in the face.

Under league rules, head butting or *attempting* to head butt calls for a five-minute penalty and a game misconduct, yet Koharski sent each player to the penalty box for roughing. "In order for there to be a penalty for head butting, there has to be contact," said Dave Newell, an NHL supervisor of officials. Not according to the rule book, there doesn't, but the call stood. What was that Melrose said about a double-standard?

General manager Nick Beverley, in what would be a futile attempt to have Gilmour suspended for Game 3, asked league officials to take another look at the incident on tape. "We felt it was important to raise the point," he said. "It's extremely important . . . that everyone be treated on an equal plane."

Not that it should have mattered, but if Gilmour did make contact, McSorley wasn't telling. But he did need seven stitches to close a fresh cut near his right eye, the one Wendel Clark pummeled in Game 1. McSorley said his face was smashed into the boards when he was struck by a high stick in the second period, but he declined to name the perpetrator. "I don't want to start another rivalry," he said.

There were plenty of those to go around even before Melrose and *Hockey Night in Canada's* bombastic broadcaster, Don Cherry, began to feud. It was Cherry, the former Boston Bruins and Colorado Rockies coach, who called Sandstrom a "chicken Swede" who deserved to have his arm broken back in November. This was hardly the first time Cherry had gone after Sandstrom, or any hockey player of European descent for that matter. Cherry all but wrapped himself in a Canadian flag when he was on the air, and his popularity was such that he probably could run for Prime Minister and win.

Melrose is Canadian, too, but he resented Cherry's constant criticisms of Sandstrom and he was outraged to learn that Cherry interrupted an interview after Game 1 to plant a kiss on Gilmour's cheek. Melrose didn't attend journalism school, but he was pretty certain Cherry's cuddling act breached all the rules of objectivity. So he objected, strongly suggesting that none of his players appear with Cherry on camera. Predictably, Cherry reacted like a juvenile. Melrose, he said, "was a candyass as a player, and he's a candyass now."

So who needed Gilmour-McSorley? Cherry's remark was idiotic but not atypical. His TV ratings were so high, the Canadian Broadcasting Corp. didn't seem to care what he said. Melrose said he "would never get into a war of words with a man who has his own television show," which probably would have been the wise move.

But Melrose can't swelter in silence, and he exploded. He accused Cherry and the CBC of slanted coverage and said they were openly pulling for a Toronto-Montreal Stanley Cup final. "It's very obvious they want Toronto to win, and they go out of their way to show it," Melrose said. "We just don't think that's professional. I don't think we're getting a fair shake. They've ripped Tomas so many times. They've ripped Marty. They've ripped so many of our players. We just took a stand and obviously we got some heat for it."

Be assured Melrose gained more satisfaction out of the Kings' Game 2 win than usual. "There's a lot of animosity between these teams," he said. Sandstrom was stoic as usual. No, the winning goal shouldn't be taken as payback. It was a lucky shot, might have grazed the post on its way in. Sure, it's always nice to contribute. "We're in the playoffs now and we can't worry about something that happened months ago," he said. "You can't worry about being pissed off. I'm not going to say anything bad about anybody."

Gilmour hurt the Kings again when he scored 2:25 into the game. The goal came after Warren Rychel, who missed Game 1 with a sore knee, was penalized for high-sticking Todd Gill. "He was holding my stick and I gave him a crack to let him know I was there," Rychel said. But except for McSorley's punch to the head, Gilmour didn't take a shot for the rest of the game, and he was on the ice when Gretzky set up Sandstrom for the decisive goal. Was it possible Gilmour hadn't skated the full 200 feet? "I made sure I took care of things on *my* side of the red line tonight," Gretzky joked.

Just about all the Kings did. Forty-eight hours after getting harpooned in the third period, the Kings limited the Leafs to six shots in the final 20 minutes, none of them especially dangerous. Kelly Hrudey faced only 23 shots — one more than he saw in the disastrous Game 1 third period alone — after Glenn Anderson gave Toronto a 2-1 lead 3:59 into the match. "Our defense has been criticized, but it's a six-man unit and when we play as a unit, we do well," Hrudey said.

The Kings caught a break in the second period when referee Don Koharski called a questionable penalty on Dave Andreychuk for bumping Hrudey behind the net. Contact was made, but it wasn't as flagrant as Hrudey made it appear. Tony Granato jammed Corey Millen's pass behind Felix Potvin on the ensuing power play to tie the game 2-2 at the 13-minute mark.

"It was a set play," Millen said after picking up his first point in seven games. "Tony told me to try and draw the defenseman out, then give it to him at the goal line. It worked out absolutely perfect." Maybe Potvin, like Vancouver's Kirk McLean, was vulnerable after all. He had allowed a total of five goals in his previous five games. "We found some chinks in his armor," Melrose said.

Two nights later, flaws were discovered in Toronto's power play. Jari Kurri and Dave Taylor each scored shorthanded goals in Game 3, a 4-2 win that put the Kings ahead in the series, 2-1. The Leafs never had a chance. The Forum crowd was whipped into a frenzy when a Smythe Division championship banner was unfurled and illuminated in the darkened arena before the game, and again when favorite son Marty McSorley skated out for his first shift. A live picture of McSorley's battered face was shown on the scoreboard's giant screens, prompting fans to break into a "Mar-ty, Mar-ty" chant. Doug Gilmour, a hero in Toronto, was a bum in Los Angeles; the fans booed and cursed him throughout the game.

McSorley definitely appreciated his reception. "I would be lying if I said the last few days in Toronto weren't a little bit taxing," he said. "I just want to play the game. So much was made out of something that I didn't think was anything at all. It was made into such a bad event."

Pat Burns was in a bad mood after the game, but he was quite the charitable fellow in the hours leading up to it. Kings fans sent 18 dozen doughnuts to Burns at the Leafs' beachfront hotel in Santa Monica, a harmless way to ridicule his weight, and he made certain the goodies were distributed to the homeless. "At least some people in Los Angeles like me now," Burns said.

Not as much as they appreciated Taylor, whose goal with Luc Robitaille in the penalty box for slashing gave the Kings a two-goal cushion 1:26 into the third period. He took a blindside pass from Pat Conacher and beat Potvin high to the glove side. "I don't think there's anyone who lifts this team more with a goal than Davey," Gretzky said.

The biggest goal belonged to Alexei Zhitnik, and Conacher had a hand in that one, too. He won a faceoff from Gilmour during a four-on-three situation, then Zhitnik accepted a return pass from Gretzky in the right circle. He smoked the puck over Potvin's right pad to snap a 2-2 tie with 1:48 to play in the second period. "Yeah, but I wasn't very good on faceoffs. I doubt if I won 50 percent of them tonight," Conacher said.

The Kings squandered the 2-0 lead they forged on goals by Rob Blake and Kurri, whose one-timer inside the near post midway through the second period gave him 100 career playoff goals, three behind the all-time leader, Gretzky. But Toronto roared back. Gilmour wriggled between Kurri and Tim Watters to stash his fourth goal in three games at 15:15 and Ken Baumgartner, who would be on unemployment if he needed to score to collect a paycheck, tied the game less than two minutes later.

But once again the Kings were solid in the third period. The Leafs were held to five shots on goal and became frustrated at their inability to attack. Gilmour, the one player they could least afford to be without, took a foolish interference penalty with 2:08 remaining and then was hit with a 10-minute misconduct for complaining. Gilmour was jeered lustily and he smashed his stick after leaving the ice.

But one thing about the Leafs, they were resilient. Toronto lost two of the first three games in each of its other playoff series and came back to win them both. "Nothing wrong with being a little bit scared," Wendel Clark said.

Trailing a Kings team whose big guns had yet to fire had to be more than a little frightening. Of the eight goals they scored in the first three games, none came off the sticks of Gretzky and Robitaille. It was Calgary all over again. Hadn't Gretzky cracked or broken a rib against the Flames? Was the injury still bothering him?

Team physician Dr. Ron Kvitne, who was being quoted as much as any Kings official, watched Gretzky get banged around in Game 3 and expressed surprise that his services were not requested. "He took a number of hits, lots of punishment, and I expected him to say something to me, but he didn't," Kvitne said. "So I think he's basically blocked it out of his mind because I think he is still playing with some pain. A rib injury — whether it was cracked or broken I don't know — tends to linger for a while. But I don't even examine him anymore, we don't even put ice on it.

"When he first got cross-checked in Calgary, he couldn't roll over in bed without experiencing pain. I'm sure he was in constant pain throughout the Calgary series, which leads me to believe he has a tremendously high threshold for pain."

Gretzky said Toronto's smothering defense was inhibiting his game more than any pain he might be experiencing. Otherwise, he wasn't concerned. At least Gretzky had three assists, two of which led to game-winning goals. Robitaille didn't have a point and his six penalty minutes exceeded his shot total by four.

"Let's face it," Melrose said, "the pace of these games has been Toronto's pace with all the whistles and stoppages. It's their tempo, not ours. I can remember some games against Vancouver when there wasn't a whistle for 10 minutes. I wish you guys would get off Wayne's case. Any time he doesn't get three points in a game people wonder what's wrong with him. Well, there isn't anything wrong with the way Wayne Gretzky is playing. I mean, Al Davis got it right when he said, 'Just win, baby.' Stats are for losers. The important thing is we've found a way to win."

Gretzky snapped out of his "slump" with a power-play goal and an assist in Game 4, but little else of a positive nature took place in Toronto's methodical 4-2 victory that sent the series back to Maple Leaf Gardens tied at two games each. Gretzky scores and the Kings lose. Gilmour doesn't and the Kings still lose. Once again they would have to win a crucial fifth game on the road.

And all because the Kings couldn't keep household names Bob Rouse, Mike Eastwood—or was it Clint?—and Rob Pearson off the scoresheet. That trio had six goals between them in the playoffs. The game-winner was supplied by 34-year-old Mike Foligno, who stripped the puck from Gretzky, passed it to Mike Krushelnyski, then got it back and scored a power-play goal for a 3-1 Leafs advantage in the first period. The only other time the Kings gave up that many first-period goals came in the opening game of the Smythe Division final, a 5-2 loss to Vancouver; at least that one was on the road.

Toronto received a huge emotional lift from Foligno, who was as popular among his teammates as Gilmour was loathed by the Kings. Foligno was benched in the previous game for his comatose demeanor in Game 2, but Burns had an inkling he would be at his animated best in a game the Leafs absolutely had to win. Burns was right. Foligno might have caused cracks in the ice the way he jumped up and down after he scored.

"I didn't have much enthusiasm in the second game," Foligno said. "I wasn't even talking on the bench like I normally do. If I'm not talking, I'm usually dead."

Rouse hurt the Kings at both ends of the ice. First he cashed in the rebound of Gilmour's wraparound attempt 2:30 into the game to open the scoring. Then he made a brilliant defensive maneuver in the second period that prevented a potential Kings goal and resulted in a back-breaking goal for Toronto. The Kings were trailing 3-1 when Rouse poked the puck from a driving McSorley to spring a three-on-two rush the other way. McSorley was caught up ice when Pearson made it 4-1. "Rouse," Burns said, "has been our anchor."

Luc Robitaille could relate to that. His stick felt light as an anvil by now. He launched five shots at Potvin, none of them went in, and he still didn't have so much as a point in the series. "Luc has got to get his nose dirty," Melrose said. "He is pushing to score because he thinks he has to score. If he would just get dirty and involved, that's all we need from him."

Robitaille's roommate when the Kings went on the road was Jimmy Carson. He had one point. Must have been a lot of positive energy in that room. "It's not like we're not trying," Carson said. "Sometimes you start to press, but you've just got to keep plugging away. The thing is, you can't let the other parts of your game falter. If you're not scoring, you've got to do other things, like making a big pass or a big hit." A big hit?

Just when the series began to calm down, Burns jump-started his spat with Melrose after the teams arrived in Toronto. It seemed Burns didn't care for Melrose's post-Game 4 remark that the Leafs "have ten 30-year-old guys who clog up the middle well," which was meant as praise for Toronto's checking game. Now Burns was taking a complimentary quote as criticism and using it to stir up controversy. What a grouch.

"Barry Melrose hasn't shown anybody any respect since the playoffs started," Burns hissed. "I don't have to like it. I have to say that he's done a great job with his team, but I don't think Barry understands that coaching is a fraternity. We should respect each other. We're alone out there. Someday he might be alone.

"I honestly think he thought he could distract me with that doughnut thing. Well, I was a cop for 16 years. I was called a pig and a dog. I had beer bottles broken over my head. I was kicked in the groin. I had a woman I was arresting try and scratch my eyes out. Calling me a doughnut is not going to distract me."

Melrose was more concerned with his team's ability to go to the well again, pull up a full bucket for the third consecutive Game 5 on the road and take command of the series. The Kings were able to do it in Calgary and Vancouver, now it would have to be done once more. It was that or be forced to win two straight games while one skate was dangling from a slippery ledge.

Jimmy Carson felt as if both of his legs had been yanked over the cliff at the pregame skate. Melrose told Carson to enjoy the view from the Maple Leaf Gardens stands; Carson was out, little-used winger Jim Thomson was in. Was Melrose serious? Thomson couldn't play regularly for the Ottawa Senators. Sure, Carson was struggling. He'd managed a mere two assists and 13 shots on goal in 10 games since his five-goal output against Calgary. But his ice time kept getting cut and, besides, none of the other Kings forwards were producing. If Melrose was looking for offense, Jim Thomson surely wouldn't provide it.

"I asked him if this was punishment and he told me not to look at it that way," Carson said. He did look embarrassed. "I'm positive about my future, what can I say? I'm not going to worry about what certain members of the press have to say. I've been taking some heat, but that's part of the game. I want to play, but I'm not going to pout. I wasn't playing much as it is, six minutes one game, eight minutes in another. Along with the power-play time I haven't been getting, it's tough to get a lot of things done."

Melrose made a fairly drastic change before Game 5 in Vancouver, when he benched Corey Millen in favor of Gary Shuchuk; all Shuchuk did was score the winning goal in double-overtime. But if this Game 5 went to overtime, Jim Thomson would have a hard time scoring from the bench. A Thomson-for-Carson swap made about as much sense as, oh, a Thomson and Marc Fortier trade for Bob Kudelski.

Shuchuk needed 86 minutes, 31 seconds to score his only previous playoff goal, but fewer than 22 minutes were required for him to give the Kings a 1-0 lead at Maple Leaf Gardens. It came at 1:53 of the second period, a slam dunk into an unprotected net after Luc Robitaille dug a loose puck from under Felix Potvin's pads. Robitaille's assist was his first point in six games.

Jari Kurri increased the lead to 2-0 at the 14:15 mark with his second goal of the season and eighth of the postseason. He lifted the puck over Potvin's glove after Warren Rychel's slap shot from the right side ricocheted off the end boards into the slot. The Kings were dominating, forcing Potvin to make big saves. Thomson had gotten in an early shift, accomplished no more than what could have been expected, and would play the part of spectator for the remainder of the game. Just like Carson.

Then, suddenly, the momentum shifted. With under five minutes to play in the period, Tony Granato was cited for high-sticking his old friend, Bill Berg, high in the Los Angeles zone. It was not a good penalty to take. "I got hit and I was falling off-balance, then my stick came up," Granato said later. "I'm smarter than that, to take a penalty like that at a time like that." No matter. Mike Krushelnyski made him pay, redirecting Rouse's point shot behind Kelly Hrudey at 16:11 to draw Toronto to within a goal.

The Kings had a slight territorial edge in the third period, but Potvin continued to excel and bought time for his team to tie the game. The Leafs did at 8:43, thanks to a couple of bounces and a non-call by referee Bill McCreary, who swallowed his whistle when Rob Pearson pulled down Shuchuk in front of the Toronto net. "He's not going to call that at that time of the game," Melrose said.

Shuchuk lost the puck when he sprawled on the ice and couldn't get back in time to prevent a four-on-three rush into the Kings zone. Doug Gilmour threw a centering pass for Sylvain Lefebvre and his shot trickled into the net off defenseman Darryl Sydor. Hrudey was inadvertently knocked down by Sydor, who was in no-man's land when he went down to block Gilmour's shot. But Gilmour passed, and Sydor took Hrudey's skates out as he slid in the goalmouth. The game was tied, the crowd roared, and the Kings were in trouble.

"I think now I should have stayed up," Sydor would say later. "(Wendel Clark) was holding me and I went down to block the shot. The puck hit my leg and after that I don't know what happened to it." It went into the net and the red light was turned on, that's what happened.

Overtime beckoned, only there would be no heroics from Shuchuk or any other member of the Kings. Some more brilliant work by Potvin — Hrudey wasn't chopped liver — proved to be the difference. The Kings peppered him with 10 of their 43 shots in the extra period, many from point-blank range, but couldn't convert. A second overtime beckoned when, 40 seconds before the intermission, Glenn Anderson used a baseball swing to swat a deflected puck between Hrudey's legs. Toronto had pulled out a 3-2 victory and was one win removed from the Stanley Cup final.

"I was thinking, 'Just get a shot on net.' I knew there wasn't much time left, and I was just hoping to get lucky," Anderson said. He nearly ended the game six minutes earlier when he cruised untouched to the net, only to have Hrudey nudge the puck off his stick. But Hrudey wasn't so fortunate the second time. "He knocked it out of the air," Hrudey said. "It was a great shot. We're desperate now, but moping and complaining won't be of any help."

And maybe it was inconsequential, but Toronto's garbage-tossing fans were at it again with 1:05 remaining in the overtime. They littered the ice with soft drinks, beer and cups—no crutches this time—to protest the Kings net being knocked off its pegs. It took a clean-up crew several minutes to clear the mess, enabling the Leafs' top line of Anderson, Doug Gilmour, and Dave Andreychuk to catch a breather. Twenty-five seconds after play resumed, Anderson scored.

Perhaps Don Cherry and the CBC would get their wish after all. The Montreal Canadiens had cooperated, having eliminated the New York Islanders in the Wales Conference bracket, now it was up to the Maple Leafs to come through.

The Kings weren't dead, of course, but Melrose had never looked so drained as he sat in a dark, dank corner outside the dressing room. This had been a heart-wrenching defeat, and all of Melrose's motivational powers were about to be put to the test.

"We'll respond," he promised. "Our heads are down, but we are competitive people. We're a little angry because we didn't get the job done. We played really hard and there are a lot of emotions running through this team right now. It really hurts now, but it doesn't matter. We've got to win the next game. They've won three and you've got to win four. We'll feel sorry for ourselves for about an hour, then we'll rebound."

Of more immediate concern was the physical well-being of defensemen Alexei Zhitnik and Tim Watters. Zhitnik suffered a concussion and cut on the back of his head 10:25 into the overtime, and he missed the balance of the game. Lefebvre drove Zhitnik's head into the glass, then Zhitnik bounced on the ice and lay there for a couple of minutes. "I didn't see it," Zhitnik said when he was asked if a penalty should have been called.

Watters was hurt midway through the second period when he collided with McSorley, whose stick came up and sliced his mouth and chin. Watters needed six stitches to close the cuts and would require extensive dental work to repair six broken teeth, three uppers and three lowers. But, other than the bitter defeat and loss of two defensemen, it wasn't such a bad night.

Finally, Melrose and Pat Burns managed to agree on something: Felix Potvin's 41-save performance had been remarkable. No question about it, the Leafs were in a fix until Felix the Cat, as he was being called, reached into his bag of tricks and pulled out a pivotal win. "I give that kid a lot of credit," Melrose said. "We had a 2-0 lead, and it should have been 4-0 or 5-0."

Only 21 and relatively inexperienced, Potvin's poise and reflexes were uncanny. The Kings scored 33 goals in six games against Calgary and 26 goals in six games against Vancouver, but they had only 12 goals in five games this series, which wasn't nearly enough even with the way Hrudey was playing. "He saved us, pulled a rabbit out of the hat," Burns said.

Apparently, it was going to take some sort of hocus-pocus for Robitaille to manufacture a goal. And what was with Gretzky? All he had was a power-play goal and five assists to show for his efforts. Sure, Toronto defensemen Sylvain Lefebvre and Todd Gill were hammering him every chance they got, giving him very little room to operate behind the net, the patch of ice that has always been considered his "office." But unless the big guy's office reopened in Game 6, the Kings would likely be shutting down operations for the summer.

Bob McKenzie, a respected columnist for the *Toronto Star*, really poured it on in a scathing article with the headline "Gretzky Playing As If He's Got A Piano On His Back." McKenzie didn't specify if this particular instrument was a Steinway, but his words were certain to strike dissonant chords with Gretzky. "What the numbers add up to is no traditional Gretzky-like jump," McKenzie wrote. "No flash. No dash. No seeing eye passes to crack a game wide open. The critics have taken some pretty good rips at the Kings' non-performing offensive stars, such as Luc Robitaille and Jimmy Carson. But the plain truth is Gretzky hasn't been much, if any, better."

The flight home on Air McNall, possibly the last one of the year, was livelier than might have been expected. Had the Kings recovered from their toughest defeat yet already? Was Gretzky tickling the ivories? "We put on 'Young Frankenstein' and everyone had a good time," Melrose said after practice the next day. "We know what the situation is, but we never want to get too high or too down. We want to stay on an even keel."

Jimmy Carson was successful in that area. His emotional state didn't change one bit at the news he would be sitting out again. At least he'd be able to commiserate with Jim Thomson, who also was being benched. He must not have impressed Melrose with the one shift he was given because Mark Hardy was going to take his spot in the lineup.

Carson revealed he often wondered why the Kings ever traded for him. Why would they dispatch a player of Paul Coffey's caliber, make such a big deal about how much they wanted Carson, then strap him to the bench? Or, in this case, force him to sit in the stands. Granted, his 12 goals in 34 games with the Kings were a major disappointment, but Carson did produce five goals in six games against Calgary before his ice time began to melt. Why not spot him on the power play? The Kings were an anemic four of 27 on power plays against Toronto.

"I want to play, and I think I can help the team," Carson said. "We haven't been scoring so, yeah, I'm surprised. Barry keeps telling me not to read anything into this, but obviously it's very disappointing to me." Melrose said he pulled Carson because he couldn't be expected to produce with the limited playing time he was receiving. Melrose would slip Hardy into the lineup, giving him an extra defenseman, he said, "because this has been a long series and Toronto is putting a lot of pressure on us down low with their big forwards. We've played a lot of hockey. We've had a lot of travel."

Sometimes sudden death can mean life. It did for the Kings in a controversial Game 6 that ended when Gretzky got the piano off his back and scored a power-play goal 1:41 into the extra period for a 5-4 win. The Kings weren't letting anyone pull the plug on the Forum ice-making machine, or their season, just yet. They were going back to Toronto for a Game 7 to determine the Campbell Conference champion and Montreal's opponent in the Stanley Cup final.

Funny, no one seemed to mind that Gretzky only had two goals now, or that both had come on power plays. "The Toronto press has had a bit of a field day with me, but that's fine and dandy," he said. "I'm not superhuman. I'm not going to get four points a night. But I have to make sure that when I do something, it's big."

On a scale of one to 10, with 10 being fairly monumental, Gretzky's redirection of a Luc Robitaille centering pass off Felix Potvin and under the crossbar was an 11. So was the performance of Mr. Robitaille, who took five shots, actually scored on one of them, and assisted on three other goals. "Attention shoppers," *Los Angeles Daily News* columnist Ron Rapoport put it, "two lost boys have been found on the ice."

Good thing, too, for the Kings' sake. They would have been sick to their stomachs all summer to have blown another two-goal lead, to have wasted a power play that finally showed more than a little spark, to have squandered the opportunity to capture the imagination of a city that had barely tolerated them for so long.

"It's not fun to be criticized," Robitaille said, "but it's fair when people ask you why you aren't producing. I didn't care if people said I wasn't scoring, but I know one thing, no one can say I wasn't working hard."

Pat Burns was beside himself. His fearless captain, Wendel Clark, singlehandedly brought the Leafs back from a 4-2 deficit with two goals in the third period to complete a hat trick, only to have the game decided by a penalty that was called and by one that wasn't.

There was little question Toronto's Glenn Anderson had to go when, with 12.1 seconds remaining in regulation, he drilled Rob Blake in the corner from behind. "Maybe he thought I was closer to the boards, but it was definitely a penalty," Blake said. Referee Kerry Fraser sent Anderson off for boarding, an infraction that carried into the overtime.

Burns had few qualms about that, but he was trying to understand why Gretzky was able to sneak to the front of the net and deposit the winning goal when, in his humble opinion, Gretzky should have been sitting in the penalty box opposite Anderson. Approximately a minute before the game ended, Gretzky caught Doug Gilmour under the chin with his stick, opening a cut that needed eight stitches. If Fraser saw it, he ignored it; ditto the linesmen, Kevin Collins and Ron Finn, who could have conferred with Fraser but didn't.

"They could have called one on Gretzky," Burns said, "but our discipline was pretty bad and our penalty killing was atrocious." The Kings scored on all but one of their five power plays, doubling their series total in just one night. Gilmour wouldn't comment on the stick foul that wasn't, but he didn't look happy wiping his bloodied chin with a towel. Barked Toronto general manager Cliff Fletcher: "They just didn't have the guts to call it."

If the Leafs had been able to hold off the Kings for seven more seconds, the teams would have been at even strength because that's how much time remained on Anderson's penalty. "When you've got No. 99 on the ice, you've got to be careful. I played with him in Edmonton and I know what kind of spirit and soul he's got," said Anderson, whose overtime goal decided Game 5. "But I've got to blame myself. If I had it to do all over again, I wouldn't have gone into the corner."

If the Kings had done an adequate job of protecting the 4-2 lead and paid more attention to Clark, there wouldn't have been an overtime. Clark whistled a 35-foot wrist shot between Kelly Hrudey's legs with 8:52 left in the third period and he beat Hrudey to the glove side with 1:21 remaining from the right faceoff circle a moment after Potvin vacated his crease for a sixth skater. "I'll still talk to him," Melrose said of Clark, his second cousin from Saskatchewan.

Burns was certain to chat with Mike Foligno, who sandwiched two second-period penalties around one Jamie Macoun took. The Kings scored on all three subsequent power plays to turn a 2-1 deficit into a 4-2 advantage. Tomas Sandstrom, who had three assists, set up Marty McSorley's first goal since Game 1 in Calgary, then Sandstrom set the table for Darryl Sydor's go-ahead goal. He nailed Macoun with a clean check and was heading to the bench when Macoun, in clear view of the referee, foolishly whacked Sandstrom with his stick. Sydor made Potvin look bad on his goal, a 40-footer from a steep angle that dipped under the shaft of the rookie's stick.

After Gary Shuchuk turned the other cheek for the team, taking a Foligno high stick well behind the play, Robitaille scooped the rebound of Rob Blake's shot over Potvin's right pad for his first goal since Game 5 in Vancouver. In case anyone wondered if the goal pleased him, Robitaille danced about 40 feet with his arms upraised. "But I was even happier when Gretz's shot went in," he said.

According to Bruce McNall, actor James Woods turned to him during the overtime and predicted a big play from Gretzky. "Look at that glint in Wayne's eyes. I think he's going to do it," Woods had said. "Then—boom—it was in the net," said McNall, who watched the game at ice level with Woods, actor Scott Bakula and actress Goldie Hawn. The bandwagon was starting to overflow with Hollywood types who wouldn't be seen dead at a hockey game if the Lakers were still alive, but at least Woods, Bakula, and Hawn could look you square in the eye and swear they knew who Teppo Numminen was.

"It was a great win for the organization," McNall said as Hawn posed for pictures with Jari Kurri in a mobbed dressing room that even included a few players. "Now we've got to take care of business in Toronto. I don't know what to think. It would be a dream come true for us to get into the Stanley Cup final."

Don Cherry's worst nightmares came to pass and he hadn't even drifted off to sleep. Watching Sandstrom rake over the Leafs was hard enough, and seeing Gilmour bleed from his cut chin undoubtedly caused more pain; maybe Cherry could kiss it and make it better? But there was Cindy Melrose, wife of the coach, confronting Cherry by waving two American flags and a "Sour Grapes" sign in a hallway outside the Toronto dressing room. Cherry, whose nickname is "Grapes," praised Cindy Melrose for "standing up for her man."

Toronto seemed to have the upper hand heading to Game 7 for two reasons: Home ice and Game 7 experience. The Leafs blew 3-2 leads against Detroit and St. Louis, too, then clinched both series with Game 7 victories. "It's our game to win," said Dave Andreychuk, who had fewer goals in the series than Ken Baumgartner, who had one. "The pressure's on us. We're expected to win."

Burns had been through worse. Coaching the Canadiens is no different than managing the Yankees or coaching at Notre Dame.

"If there were two Stanley Cups a year, in Montreal you'd have to win them both," he said. "It's tough on your personal life, on your family life, and on your health. It's a strenuous situation."

Burns sure was acting strained. When he saw Melrose quoted in the papers as saying "Pack extra underwear, we're going to Montreal," he blew a gasket. Melrose made the statement while answering a Los Angeles sportscaster's loaded question and mugging for the gentleman's camera, but several writers were listening and used the quotes in their stories. Maybe Melrose should have known better, but he wasn't making a prediction.

Burns saw the quotes and smiled. "Oh, that's perfect," he said. "We heard that. We heard they were packing their things for Montreal. They're allowed to do that, to think positive. We're thinking positive, too, but we're not thinking about Montreal." Burns apparently expected the Kings to wait until after Game 7 to see if they would need to fly back to the West Coast for extra clothing.

Finally, the long, grinding road to the Stanley Cup final was about to reach the climactic stage. The game would be the 21st in 41 days for the Maple Leafs, who had traveled to three states in two time zones during the playoffs. It would be the 19th game in 42 days for the Kings, who traveled to three Canadian provinces in three time zones. With the jet lag, all the miles skated on bone-weary legs, the gallons of sweat poured . . . players from both sides were exhausted.

There was little to choose between the teams in terms of mental toughness. The Kings had rebounded from what could have been a devastating overtime loss in Game 5 to force the decisive match, while the Leafs won both of their previous series after losing Game 6.

And now it came down to this. One game, winner take all.

"You never want to take a chance on a Game 7 because there are so many variables on any single night," Gilmour said. "Anything can happen. But other than that, I don't mind because I prefer playing every other day. I'd sooner keep the momentum going than take a chance on losing it. Once it's gone, you might never get it back."

If the Kings were tight, they didn't show it. Buoyed by the reappearance of their top three scorers—Gretzky, Robitaille, and Sandstrom—the Kings were confident they had at least one more big game to give. After the team meal, Gretzky turned to his agent, Michael Barnett. "I think the Piano Man still has a tune to play," he told him.

The recital before 15,720 inside steamy Maple Leaf Gardens began at precisely 9:48 of the first period, 63 seconds after the Kings were penalized for having too many men on the ice. Four skaters were plenty when Gretzky, on a shorthanded, two-on-one foray into the Toronto zone, accepted Marty McSorley's last-second return pass and skimmed the puck inside the goal post for a 1-0 Kings advantage.

Gretzky, his aluminum stick a music machine, passed to Sandstrom for another goal and a 2-0 lead at 17:30. The crowd hushed. "I was frightened before the game," Bruce McNall said. "Wayne came up to me and he said, 'We're going to win, Bruce. We're going to win.' "

If the Kings were going to win, they would have to start paying more attention to Clark, who burned them for three goals in Game 6 and scored again at 1:25 of the second period with Tony Granato off for hooking. Hadn't Toronto scored a momentum-changing power-play goal in Game 5 with Granato sitting in the penalty box? The Kings were essentially two men down when Clark scored; Gretzky didn't have enough time to skate into the play after he replaced penalty-killer Dave Taylor, who lost his stick.

When Anderson busted down the slot and around Tim Watters, took Gilmour's perfect pass and snapped the puck over Kelly Hrudey's glove at 7:36, the Leafs were back in the game and so was the crowd. The score was 2-2. The Kings had frittered away a two-goal lead for the third consecutive game, for the fourth time in five games. Melrose, his troops rattled, called a timeout.

Shrewd move. Gretzky used the break to re-tune his stick and ripped a 25-foot shot by Potvin's glove at 10:20 to put the Kings ahead again, 3-2. Sandstrom, with his fourth assist in five periods, slid a pass behind Toronto defenseman Sylvain Lefebvre, Gretzky took the puck and then he cut around flat-footed Kent Manderville for his third goal in three periods.

The Piano Man was doing all right, but the Kings continued to live dangerously. Rob Blake did more than finish a check and was penalized for roughing Dave Andreychuk with 53 seconds remaining in the period, giving the Leafs their fifth power play of the game.

The Kings killed it off, but Kings' killers Clark and Gilmour teamed up for the tying goal 18 seconds after Blake returned to the ice, just 85 seconds into the third period. Gilmour still hadn't registered a shot, but he drew his third assist from Gretzky country, behind the net, hitting Clark in front for a 10-foot chip shot that beat Hrudey to the glove side. A team can usually feed off such an early goal, and Clark had delivered one in back-to-back periods.

The pace slowed as the period wore on. The conservative nature of playoff hockey, one team waiting for the other to make a critical mistake, dictated the flow more than exhaustion. Sure, the players were dragging and the stale, muggy air was almost unbearable, but adrenaline would carry them through.

Finally, with 3:51 to play in the period and overtime calling once more, the tie was broken. Fortune, not error, played a part in the goal Mike Donnelly won't soon forget. Alexei Zhitnik, his head clear despite all of the ferocious hits he'd been taking, took a shot that acted like a billiard ball. The puck banked off two Toronto defensemen, Bob Rouse first and then Sylvain Lefebvre, and came to Donnelly. He slam-dunked the puck inside the right post to give the Kings a 4-3 lead, then spun around and leaped into McSorley's arms. "I almost jumped over his head," Donnelly said.

Thirty-seven seconds later, the Piano Man struck again. Or was it the Pool Man? Like Zhitnik, Gretzky threw the puck in front and it ricocheted off the skate of a Leafs defenseman, Dave Ellett. Unlike the puck cued by Zhitnik, Gretzky's bounced up and sailed over Potvin's left shoulder. "I didn't even feel it," Ellett said much later. "I felt like everyone else. Kind of numb." Not everyone. Gretzky pointed to his father, Walter, sitting in the stands and he pumped his fist in the air.

The Kings had a 5-3 lead. Not that it would last. "Nothing comes easy for this team," Melrose said. "That's been a characteristic for us all year." Dave Taylor, who had waited so long for this kind of moment, had a chance to put the Leafs away but watched his shot slide wide of a gaping net.

Then, with 67 seconds to go, Ellett scored to trim the gap to 5-4. With 45 seconds left, Burns yanked Potvin for a sixth attacker and the Leafs buzzed furiously around Hrudey. "We were pressing, we had a lot of chances," Clark said. Gilmour, still looking for his first shot, might have had another as he cradled the puck at the side of the net, only to be bulldozed to the ice by Tim Watters. "It was hairy," Hrudey said, "but the guys were on their knees, working like dogs."

When the puck was cleared to center ice with five seconds left, the Kings were in the air, leaping and exulting like giddy schoolchildren. Players and coaches poured over the boards. Time had expired but the Kings hadn't. They embraced and hollered even as Toronto's disgusted fans heaved yet more junk onto the ice, some of which was fired back into the stands by Zhitnik's accurate slap shots.

It had taken 26 years, but the Kings were Campbell Conference champions. The suffering, the insults, the infamy, were forgotten. They were going to the Stanley Cup final.

Melrose and Burns, who feuded throughout the series, shook hands vigorously before the teams lined up for the traditional congratulatory ceremony at center ice. "He said if I wanted to know anything about Montreal to call him," Melrose said. "He's cheering for us now. I said a lot of stupid stuff, but most of it was bull. I hope he doesn't hate me, because I respect him a lot."

The Kings dressing room, and the area immediately near it, was jammed with beer-drenched players, coaches, staff members, family members, friends, hangers-on, and the media. The room was a steambath, a madhouse with the Campbell Conference trophy serving as a glistening centerpiece, a prize to touch, to be photographed with.

"This is too exciting for words," Bruce McNall said for probably the 50th time in a 10-minute span. "I hear they're going crazy back in L.A. It sends a chill up your spine to think people care so much about hockey right now. And what about Wayne, huh? Did he have some game or what? I guess he still has a little bit of hockey left to play."

Presumably, without the piano. The Kings certainly would not be heading to Montreal — no packing required — without Gretzky's eighth playoff hat trick and four-point night, which gave him five goals and four assists for the series and 13 goals and 33 points in 19 playoff games overall.

"There were a couple of articles written about my play and they really motivated me," Gretzky said. "The articles fueled the fire, made me mad. When you take the roses, you also have to take the heat, but tonight I stood up and answered the bell. I don't think I've ever been more personally satisfied at winning a series. It's the sweetest moment of my career. I've played 14 years, and I didn't want to be remembered as the guy who didn't play well in the Stanley Cup semifinals against Toronto."

That certainly wasn't going to be the case now. "Wayne came to play tonight," said a glum Gilmour, who was hardly a slouch himself. Gilmour had four goals and nine assists in the series, 10 goals and a playoff-leading 35 points overall. He and his linemates, Wendel Clark and Glenn Anderson, scored 13 of Toronto's 23 goals against the Kings. But for all the grief he caused, Gilmour was gracious in defeat. "Wayne Gretzky is a great player, an opportunist, and I wish them all the best."

Maybe Kelly Hrudey wasn't a great goalie, but no one was going to be ripping his play apart now. In the end, Hrudey's clutch work in the crease surpassed that of the more critically-acclaimed Felix Potvin, and this victory meant sweet vindication. "I wasn't in a hole," he said of the season's darker days, "I was in an abyss."

More than a few times in his career Dave Taylor felt like he had been dumped into a black hole. He was one of the few Kings remaining who knew what it was like to wear a purple and gold uniform, who knew what it was like not to make the playoffs at all. Taylor was a scratch for the season opener in October, now he was considered an integral cog of a championship contender, preparing to skate into June. "This is what I've been striving for my whole career," he said softly. "To go now into the Montreal Forum and play for the Stanley Cup, it doesn't get much better than that."

Pete Demers could relate. The Kings' trainer since 1972, he had been around longer than anybody and admitted to doubting this day would ever come. "We were standing there near the bench at the end congratulating each other, then all of a sudden it was 5-4," Demers said. "I was frightened, really frightened."

Couldn't blame him. Two weeks earlier, after the Kings knocked off Vancouver, Demers finally was able to pull out a dusty and dented can of beer he'd been saving for nearly a decade. He finally was able to make a little speech to the team, then pop open the can and take a few swallows. Demers intended to drink the beer in 1982 to celebrate a second-round series win over the Canucks, but the Kings fouled up his plans and he decided to put the can away. It sat on a shelf in the equipment room at the Forum for all those years.

"Every so often I would think about it, even look at it," Demers, a non-drinker, said with a grin. "I didn't drink all of it, though. I saved some for the final. Now it's showtime and we're going. If we win the Cup, that's when I'll drink the rest."

Thirteen

Leader of the Pack

The most popular person in the Los Angeles organization is the owner, Bruce Patrick McNall.

The players adore him because he is generous with a dollar and hands out perks like the $5 million Boeing 727 he bought three years ago to help ease their murderous travel schedule; the players were as happy for McNall as they were for themselves to be heading to the Stanley Cup final.

The fans like McNall because, despite his substantial net worth ($200 million, give or take a few million) he really is one of them. Reporters flock to him because, as the powerful chairman of the NHL's Board of Governors, he is an overflowing fountain of information; the fact that McNall also happens to return telephone calls and is quotable doesn't hurt his relationship with the press.

"If you begin to believe that you're something big," he once said, "then I think you've got a problem."

Like it or not, McNall became somewhat of a Hollywood celebrity overnight when he engineered the August 9, 1988 deal that turned Wayne Gretzky into a King. In exchange for $15 million in cash, Jimmy Carson, the rights to Martin Gelinas and three first-round draft picks, Edmonton Oilers owner Peter Pocklington sent the greatest player of our time, perhaps of all time, to Los Angeles. Mike Krushelnyski and Marty McSorley also headed south.

McNall made quite a splash 14 years earlier when he spent a then-world record $420,000 at auction on an ancient coin called the Athens Decadrachm. The silver dollar-sized coin, which McNall sold to a movie producer named Sy Weintraub, was struck in 460 B.C. to commemorate an important battle between Persia and Sparta. McNall, who had formed Numismatic Fine Arts Antiquities, a Beverly Hills-based firm that is the largest privately-owned ancient coin operation in the world, outbid representatives of the late Aristotle Onassis and the French government, which was represented by finance minister (and later, president) Valerie Giscard D'Estaing.

Problem was, only an elite few could relate to a 2,500-year-old coin that would be stashed in some rich fellow's private collection. (McNall eventually sold the Athens Decadrachm for Weintraub and it fetched $1.5 million.) The same couldn't be said of Gretzky, who became huge news even in Los Angeles, which essentially was a hockey wasteland when McNall arrived on his white horse.

McNall, a native Southern Californian who grew up in Arcadia, came aboard in September 1986. He handed Jerry Buss, who also owned the National Basketball Association Lakers as well as the Forum, a $4 million check for a one-quarter interest in a team that was a flop on the ice and at the box office. Talk about a dangerous combination. Sure, McNall had amassed a fortune in ancient coins and he eventually formed several other multimillion dollar businesses that included a movie production company and a thoroughbred horse racing stable.

But the Kings? They were a mess. Most folks whose IQ surpassed that of a vulcanized rubber puck looked at McNall and saw a sap; his hockey investment would melt away right along with the Forum ice, which usually disappeared four or five games into the Stanley Cup playoffs. If the Kings were fortunate enough to qualify for the playoffs at all.

Los Angeles' track record didn't exactly mirror that of, say, the Montreal Canadiens. Maybe the Winnipeg Jets. Anyway, they were coming off a typical, miserable season (23 wins, 54 points, last place in the Smythe Division) when McNall, a season ticketholder for 10 years, put his money where his heart was.

"I used to sit and scream about players and coaches, just like everybody else does," McNall said. " 'How can they keep this bum?' Or, 'Fire that guy.' That sort of stuff. But even now I would like to be perceived as a people's owner. I don't sit in an ivory tower, unaccessible to the rest of the world. In a way, all the fans are my partners. They're all on you, they all have questions, and they all want to win. People will live and die with that. Even I might. It gives you a certain responsibility. It's a public trust, I guess."

McNall bought into the Dallas Mavericks when that team joined the NBA in 1980, and he would see Jerry Buss at various basketball-related functions. McNall and Buss had other common interests: Coins, stamps, and hockey.

"Jerry knew I was a hockey fan, but I never knew he was interested in selling any of his teams," said McNall, who kept his piece of the Mavericks for three years. "We began to talk a little bit about the Kings in 1985 and it piqued my interest. But I wasn't interested in having just a little bit of something. I wanted half, at least.

"One thing I've always had is a pretty good feel for knowing when to make a buy," McNall said. "That's the whole key, getting into something that appears to have hit rock bottom but in your mind is actually just about ready to take off. Even when I was a kid collecting coins, I'd buy things nobody else wanted or cared about. Every endeavor doesn't pay off, but I think I've done pretty well for myself."

McNall continued, "This team was so bad there was nowhere for it to go but up. You might have called it a depressed marketplace."

The depression turned into a gaping canyon by the time McNall decided to pick up his option to purchase an additional 24 percent following the 1986-87 season. The Kings won 31 games and lost a head coach, Pat Quinn, to a league-imposed suspension that year. Quinn, whom Buss later described as "the best hockey person I ever met," had signed a contract that would make him the future president and general manager of the Vancouver Canucks after the season, but he was still under contract to Los Angeles when he inked the deal.

Then, in 1987-88, while the Kings were slipping to 30 wins and 68 points, and making yet another coaching change (Robbie

Ftorek replaced Mike Murphy a mere 28 games into the season), McNall became team president and sole owner. The good news was that home attendance reached 11,667. Don't snicker; this was an *improvement* from the previous year. The final bill of sale came to about $20 million, with $4 million of the total being used to cover some debts.

"I just felt I could turn it into a profitable business," McNall said. The Kings were losing between $3 and $4 million per season at the time. "I knew I would have to put a lot of effort and money into it, and I was willing to do it," he said. "Naturally, I didn't know it was going to be Gretzky, but I knew that something had to be done. I mean, I'd go to hockey games and friends of mine who knew nothing about the game would say, 'What about this guy Gritsky?' I'd laugh, but they at least had an idea of who he was."

It didn't take long for the other NHL owners to discover who McNall was. For one thing, he showed up for league meetings. Buss had been very visible for a while, but it got to the point where he began to send other people to do his bidding. This alienated some owners who otherwise might have shown more concern for the Kings' problems, not the least of which was a horrendous travel burden that remains difficult today but has been eased by realignment and the additions of two California neighbors, the San Jose Sharks and the Mighty Ducks of Anaheim.

"Jerry for all those years had basketball and hockey going at the exact same time," McNall said. "One was a world champion and one was a doormat. I think what was needed was somebody who only had the Kings as an interest."

A plan to pique Los Angelenos' interest in the Kings also would be helpful.

One of the first things McNall did was to change the team's color scheme from purple and gold to black, silver and white. The new colors would undoubtedly be more popular at souvenir stands and sporting goods stores — the Kings have become big-time merchandisers — but the move also served as a symbolic break with the club's pathetic past.

Naturally, success or failure on the ice would hinge solely on the players who would wear the redesigned uniforms, which closely resembled those of the Hull Olympiques, a Quebec Major

Junior Hockey League team that Kings all-star left winger Luc Robitaille played on for three seasons.

Imagine the fashion statement McNall could make if Wayne Gretzky was available to model?

"I kept asking myself, 'What can I do to try and make everyone pay attention to the team, to really stand up and take notice?'" McNall said. "There was only one way to do it, and (acquiring Gretzky) was it." McNall credits Buss for "planting the seed" in the head of Edmonton owner Peter Pocklington. "That happened a couple of years before," McNall said. "The seed was there and we germinated it."

The way McNall tells it, Buss had visualized Gretzky in a purple and gold uniform well before he began to fantasize about the possibility himself. Shortly after McNall entered the picture in 1986, Buss told him, "I'm trying to get Wayne Gretzky." McNall responded to Buss the way television viewers do when they are watching Ralph Kramden and Ed Norton make fools of themselves in "The Honeymooners."

Regardless, McNall was curious. "I began to see Peter at league meetings and I would always bring the matter up," McNall said. "He said he wasn't interested, but if he was he would take the Lakers *and* the Kings in return. He had a long list of what he would take."

Pocklington would be required to settle for considerably less. According to McNall, Pocklington telephoned him two days after Gretzky married actress Janet Jones in July 1986. If Pocklington had called collect from Yellowknife, McNall would have accepted the charges. Gleefully. "The subject is No. 99," Pocklington told McNall. "If you're serious about him, I think there's an opportunity to discuss it a little bit."

You might say McNall was reasonably interested. He said that Buss, during his original conversations with Pocklington, had offered "something like any three players he wanted, some draft picks and $15 million (in exchange for Gretzky). We used that as a starting point. I never did get Peter off the $15 million."

McNall received permission from Pocklington to speak to Gretzky about two weeks before the deal was completed. McNall needed to know if Gretzky would be interested in playing for the Kings. He also had to find out if Gretzky would be interested in signing a long-term contract. Gretzky had four years left on his

Edmonton contract and could become a free agent after the 1991-92 season.

Gretzky was already in Los Angeles with his wife, who had a home in suburban Sherman Oaks, and he met with McNall several times. "He almost couldn't believe it was really happening, even though a million times he knew we were close to something," McNall said. "To tell you the truth, I was almost in shock when I began to realize that we actually were going to pull this off."

McNall wasn't enthusiastic about dealing Jimmy Carson, though. The rarest of Kings in that he was (a) a first-round draft pick, and (b) a first-round draft pick who didn't turn out to be a complete bust, Carson was coming off a sophomore season in which he had scored 55 goals as a 19-year-old. Carson and Gretzky were the only teen-agers in NHL history to score 50 goals in a season, and the Kings were planning to build with young players like him, Luc Robitaille and Steve Duchesne.

"I was really concerned about Jimmy Carson," McNall said. "I am extremely close to Jimmy and his family. I did not want to give him up. I would rather have paid more in hopes of keeping Jimmy, but that just wasn't possible. It was my biggest stumbling block, my biggest heartache."

On August 8, 1988 — 24 hours before the most significant trade in hockey history was completed — McNall felt compelled to call Carson at his home outside Detroit. "I told him, 'I don't know if this is going to happen, but I want you to know beforehand in case it does,' " McNall said. "I felt I had to do that."

Gretzky and McNall flew to Edmonton in the owner's private jet for an emotional farewell news conference the next day, then they returned to Los Angeles for a festive, evening introduction in the ballroom of the Sheraton Plaza La Reina, near the airport. Gretzky had been a King for only a few hours and already McNall was being touted as the man who saved hockey in the Western United States.

"It's impossible to predict the economic ramifications of this," McNall said then. "I could lose my shirt or I could break even. I can maybe even make a little, though certainly not over the short term."

Quick, fast-forward to last spring, when the Kings made their unlikely march to the Stanley Cup final, when the value of the franchise was estimated to be $70 million — more than three times McNall's original investment. The Kings sold out the 16,005-seat Forum for 31 of their final 33 regular-season games and for all 11 playoff games.

"If only we had more seats," McNall thought. Eventually, he hopes to form a partnership with his old friend, Jerry Buss, and build an arena that is capable of accommodating the Kings' ever-expanding following.

Though one media critic described McNall as a "thick-skulled fool" as recently as the summer of 1992 for pampering his players, he has not been called a sap recently for taking on the Kings. In fact, eyebrows were barely raised in March 1991 when McNall and Gretzky teamed up to buy a 1910 Honus Wagner baseball card at Sotheby's auction house in New York. Purchase price: $451,000.

"I've been collecting things all my life, and my approach has always been to buy the best," he said. "I've always felt, if something is the best in the world, it doesn't matter what you pay for it. We were told it was the best there is, so we bought it."

McNall is also in the business of selling. But the hockey team, he has said, is not for sale. Contrary to some of the whispers making the rounds, McNall isn't planning to put the Kings on the market five minutes after Gretzky plays his final game.

"In any business," McNall said, "one of the theories is to maximize your investment and then sell it prior to it becoming worth less money. But I don't think sports teams are ever worth less money. Even after Wayne is gone, we should be able to maintain a certain level of what we have. So I don't think I'll ever find the need to sell. I don't think I ever would.

"I love the sport and I love the ambience about it. I love the people. Besides, what would I do with the money? I would think I would own the Kings forever. I'm too emotionally involved with the team."

"We all feel happy for Bruce," Gretzky said. "He has put a lot of money into this organization. He's into this team for probably $40-50 million. He's taken a lot of financial risks. He's put a lot of money and time in this. It's sort of funny, isn't it? We take it for granted now that there will be 16,000 in our building every night when there used to be 8,000 or 9,000. These are exciting times."

Certainly McNall was excited about the attention his attention-starved team was receiving. "I'm saying to myself, 'I can't believe it.' I feel like a little kid," he said. "I think back to when I was a kid sitting in the stands and there were a few thousand fans there. Now we're in the Stanley Cup finals. I'm telling you, it's wilder than when Gretzky first came here, just out of control.

"It's just absolutely unbelievable what is happening. Everybody wants a ticket, everybody in town. You ought to see the list. It's a mob scene. Honest, I don't know what we're going to do. Maybe we can stack these people in. It's wild, just wild."

Fourteen

Thrown for
a Curve

Skating through the Maple Leafs' tenacious checks and swarming defense was only a little more difficult for the Kings than getting past a gantlet of belligerent Toronto fans outside who shook Bruce McNall's limousine and pelted players with eggs, tomatoes, and other assorted leftovers from the game.

The most unsettling part about the whole ordeal was the thought that hockey is taken even more seriously in Montreal. Simply qualifying for the privilege of competing for the Stanley Cup, the oldest and most revered trophy in North American professional sports, wasn't such a big deal for Canadiens fans. That much was expected. Win the damned thing, then we'll talk.

The Canadiens had won the 100-year-old bowl on 23 occasions, which in most National Hockey League cities would have been more than enough to spark a decent conversation. But in Montreal, perhaps because French and English is spoken there, fans were feeling the effects of the seven-year itch. The *bleu, blanc et rouge* hadn't won a Stanley Cup since 1986. In the old days, a Canadiens captain — maybe Maurice Richard or Jean Beliveau — was parading the 35.5-pound prize around the Montreal Forum every year.

It is this mystique that drew Jacques Demers, 49, back to Montreal, the hometown he left to take coaching jobs in St. Louis and Detroit, places where he had success but didn't win the really big one. After the Red Wings fired him in 1990, Demers hopped on an air bus and landed in Quebec City, 145 miles up the mighty St. Lawrence. He worked as a radio analyst on Nordiques games for two years. Then, somewhat surprisingly, Pat Burns left Montreal for Toronto. Demers didn't think twice when the Canadiens telephoned to offer him the position. "They don't just pick anybody," he said.

The Canadiens looked for a better balance between offense and defense under Demers, a strategic change that was reflected in the club's improved goal production, up 59 from the previous season; but Montreal permitted a staggering 73 more goals than it did in Burns' final year, and it didn't seem likely the Canadiens would be able to inflict much damage in the playoffs.

They finished third in the Adams Division with a 48-30-6 record and 102 points, two behind archrival Quebec and seven behind the Boston Bruins, who were red-hot down the stretch. Once the playoffs began, though, Montreal went back to its strong suit, which is preventing goals and scoring just enough to get by.

Riding the exceptional goaltending of Patrick Roy, the play-off MVP as a 20-year-old rookie in 1986, the Canadiens were 12-3 heading into the Stanley Cup final. They spotted Quebec the first two games in the opening round, then won four straight. They swept the Buffalo Sabres, who stunned Boston in the first round, and then the Canadiens dispatched the New York Islanders in five games in the Wales Conference final.

"We've been playing well defensively all through the play-offs," said center Kirk Muller, the Canadiens' best all-around player. "Everyone here is pretty well aware of how to play defensively, even though we spent a lot of time on offense during the regular season. But this is different, it's the playoffs. If we hadn't played so well defensively, we wouldn't be here."

As they did with Toronto, the Kings had their hands full with Montreal in the regular season. Their only loss in three meetings was the 7-2 drubbing in February, the last game before the All-Star break, a point in the season when the Kings were at their worst. The other two games ended in 5-5 ties; Vincent Damphousse scored three goals for the Canadiens in the final eight minutes of the game in December, and Rob Blake scored for the Kings with 46.8 seconds left in January after they squandered a two-goal lead.

No question, the brand of hockey the Kings were playing now could not be compared to the dime-store variety they put on display when these teams last met, but the smart money was still on the Canadiens. The teams were pretty much evenly matched, but the Kings were whipped physically while the Canadiens had had eight days to relax and to allow the usual assortment of bumps and bruises to heal.

Happily, there was no reason to believe Barry Melrose and Demers would carry on the way Melrose and Burns did in the Campbell Conference series. Demers coached Melrose with the Cincinnati Stingers in the old World Hockey Association in 1977, and he was working in Detroit in 1989-90 when Melrose was in his first season with the Red Wings' farm team in Adirondack. Their paths had crossed many times since and they respected each other.

Demers, who had his own little feud with Burns in the regular season, suggested the daily Melrose-Burns shenanigans became embarrassing, but he did not blame his one-time pupil for that. "It wasn't Barry Melrose who started it," Demers said. "When a coach lunges at you . . . I thought Barry kept his cool. Pat Burns is tough, but Barry Melrose is tough, too. For coaches to insult each other . . . we're not here to put on a show. The show is going to be put on by Wayne Gretzky and Marty McSorley and Patrick Roy. We're just coaches."

Other than the weather — rain and humidity had replaced snow and freezing winds — probably the biggest difference between this visit to Montreal and the previous one was Gretzky's state of mind. He was a miserable wretch four months earlier, playing poorly for a team in the toilet and the subject of an absurd trade rumor. He was a different person now, at the top of his superior game and anxious about playing in a Stanley Cup final for the first time since leaving Edmonton. Is there such a thing as a five-year itch?

"The whole reason I play this game is for the opportunity to win a championship," he said on the eve of the series opener. "This is my sixth final, and I'm probably more excited about this one than any of the others. The last time I was here, things didn't look so good for me. That's why I'm so excited. I just feel very fortunate to be here. I've been doing a lot of smiling lately."

Gretzky might have smiled just a little bit more when he discovered the Canadiens did not plan to assign a checker to shadow him. Muller and Guy Carbonneau, a former Selke Trophy winner as the NHL's best defensive forward, were certain to get in his face as much as possible, but Demers wasn't going to play a juggling act with his lines every time Gretzky skated onto the ice.

"We like to play four lines and three sets of defensemen," Demers said. "When you play everybody, like we do, everybody plays a part in it. I'll say this over and over: I have an enormous amount of respect for Wayne Gretzky, but he's not the only guy on that team."

Those words proved to be prophetic when the Kings coasted to a shockingly easy 4-1 victory in Game 1 before 17,959 who could not have possibly fathomed what was going on. It's possible the Kings didn't, either, during or after the Canadiens' first home defeat in nine playoff games. Gretzky was dominating, drawing assists on the first three goals, scoring into an empty net with 1:58 remaining, and helping to kill off all five of Montreal's power plays. "Gretzky toyed with us. He did what he wanted," snapped a visibly-shaken Demers. "We saw the Great One at his best."

Luc Robitaille, a native Montrealer who grew up 25 minutes from the Canadiens' famous pond and skated on it as a young boy, frolicked right alongside the captain. He took nine of the Kings' 38 shots, seven in the second period when he delivered his second power-play goal of the night on a 15-foot snap shot from the base of the right faceoff circle. The goal, which slipped between Roy's skates at 17:41, broke a 1-1 tie.

The Kings were overpowering, at their explosive best. They peppered Roy, who carried a 2.15 goals-against average into the game, with 13 consecutive shots in the second period and prevented Montreal from generating much of anything in the way of offense. It was Gretzky, in fact, who spoiled Kelly Hrudey's bid for a shutout. With 1:51 to play in the opening period and the Kings protecting a 1-0 lead, Gretzky inadvertently tipped Ed Ronan's attempted centering pass into his own net, a faux pas that motivated him much as the Piano Man column did in Toronto.

"I have to admit I was pretty embarrassed about it," Gretzky said. "I didn't just tip it, I fired it. I know I've done it three or four other times, but I never shot one as hard as that. It went in pretty quick. I really think, I don't know what the right word is, after I scored that goal for them, I wanted to redeem myself."

No problem, Hrudey said. "He can score on me all night as long as he has a night like he had at the other end," said Hrudey, who stopped all 31 of the shots actually taken by Canadiens players. Even Pat Burns would have been proud, seeing Gretzky skate 200 feet the way he did. "He was backchecking, those things happen," Melrose said. "It's okay because Gretz was working. Mistakes out of aggressiveness and trying have never been a problem with us."

Even on his worst night, when he is skating as fast as he can and going nowhere, no one has ever accused Robitaille of slacking off. He wasn't about to set a precedent in the Montreal Forum. "A lot of legends have played in this building. It's special," said Robitaille, who has a sense of history and often dreamed of playing in this shrine. During the morning skate, his feelings for the place were enhanced when he looked into the stands and spotted Henri Richard, the Pocket Rocket. "Henri Richard," Michael Farber wrote in the *Montreal Gazette*, "is the reason Montreal children learn how to count from one to 11. To stop at ten would miss one of his Stanley Cups."

For the time being, just one would satisfy Robitaille's appetite, and he would do whatever it took to get it. "Before the game I was thinking, 'We're a part of history here. A team from L.A. has never been here before and who knows if we'll ever get another chance to play for the Stanley Cup,' " Robitaille said. "I told myself, 'Work hard and go out there and have fun.' I want to enjoy this. I don't want to put any extra pressure on myself."

The Canadiens, perhaps rusty from their eight-day layoff, were outclassed from the start. Montreal's Lyle Odelein went off for holding Tony Granato, who spent much of the game drawing penalties, at 2:42 of the first period and the Kings responded with a power-play goal 21 seconds later. After Gretzky hit Alexei Zhitnik with a pass at the right point, Robitaille moved in front and knocked down the rookie's shot with his stick. He corralled the loose puck at the side of the net and banked it in off Roy's skate.

That power play, which runs hot and cold but never lukewarm, clicked again late in the second period. Gretzky ripped a slap shot that hit the post and bounded to Zhitnik, who fired it at the net. Roy made the save, but he steered the rebound to Gretzky near the right-wing boards. Gretzky gave the puck to Rob Blake, who slipped it around Carbonneau down low to Robitaille. Boom, it was in the net, and the Kings were ahead to stay.

"Lucky is a guy who really gets excited about this building," Melrose said. "The rest of us aren't from Montreal, aren't from Quebec. Lucky is just fired up being here. He's not sleeping, he's dreaming. I haven't seen him speaking this much French all season. I didn't know he remembered it." Robitaille would not have minded saying the words *truc du chapeau* — hat trick in French — but two goals were better than none, the number he scored in Game 1 in each of the previous three series.

Jari Kurri scored an important goal at 1:51 of the third period, increasing the Kings' lead to 3-1 after the Canadiens bungled a clearing attempt behind their net. Roy and Patrice Brisebois failed to communicate, and, following some hesitation, Granato swooped in and checked the defenseman off the puck. Gretzky gained possession and passed to an uncovered Kurri for a point-blank shot.

"Absolutely no excuses," Demers said. "They outplayed us, came in on a high. If you make mistakes, they capitalize, and we made a heck of a lot of mistakes. We made more mistakes tonight than we did in the last four-five games combined."

Roy said the impending birth of his third child—his wife, Michele, was due to give birth the next day—was not a distraction for him, and he hoped his teammates were smart enough not to look for excuses of any kind. "Listen, we didn't do anything for eight days," Roy said. "Everybody was saying how great we were. When everyone is saying you're doing well and you receive pats, you start to believe it."

Jimmy Carson, benched for the fourth consecutive game, was starting to believe he had played his last hockey of the year. "It's tough mentally. You come to the rink, watch the games and wish you were down there on the ice, but you also desperately want the team to win," he said. "The focus now is to win the Stanley Cup. I could sit and pout and complain and be a disruption, but I'm not going to do that."

If it hadn't been for the Kings' stirring win, Carson's second day in town would have been a total wash. Earlier, he reported his passport and a Campbell Conference championship T-shirt as being stolen from his hotel room. A suspect was apprehended at the Forum after he told guards he was Carson's brother. "I don't have a brother," Carson said. Suspicious, the guards summoned police. Strangely, Carson's passport was returned anonymously.

Melrose replaced Carson with defenseman Mark Hardy, and he wound up skating a regular shift in the first period because Darryl Sydor was injured eight seconds into the game. Sydor needed 32 stitches to close gashes on his mouth and under his nose after he was struck by a puck that came off the stick of Lyle Odelein. "He wasn't hurt much, just got his lip sliced in half and he lost two teeth," Melrose said. Sydor, whose only dental damage was one chipped tooth, played the final two periods with a full face shield. "This is the Stanley Cup final," a barely audible Sydor said through swollen and bloody lips. "I didn't care what was wrong with me, I was going back out there. It's only a cut."

The Kings knew the task of winning Game 2 was going to be a difficult one. The Canadiens were angry at themselves for playing so poorly in the opener and embarrassed for doing it before their home fans. Besides, Game 1 served as a wake-up call that knocked out the rusty kinks from eight days of inactivity. Carbonneau actually volunteered to check Gretzky, and another strong defensive forward, Mike Keane, was ready to pitch in after sitting out the first game with a sore back. As if all that wasn't enough, Roy could concentrate totally on hockey now that his wife had given birth to a healthy baby girl.

In the meantime, though, the first controversy of the series surfaced when the *Journal de Montreal*, a French newspaper, published a story claiming Bruce McNall had offered his players a $1 million bonus for winning the Stanley Cup. The offer was made, the story said, in the dressing room following the Kings' Campbell Conference series-clinching win in Toronto. Such an offer would be in violation of NHL by-laws and could result in a fine as high as $1 million.

McNall denied the report, but he had to answer to league commissioner Gary Bettman, who saw the story and called him. "They've been accusing me of trying to buy the Stanley Cup for five years," McNall said. "I have no idea where this story came from or how it got started. With the press in Canada, you never know how something like that gets started. It's a totally dead issue. Look, this is a great hockey town and they have lots of sports pages to fill. I guess it's better to make something up than to ask somebody."

It would have taken someone with a much wilder imagination to dream up the bizarre finish to Game 2, which was decided as much by an obscure rule as the *truc du chapeau* defenseman Eric Desjardins delivered in Montreal's 3-2 overtime victory, the Canadiens' eighth consecutive overtime decision of the playoffs.

Despite being outskated, outhit, and outshot by a mile, the Kings managed to build a 2-1 lead on goals by two of the oldest players on the team, Dave Taylor and Pat Conacher, and used the exceptional play of Hrudey to nurse it into the final two minutes.

Taylor scored his second shorthanded goal of the playoffs at 5:12 of the second period to tie the game, 1-1, after Patrice Brisebois, who didn't look good in the opener, fell down. Taylor chugged down right wing as quickly as his 37-year-old legs could carry him, and he rifled the puck between Roy's skates.

The Kings spent the rest of the period playing spectator, watching Hrudey drop to his knees or stack his pads or kick out his legs and make one spectacular save after another. The score remained tied after two periods even though the Canadiens, who pressed the attack from the beginning, had a 28-14 advantage in shots.

Los Angeles' play in the third period was considerably better, though Montreal maintained a slight territorial advantage. Carbonneau, with some help from Muller and several hits from the Canadiens' defensemen, effectively shut down Gretzky; his only shot of the game came in the first period and his streak of collecting a point or more in Stanley Cup final competition would end at 17 games.

Still, the Kings plugged on. When they grabbed the lead, 2-1, when Taylor threw the puck in front and Conacher banged a backhanded shot behind Roy at the 8:32 mark for his sixth postseason goal, the Kings on the ice as well as those on the bench were jumping with delight. The Canadiens sagged. It seemed quite possible, almost certain, that the Kings were going to steal a win in the Canadiens' building and head home with a commanding 2-0 lead in the best-of-seven series.

There was little reason to think otherwise as the game wore on, and especially after they finished killing off a Taylor interference penalty with six minutes left; the Canadiens were 0 for 11 on power plays in the series and had failed to produce a goal on 32 power plays in a row, an indication they probably wouldn't break through after pulling Roy for an extra skater in the final minute. If the Kings could just hang on a little longer, Roy would be out. They'd have a chance to put the game away, maybe the series, with an empty-net goal.

The Kings were gaining confidence in their ability to repel every Montreal rush into their zone, forays that were becoming less frequent and less dangerous. The Kings were doing a much better job of supporting Hrudey, clearing the puck out of danger with little resistance as Melrose kept the shifts short, changing lines often to keep fresh bodies on the ice.

And then it happened.

One minute, 45 seconds remained when a puck was frozen along the boards in the Kings end. Referee Kerry Fraser blew on his whistle to stop play and the teams began to line up for a faceoff in the circle to Hrudey's right. Except Jacques Demers had some other business in mind, and the puck wasn't going to be dropped until he was finished.

Demers motioned to his team captain, Carbonneau, who in a matter of seconds was conversing with Fraser. "We'd like you to check out McSorley's stick," Carbonneau told him. The curvature of Marty McSorley's stickblade. In a flash, McSorley, who was on the ice and thus fair game, was ordered to surrender his stick. Fraser carried it to the timekeeper's bench, used a stick gauge to measure the top, middle, and bottom of the blade.

Among other things, NHL rule 20 (b) states: "The curvature of the blade of the stick shall be restricted in such a way that the distance of a perpendicular line measured from a straight line drawn from any point at the heel to the end of the blade to the point of maximum curvature shall not exceed one-half inch."

A curved stick enables a player to get off a more powerful shot. It is much easier to lift a puck while shooting or passing — the latter is necessary when chipping a pass over another stick — with a curved blade than it is with a straight one, or to make a shot dart and dip on its way to the net. Virtually every player uses a curved blade; generally speaking, the more prolific goal-scorers own the biggest curves.

The use of curved sticks began to multiply in the mid-1960s when players saw what they did for powerful shooters like

Bobby Hull of the Chicago Blackhawks. Sticks are manufactured to players' personal specifications and usually arrive from the factory with a slight curve. Players modify their own curves by bending the blade after heating the wood with a small blow torch.

The Kings were concerned about McSorley's stick now. "Marty likes a big curve," Gretzky said. "It's pretty obvious. It's easy to see. It's no big secret." If McSorley used an illegal stick — many players do — had he remembered to put it away, to make absolutely certain the stick he took onto the ice at such a critical juncture would pass inspection? Every player keeps a batch of sticks in the stick rack behind the bench. If he's been careful, he knows that at least one of them is legal.

For if Fraser found the stick was illegal, it would be confiscated for the balance of the game, McSorley would be fined $200, and he would be assessed a minor penalty; Montreal would go on the power play and probably pull Roy for a six-on-four skating advantage. The same penalties would have applied if McSorley refused to surrender the stick, with a 10-minute misconduct tacked on for good measure, so it was pointless to be stubborn.

The Kings prayed the stick was legal. The Canadiens would just about be through if it was because they'd be assessed a minor penalty for delay of game, putting the Kings on the power play. If the stick was okay, the Kings were virtually guaranteed a 2-0 lead in the series.

But McSorley's stick wasn't legal. Wasn't even close. According to Bryan Lewis, the NHL's director of officiating, the curve was off by a good quarter-inch. Neither the Kings nor McSorley were pacified to learn the stick would be returned after the game, that he could legalize the stick and use it again.

Under two minutes remained in a Stanley Cup final game that might be decided because of an illegally curved stick. At least McSorley hadn't covered it with pine tar or hollowed it out and stuffed it with cork. The Kings could complain all they wanted, but rules are rules. It was another "McSorry Incident!" He was escorted to the penalty box and, as expected, Roy stayed on the Canadiens bench. The Montreal net was empty, but the Kings would have to kill off a two-man disadvantage for 1:45 to win the game.

They couldn't do it. Eric Desjardins, who had scored the only goal for either team in the first period, was high in the slot when he blew a slap shot into the net with 73 seconds to go. Hrudey, hopelessly screened on the play, never had a chance. The crowd, so silent before, erupted. The Canadiens had broken an 0 for 32 schneid on the power play and the game was tied, 2-2.

Fifty-one seconds into overtime, the crowd went crazy again when Desjardins, who had one goal in Montreal's previous 16 playoff games, became the only defenseman in Stanley Cup final history to score three times in a game. Desjardins' original shot was high and wide of the net, but instead of hitting the glass flush and bounding away harmlessly, the puck struck a metal partition that keeps the glass in place. It bounced right onto the stick of Benoit Brunet at the side of the net and he passed to Desjardins, who was left uncovered, steaming down right wing. He drilled the puck between Hrudey's skates.

Hrudey, his marvelous 38-save performance wasted, looked skyward in disgust, then trudged off. "Stupid, crazy bounce," he muttered. Desjardins is a fine defenseman, but he never reminded anyone of Bobby Orr at any time in his six NHL seasons. Nevertheless, he had accomplished something Orr could only dream about. "I was a little bit lucky on the last one," he said. "I tried to go too hard and it hit the bar, the middle part, and then the glass and came back on Benoit's stick. He made a great play to give it back to me."

Once again, though, Marty McSorley had squeezed his way into the spotlight. The guy sure had a way of making news. First the melee-triggering hit on Doug Gilmour in the Campbell Conference series, and now this.

The Canadiens had used the rule book to their advantage, nothing wrong about that, yet many of the Kings expressed nothing but contempt for Demers, whom they saw as having broken some sort of unwritten code. In their view, Montreal's victory was somewhat tainted. "First of all, we should have killed the penalty off," Rob Blake said. "They didn't have a goalie and we should have iced it, anything. It was a nice goal, a nice win for them. It's in the rule book so we have to pay. But I thought it was kind of cheap. This is the Stanley Cup final and it should be decided on the ice."

Warren Rychel's reaction was less subtle. "It's bullshit," he said. Gretzky said, "It's in the rules, part of the game." Darryl Sydor thought Demers' move was a "gutsy" call. "It could have backfired on him, too," he said.

Melrose, furious that the opportunity to win two straight games in Montreal had slipped away in such a strange manner, laced his postgame remarks with heavy doses of sarcasm. When someone wondered how McSorley was handling his disappointment, Melrose snapped, "He broke down and cried for about two minutes." He said he would be sure to check "the length of skate laces" as well as the curvature of stickblades before Game 3. "I found out we've got two urinals in our building that are four inches too high. I guess we'll have to get them fixed, too," he said.

Melrose went on to say he did not want his comments to be taken as criticism of Demers. "But I wouldn't have done it. I'm very good friends with Jacques Demers. It's nothing against him, but Barry Melrose wouldn't do it. I have never called for a stick penalty and I never will," he said. "Yes, it's my fault. It's the coach's responsibility. But, no, I don't believe in winning that way. This is a pressure-packed place, Montreal. Pressure breeds things." But no, he wasn't criticizing Demers.

Not that Demers was about to apologize. He vigorously defended the move, which happens occasionally in the regular season but had never been attempted in a Stanley Cup final as far as anyone knew. "It's the rules," he said. "I never like to embarrass a man who has so much pride like Marty, but it was visible. I asked three of my players to look in Game 1 just to be sure. One thing I always tell my players, if one of my players ever has an illegal stick, he's fined terribly."

Melrose said he did not have such a policy, but it's questionable how much blame a coach should be given when a player is caught. He can't be expected to inspect all of his team's sticks, which would number over 100.

"We're not talking about stuff that anyone goes to jail for, but if you cheat, you have to be smart enough not to get caught," Montreal's Denis Savard said. "You cheat because you think it's going to make you a better player, and maybe Marty decided that stick made him a better player. I'm sure every team in the league has four or five guys who use illegal sticks. It's all a question of timing."

Demers didn't mind acknowledging the unusual measure was borne out of desperation. He was going to pull Roy for an extra skater anyhow, but the Canadiens' ineptness on power plays convinced him a simple one-man advantage would likely end in futility. "Our five-on-four has been zilch, zero," Demers said. "The only thing that could go for us is six-on-four. Our power play has simply been non-existent. We just did a job. If not, we'd be down 2-0."

Demers said the Canadiens "suspected" McSorley and Robitaille were using illegal sticks. Carbonneau, whose vision must be uncanny, said he thought McSorley used an illegal stick in Game 1. "I saw it in the first period of the first game," Carbonneau said. "I talked to Jacques about it. Tonight I kept reminding him." Carbonneau claimed Robitaille didn't switch to a legal stick until there were about four minutes to play in Game 2. Robitaille denied the charge. "The only time I ever change my stick," he said, "is when it's broken."

McSorley, as you can well imagine, was not the happiest man in Montreal this night. He undoubtedly would have permitted Wendel Clark a free swing or two at each of his eyes in exchange for wiping away the penalty. But that was not going to happen. McSorley took a few gentle jabs at Demers — "He's a great coach, isn't he? How did he know I was going to be out there then? They had a power play earlier, you'd think that's when he would have called it" — but unlike Melrose and so many of his teammates, McSorley did not accuse the Canadiens of breaking with hockey etiquette, as if such a thing exists.

McSorley said the bad stick was included in a batch of six new sticks he received that morning, and he actually worked on taking some of the curvature *off* the sticks. "I guess I didn't take enough off that one," he said. "Gretz is the only guy whose sticks are absolutely perfect." McSorley's other error was to become so involved emotionally that he forgot to double-check the stick he carried onto the ice. "I should have thought about it," he said. "I should have gone to the rack and made damn sure. I'm a veteran. It's never been called against me, and I don't feel good about it. I made a mistake."

Fifteen

Big Mac Attack

All the Kings felt badly for Marty McSorley, whose Game 2 gaffe was certain to become a part of Stanley Cup playoff lore, and not the kind any of them would particularly care to remember. Besides, he was sort of like a Big Brother on skates, a teammate they looked up to because of the role he played on the club.

In the euphemistic vernacular of the NHL, McSorley was an enforcer. Basically, this meant he was supposed to ensure that smaller, more skilled and peaceful teammates were given adequate room on the ice in which to operate. A jolting body check, or a well-placed punch, usually were more effective ways to get the job done than, say, a glare from a pair of steely eyes. But whichever tack McSorley decided upon, he could intimidate with the best of them.

"Any time I'm on the ice," he said, "I want every opponent to look at me as being a tough guy." Being "tough" in the NHL carries a number of connotations, all of them related to violence; goon, thug, bully, and hooligan are just a few. McSorley, who stands 6-feet-1 and weighs 225 pounds, was called those and worse, especially in Calgary, where he is still disliked for spearing Flames center Mike Bullard during a 1988 playoff game when he was still playing for Edmonton.

Not that Oilers fans cared for McSorley anymore. Nor did he gain many friends in Toronto after he smashed Maple Leafs star Doug Gilmour to the ice with an elbow to the face in the opening game of the Campbell Conference final.

Come to think of it, the man was pretty much disliked in every city in North America, provided there was a 200-foot patch of ice.

McSorley would be the first person to agree he doesn't play with a halo surrounding his helmet. The Lady Byng Trophy, which annually is awarded to the league's most gentlemanly player, will never sit atop his mantle. He piled up a Kings record 399 minutes in penalties in 1992-93, when he was suspended or fined three times, punishment that cost him $21,995 of his $650,000 salary.

The most expensive disciplinary action was meted out by then-NHL president Gil Stein, who handed McSorley a six-day suspension after he received a match penalty October 29 for cross-checking Boston's Darren Banks in the face. Banks needed six stitches to close two cuts near his left eye. Banks eventually returned, but McSorley did not; he was banished for the rest of the game.

McSorley repeatedly claimed the incident was an accident. "I was trying to drop my gloves to get ready to square off," he said with a straight face, "and Banks ducked." Not surprisingly, Stein didn't buy the explanation. His subsequent ruling, which included a $500 fine, cost McSorley $14,130 in lost wages.

McSorley suspected the No. 33 on his sweater looked like a bull's eye to the referees. "Certain guys get more calls than others," he said. "I would just like to see the sweater colors called and not the numbers."

He made those comments following a March 12 game with the Flames. Referee Don Koharski had given McSorley a major penalty for cross-checking 5-foot-6 Theoren Fleury during a last-minute scramble around the net. McSorley protested. "I'm willing to take what's coming to me if I deserve it, and I have no problem with the league setting strict rules," he said, "but it isn't right if I'm forced to sit on the bench in the last five minutes of a physical game because a major penalty may be called if I'm out there. If the league doesn't look at the video and take back the stick infraction call, I'll have serious questions about how they come about their policies."

If the penalty had been allowed to stand, it would have been McSorley's third major stick foul of the season and cost him a three-game suspension and another $7,065 of his rapidly-disappearing salary. McSorley is a generous fellow, but this was getting to be a bit much even for him.

"There's no way I hit Fleury with a stick," he said. After viewing videotape, Kings assistant coach Cap Raeder agreed. "Marty shouldn't have put himself in that situation, but it was not a stick infraction," Raeder said. "He only had one hand on his stick." The other hand, apparently, was planted squarely in Fleury's face. But a fist is not a stick. The Kings sent a tape to the NHL office, the cross-checking penalty was rescinded, and McSorley held onto his wallet.

McSorley worked hard to become a useful player who could contribute whether or not he punched out an opponent. His ability and willingness to fight kept him in the NHL long enough for him to develop his playing skills to efficient levels. And yet he would make no apologies for playing the part of Sluggo from time to time.

"I know a lot of people won't agree with this," he said, "but when two guys drop their gloves and go to the penalty box for five minutes, it can help quicken a game. That's because there probably was a series of chippy events before that otherwise would probably continue. Guys see a fight and they say, 'Okay, now we can get back to playing.' A fight can settle things down."

McSorley could settle down when the spirit moved him. And even though he was still regarded as a musclehead and a caveman in some quarters, the truth of the matter was he could do a lot more than bash in someone's face. McSorley was coming into his own as a legitimate, honest-to-goodness *player*.

"You want respect as a player," he admitted. "You really do want that. At the same time, you can get caught up in a 'Catch-22' type situation that's tough to get out of. I want to be known as a tough guy so teams will leave Wayne Gretzky and Luc Robitaille and our other big scorers alone. On the other hand, because of my reputation, I'm going to get more penalties. And I still hear people say, 'What's that guy doing on the power play?' They're surprised at the amount of ice time I get. Hey, I just want the respect I think I've earned. But I guess that's all in the eye of the beholder."

Different cities, different eyes. McSorley remained a villain on the road, where he was booed, jeered, and mocked. In Los Angeles, he was considered a hero, the most popular player on a team that included half a dozen or so marquee names.

McSorley was "comfortable" with being popular, he said, "Because I don't think I did it with any gimmicks. I'm just happy when people show they appreciate the work you've put in. I just think people want to see a good, honest effort. I think they like seeing a player play hard and get involved."

For McSorley, this could mean fighting Wendel Clark and visiting a sick child in a hospital. If he ever turned down a charitable request, no one had ever heard of it. In many ways, McSorley was a living, breathing contradiction. Off the ice, he flashed a killer smile, was soft-spoken, thoughtful and gentle. On the ice, sneers often exploded from an angelic-looking face that sat beneath long, golden hair.

Autograph seekers waited after practices and games to meet him, and the wait was often quite long. McSorley probably spent more time at the rink and in the dressing room than he did in his own living room. He worked on puck handling and shooting well after most practices ended and countless hours were spent in the weight room to keep his body chiseled. "I also watch myself a lot on tape," McSorley said. "It's the only way I'm ever going to get any better."

During the playoffs, Kings coach Barry Melrose was calling McSorley "the best defenseman in hockey" every chance he got. Okay, so Melrose was biased. He also was prone to exaggeration. But few observers were questioning McSorley's value to one of the smallest teams in the league. Whenever the subject of McSorley's impending free-agent status was mentioned, even Gretzky would smile and say, "I'd like to be his agent." Like Gretzky, McSorley is represented by Michael Barnett.

McSorley was grinning often, too, especially when Melrose's "best defenseman in hockey" statement was brought to his attention. "I never second-guess the coach," he responded. "But do you remember training camp? There were a lot of rumors I'd be traded even before the season started."

Most of the rumors were based on speculation that his union activities of the previous season — the NHL Players Association staged a 10-day strike, the first walkout in hockey history — had enraged Bruce McNall. The Kings owner treated his players well and was stung when they voted to join ranks with their brethren on picket lines. "We did it very regretfully, very reluctantly," said McSorley, who remained the team's union representative.

McSorley wound up playing in 81 games, easily a career high. The season before, when he missed six games with a throat virus and three with a shoulder injury, marked the only time in his Kings career he did not lose a game to some sort of NHL suspension; he tied Fleury for the best plus-minus figure (plus-48) that year, a sign he was maturing as a player.

Despite shuttling between right wing and defense for good chunks of the 1992-93 season, McSorley tied his career high for goals (15) and set a personal best for points (41). But he continued to play tough; his 16 fights were second on the team to Warren Rychel's 29, and his franchise record 399 minutes in penalties gave him 1,560 minutes — 26 hours — in his career as a King, one minute shy of Dave Taylor's all-time club record for time spent in the penalty box. Taylor needed 1,078 games to reach his total, McSorley a mere 354 games.

But McSorley played with more discipline once the playoffs began. "You have to," he said. "Everybody does. The games are close and you don't want one decided on a power play." McSorley would finish with 60 penalty minutes, a relative pittance for him, in 24 playoff games; he would score four goals and add six assists. Melrose had enough confidence in McSorley to use him on power plays, to kill penalties, and even in four-on-four situations, a tribute to his improved skating ability. He was probably logging 25-30 minutes of ice time per game, generous minutes usually reserved for players like Gretzky.

"Barry sat me down early this year and he told me he believed in me as a player," McSorley said. "He asked me about the hockey team, showed me a great deal of respect. Because we're not a big team, we were in a lot of out-sized situations and I had to be there. Let's face it, that's still a big part of my job. Sure, over the course of the five years I've been in L.A. I've gotten a lot of penalty minutes and I certainly haven't broken any scoring records. But I'm also not a guy who just sits in the penalty box. I believe I can play."

More people will agree with that statement now than would have, oh, a dozen years ago when McSorley, who was born in

Hamilton, Ontario, showed up for a tryout with the Belleville Bulls. An Ontario Hockey League team, the Bulls were owned by a 20-year-old named Gretzky. "My dad's best friend brought Marty down for a tryout and told everyone he could make the team," Gretzky said. "My dad's friend was so proud. He always felt he was the guy who put Marty in the National Hockey League.

"I remember Marty was always the last guy off the ice, just like he is now. He made himself a hockey player strictly by hard work and a love of the game. He's one of the best defensemen in hockey right now and he might be the toughest player, so that's a pretty good combination."

McSorley wasn't drafted by any NHL team following his 10-goal, 183-penalty minute season with Belleville in 1982-83, which is when he vowed to do whatever was necessary to get into the show. "I probably ran six miles a day that summer and I didn't even know how to run," McSorley said. "I worked out with weights and I gained 15 pounds."

He worked hard enough to gain an invitation to the Pittsburgh Penguins training camp on a free-agent tryout basis. "There were a lot of people who didn't think I deserved to be there," McSorley said. "But I didn't care. I was in great shape, really strong. And once I got there I never dropped my gloves. I was scared because I was going into unknown territory. I had put in the work out of fear. But it was worth it because they signed me to a contract."

McSorley spent parts of two seasons in a Penguins uniform and he caught a break in 1985 when Pittsburgh general manager Ed Johnston traded him to Edmonton in exchange for goaltender Gilles Meloche. "Eddie did me a favor," McSorley said. "I think he saw some talent in me and he wasn't afraid to send me somewhere where I would get a chance to get better."

Maybe McSorley didn't blossom in Edmonton, where the explosive Oilers were emerging as a powerhouse, but couldn't a claiming horse have improved by rounding the track with Secretariat? McSorley should have been able to learn something by skating with Gretzky, Mark Messier and Paul Coffey.

"The whole thing about Edmonton," Gretzky said, "is the way the game is taught. You move the puck, you skate, and you learn how to pass. The fundamentals of hockey are taught there and Marty learned and observed and he got to work on them every day. There's no question he became a better player because of it.

"Honestly, I've never known a man quite like him, and I'm very proud of him. I'm happy for him and I'm happy that people are starting to give him some respect, give him some due, for being a good hockey player and not just talking about the bad reputation that some people want to put on him."

McSorley was not a star in Edmonton, but the Oilers were blessed with a whole galaxy of stars and they didn't need him to be much more than a little meteorite. He stayed there for parts of three seasons before he was included in the trade that sent Gretzky to the Kings. McSorley's acquisition — the Kings also picked up Mike Krushelnyski from Edmonton — merited about one paragraph in each of the Los Angeles newspapers.

"If given the opportunity, I'm sure the Kings would have taken a Glenn Anderson or a Grant Fuhr," McSorley said. "But I think I was on the list of people they thought they could get. I guess Wayne thought enough of me that he talked to Bruce about putting me in the package. I've never really talked to Wayne about it, but it makes you feel good."

If Gretzky wanted McSorley, cynics suggested, it was solely to ride shotgun on his line. For bodyguard purposes. Yet, even now, McSorley does not try to dispel his image. "When a guy is harassing one of your best players, well, sometimes you have to step in and send a message," he said. "I mean, the goons are already outdated. There are very few of them left, and I think that's good because you want to magnify the skill players. But you still need tough guys. If you eliminate fighting, the threat of repercussions will be gone and the cheap stick stuff will just get worse.

"I think it's important to remember that the tough guys are there to protect the stars. It's the small guys who make a living by harassing Wayne Gretzky and Mario Lemieux. I think the league ought to be more concerned about the hooking, holding, slashing and shadowing that goes on. You don't see me or a Rob Ray or a Joey Kocur taking a Mario Lemieux or a Steve Yzerman out of the games. We deal with people like a Garth Butcher. You can't let a guy take a whack at a star player. We're there to protect the stars, not to hurt them.

"Look, I don't see too many fans going to the concession stands during a fight. And you know as well as I do that no matter what I do, that if I play well and score a goal and we win, or if I've been doing a good job killing penalties and playing great defense . . . it doesn't matter at all what I've been doing sometimes because there are always going to be some people who will only want to talk about a fight."

And that was fine, too. Especially now. The illegal stick incident had left Marty McSorley in a particularly ornery mood.

Sixteen

Overtime
Doesn't Pay

The very first hockey game to be played inside the Forum, the house that Jack Kent Cooke built, took place on December 30, 1967. The Kings were beaten — and probably beaten up — that day by their tormentors from the East, the Philadelphia Flyers. The final score was 2-0 and the game attracted 14,366 fans, many of whom were probably more interested in touring Inglewood's splashy new sports venue than in watching players named Eddie Joyal and Bill "Cowboy" Flett hitting a black disc with crooked sticks while skating around an ice rink in purple and gold uniforms.

The Kings played a handful of games at the Sports Arena in downtown Los Angeles and also in Long Beach, often before crowds of under 5,000, during that inaugural season while the Forum was being constructed, but even after it was finished attendance hardly skyrocketed; the Kings averaged a little more than 8,000 fans per home game.

Twenty-six years later, in sweltering June heat, hockey was the hottest ticket in town. Fans fortunate enough to have one to Game 3 of the Stanley Cup final were tempted by have-nots to give it up for as much as $500, to go home and watch for free on television. Stretch limousines carrying the rich and famous were stacked up, one behind the other, outside the Forum on June 5, an historic date in the annals of Kings hockey. Spotlights danced across the sky, and across the bright sheet of ice inside the darkened arena. It would be full — all 16,005 seats sold long ago — for the 35th consecutive time.

The Kings sure had come a long way, baby. Playing for the Stanley Cup on home ice against the Montreal Canadiens, it didn't get any better than this.

"I can remember not long ago, maybe five or six years ago, we'd go to the hotel in L.A. and then we'd go to the rink and nobody would recognize us," said Montreal captain Guy Carbonneau, who might have preferred not to be identified on this particular day. "We went for a walk today and a lot of people recognized us. It's obvious they're very enthusiastic about the game. You have to give credit to Bruce McNall. He went out and got Wayne Gretzky and made a commitment to make hockey exciting here."

The crowd definitely was wired. First the silver Cup itself was brought to center ice, carried over a red carpet, and with great care placed on a table. The fans cheered. Then a Campbell Conference championship banner was uncovered on the north wall, where not very long ago the Smythe Division championship banner was put up. The fans roared. Next, coaches and players from both teams were introduced under multi-colored spotlights, first the Canadiens and then the Kings. The fans booed, then they cheered again. Jacques Demers' reception was cooler than the one Doug Gilmour received.

Too bad the Kings couldn't capture the crowd's spirit. Maybe they were too busy star-gazing, checking out Michelle Pfeiffer, Goldie Hawn, Mick Jagger, Dyan Cannon and James Woods in the stands when their eyes should have been glued to Kirk Muller, Brian Bellows, Mathieu Schneider, Stephan Lebeau and Vincent Damphousse on the ice.

Five seconds after Tim Watters went off for tripping, the suddenly-rejuvenated Montreal power play burned the Kings again. Muller won a faceoff from Pat Conacher, drawing the puck back to Kevin Haller at the point. Haller shot and Bellows tipped it in for a 1-0 lead at 10:26 of the first period. It was the sixth playoff goal for Bellows, a 40-goal man in the regular season who was benched for the entire second period in Game 2. "Wasn't playing Brian Bellows hockey," Demers explained.

Barry Melrose might have considered strapping all 20 of the Kings to the bench in the opening three minutes of second period of this game after Gilbert Dionne and Schneider scored goals 21 seconds apart to give Montreal a 3-0 lead. The streak marks left by the Zamboni machine during the intermission were still visible and already the Kings were in serious trouble.

Enter Mark Hardy, the 34-year-old defenseman who again was sitting in for Jimmy Carson. Hardy played nine years for the Kings, wore purple and gold for all of them and was on three non-playoff teams before a trade in 1988 sent him to the New York Rangers. Nick Beverley reacquired Hardy in March, and he was turning out to be quite a useful utilityman. He might not have gotten into this particular game if Charlie Huddy hadn't been forced to leave with a torn ligament in his right knee, possibly a season-ending injury. But Hardy was out there now and enjoying every shift.

Then — pow! — Hardy lined up Mike Keane for a check and drove him into the sideboards with such power that a pane of glass was knocked out. Keane was shaken, not hurt, but the crowd was recharged and the Kings began to feed off that energy.

A little over two minutes after Hardy's crunching hit, Luc Robitaille took a return pass from Tomas Sandstrom and slid the puck to Wayne Gretzky behind the net. Gretzky waited, and waited some more for Robitaille to get open in front, then he got him the puck for a shot that skipped past Patrick Roy. The time was 7:52. The Canadiens had a 3-1 lead, but the Kings had gotten on the board.

They struck again at 11:02. Tony Granato, with just one goal to show for his previous 13 games, chopped the puck away from Dionne in the Montreal end, moved to the right circle and snapped the puck home. The Kings were back in the game.

Los Angeles' confidence soared from there. The Kings picked up the pace, began to put more pressure on Roy. Finally, with 2:53 to go in the period, they tied the game. Hardy hit Mike Donnelly with a clearing pass and Donnelly used his speed to break across the red line. The Kings had their skating legs back, were playing aggressively, pounding the boards and making things happen. Donnelly passed to Gretzky moving across the blue line and Gretzky leaned into a slap shot. Roy flailed at the black blur with his catching glove . . . and missed. It was Gretzky's 15th playoff goal, his second of the series.

The second half of the third period was a repeat of the final 10 minutes of the second period for the Kings, except for one minor detail. They couldn't score. Roy made up for his earlier play by making big saves, but Kelly Hrudey was in a groove, too, and overtime beckoned again. There were under seven minutes to go when Sandstrom caught Montreal napping and fed Robitaille with a breakout pass. Robitaille isn't a swift skater, but he had a head start and chugged into the Canadiens zone alone. And he *is* one of the most dangerous goal-scorers in the NHL. Robitaille broke in on Roy, forced him to lean to the right, then he ripped a shot for the opposite corner. Wide. The puck missed catching the inside of the left post by inches.

And then it happened again. More controversy. More debate. Time was running out in the third period and the Kings were swarming in Montreal's end when Sandstrom attempted to sweep the puck into the net. It might have gone in if Guy Carbonneau, who spent Game 2 eye-balling sticks and checking Gretzky, wasn't stretched out in the crease. Warren Rychel had put him there with a nice little cross-check, and then Carbonneau's arm reached out and the puck disappeared. Referee Terry Gregson blew his whistle. Was he going to award a penalty shot to the Kings with 12.9 seconds remaining?

No. Gretzky argued with Gregson behind the net, pleaded with him to call a penalty shot. Carbonneau had covered the puck in the crease, Gretzky complained, and as far as he could tell the Canadiens hadn't dressed him in a goalie's mask or pads.

While the Kings pulled out their hair, observers pulled out NHL rule books again, flipped past the part about illegal sticks and stopped at rule 53 (c). "No defending player," the rule stated, "except the goalkeeper, will be permitted to fall on the puck, hold the puck or gather the puck into the body or hands when the puck is within the goal crease. For infringement of this rule, play shall be immediately stopped and a penalty shot shall be ordered against the offending team."

But Gregson's interpretation was that Sandstrom shot the puck into Carbonneau, who already was down, and therefore a penalty shot was not warranted. Bryan Lewis, the league's director of officiating, supported Gregson and said, "If a player is down and the puck is shot into him or under him, it is a stoppage, not a penalty. Terry saw that the player was down and the puck was underneath him, causing a stoppage in play."

Gretzky was flabbergasted. "I learned a new rule tonight, that if you shoot the puck into a guy in the crease, it's not a penalty shot," he said. "All I know is there was no doubt the puck was under Carbonneau. The puck was 100 percent under him, but the interpretation was it's not a penalty shot. I never, ever heard of that. The only times I've ever seen guys in the crease like that, they've thrown the puck away so there isn't a penalty shot."

The Kings claimed Carbonneau was more than an innocent victim of a cross-check. They said he used a sweeping motion with his arm to gather the puck into his body, and they were even more furious when Montreal's John LeClair scored 34 seconds into overtime to deal them a bitter 4-3 defeat.

"We should have had a penalty shot, that's the rule," Melrose said. "But we're not using that rule tonight. (Gregson) already had given each of us a power play (in the third period) so I knew there wouldn't be anything else called . . . unless there was an illegal stick." When asked if Gregson might have decided against calling for a penalty shot after letting Rychel's obvious cross-check slide, Melrose responded, "Did they say Rychel picked him up and put him on top of the puck?"

Carbonneau, playing coy, said he didn't know where the puck was but admitted to moving his hand. "Once I was down, I tried to grab the post and pull the net off," he said. Ironically, had Carbonneau succeeded, Gregson would have been forced to make another judgment call. Under rule 50 (d), a penalty shot can be awarded if the net is deliberately dislodged with under two minutes to play in a game.

Rychel appeared to have an excellent view, considering he was standing right over Carbonneau after clubbing him into the crease with a two-handed smash to the back. "It looked to me like he brought (the puck) into himself," Rychel said. "The puck was about a half-foot away from him, I was going for it, and he pulled it in." No one was surprised when Sandstrom, the guy who shot the puck into the crease in the first place, said he "didn't see" the play well enough to make a comment.

So now the Kings were down 2-1 in the series, and it was obvious they would need to win Game 4 or forget about winning the Stanley Cup. The Canadiens were not going to blow a 3-1 series lead, not with as many as two more games at the Montreal Forum. The Kings were going to have to forget about yet another heart-wrenching defeat and go on.

"Why torture yourself over something that wasn't called?" Kelly Hrudey said. "You've got to stay on an even keel." The

Kings definitely were going to have to start causing some damage on a power play whose fuses had blown again. Since Game 1, when Robitaille scored two power-play goals, the Kings were 0 for 13 with an extra man.

While they were at it, exhibiting a little emotion from the opening bell would be a good idea, too. Several players vowed to take a cue from Mark Hardy, whose crushing hit sparked the three-goal comeback that made Montreal sweat. The Canadiens didn't have a habit of frittering away such leads and it would be wise for the Kings not to fall so far behind again.

"We've got to be more physical," Gretzky said. "If we don't hit them, we're not going to win this series. We disliked Calgary, a team in our division, and we disliked Vancouver for the same reason. Then Marty (McSorley) sort of got things going against Toronto, but so far in this series everybody is in love."

Demers didn't agree. "They're an aggressive team and there's nothing cheap, but there are good hits and we keep bouncing back," he said. Demers was particularly pleased with his young defense corps; J.J. Daigneault, 27, was the oldest of the six regulars, with the rest of the group ranging in age from 22 to 25. Daigneault's most impressive move in the series so far was taping the following note for Goldie Hawn on his stick: "Hello, Goldie, I love you. Can we meet after the game?" But in general the Canadiens' defensemen were playing very well.

The Kings would have to find a way to cope without defenseman Charlie Huddy and right winger Dave Taylor in Game 4. Huddy suffered a Grade 3 tear, the worst kind, of the medial collateral ligament in his right knee and could barely walk. Taylor strained his right shoulder when he was hammered into the boards in the second period, and he couldn't stickhandle or shoot.

Huddy was hurt on his first shift when he planted his skate, delivered a pass, then was checked by Keane. He took three more shifts, then called it a night. "You play 100-plus games to get this far and then you can't play," Huddy said. "It's depressing." Dr. Ron Kvitne said it was possible Huddy could play with a brace in Game 5 provided the pain subsided and he could move well enough to be effective. "He can't tear it any worse," Kvitne said.

With Huddy gone for at least one game, Melrose would turn to the Kings' forgotten men of the playoffs, Jimmy Carson and

Lonnie Loach. "He's fresh and he's a guy who can score goals," Melrose said of Carson. All Carson had done since Game 3 of the Toronto series was watch from the stands, and have his passport and a Campbell Conference championship T-shirt stolen. Other than that, he was having a wonderful first Stanley Cup final. "Barry insists he wanted me, but it's tough to believe at times, under the circumstances," Carson said.

More improbable was the manner in which the Kings played after referee Andy van Hellemond dropped the puck to begin Game 4, a game they absolutely had to win. If the Canadiens weren't skating so smoothly, you would have thought someone came along after the morning workouts and dumped gallons of molasses on the ice. The Kings were stuck in neutral and looked even worse than they had the other night.

It took the Kings 6 1-2 minutes to register a shot, a harmless 40-footer by Alexei Zhitnik, and they misfired on two more power plays to run the slump to 15 in a row. When the period ended, the Kings had six shots and no goals, the Canadiens 13 shots and one goal. It was scored by Kirk Muller on a faceoff at the 10:57 mark. Muller won the draw from Jari Kurri, then he stepped around the Kings center and fired a 25-footer that beat Hrudey down low.

The already restless crowd grew more impatient in the second period when Vincent Damphousse scored with eight seconds to go on a holding penalty to Hardy, giving Montreal a 2-0 lead at the 5:24 mark. The goal by Damphousse, who murdered the Kings in the regular season but was held to three assists in the first three games of this series, gave the Canadiens three power-play goals in seven chances since they snapped a 0 for 32 skid in Game 2. Keane ripped a shot wide of the left post, but the puck came around to Damphousse deep in the right circle and Hrudey couldn't slide over in time to get a piece of his quick shot.

But, just as they had throughout the playoffs, the Kings recovered when the hour seemed darkest. The so-called Smurf Line of Mike Donnelly, Corey Millen and Tony Granato produced the breakthrough goal. The unit was applying pressure in the Montreal zone, lost possession, then regained it when Granato bumped Paul Dipietro off the puck. He threw a quick centering pass to Donnelly, who put in his own rebound before Roy could smother it with his glove. Donnelly's goal, his first of the series, came 69 seconds after Damphousse's and trimmed the deficit to 2-1. The Kings were back in the game.

The momentum changed totally in their favor much later in the period when Bellows took a hooking penalty with 50 seconds to go before the intermission, with the Kings' power play finally delivering. Gretzky, who moments earlier picked up his first shot of the game, came from behind the net and slid the puck between the post and defender Benoit Brunet. It came to McSorley in the slot and he drove a bullet over Roy, who was stretched across the crease, to tie the game with five seconds left in the period.

It stayed that way through a scoreless third period in which Roy and Hrudey put on a masterful clinic in goal. The Kings fired 15 shots at Roy, and the Canadiens launched 12 shots at Hrudey. There was Roy, with a minute to go, on his belly and eating ice, somehow getting a piece of the puck just when it appeared Sandstrom would break the tie. He didn't need Carbonneau's help this time. There was Hrudey, sprawling to kick out a drive by Dipietro halfway through the period, snaring Bellows' point-blank slapper two minutes after that.

Then came overtime, winning time on nine consecutive occasions for Montreal and, in this series anyway, not a good time for the Kings. But how much longer could that go on? Wasn't the law of averages stacked heavily against the Canadiens?

Carson nearly won it for the Kings 4:46 into the extra period, and what an interesting little story that would have made. Banished for the previous six games, Carson was permitted two brief shifts in the first period, none in the second, and a handful in the third. But now it was overtime and Melrose was letting him play. When Carson won a draw from Dipietro in the right faceoff circle and took a quick shot, he caught Roy by surprise. "I hit it clean and I thought it was going in," Carson said. But the puck hit the near post and bounced away.

Play continued for nearly 10 minutes more, and the end-to-end action was fierce. The Kings threw everything they had at Roy, peppered him with shots from every conceivable angle, forced him to flop all around his crease. "We played our hearts out," Granato said. But nothing would go in.

Until the 14:37 mark. That's when LeClair, the strapping Canadiens center who ended Game 3 by taking three whacks at the puck as the Kings scrambled around their net, put in the rebound of his own shot to give Montreal a 3-2 victory and a 3-1 stranglehold on the series.

The Kings had been beaten by a dog. LeClair, a 6-foot-2, 205-pounder from St. Albans, Vermont, was nicknamed "Marmaduke" by his teammates. "Because," Mike Keane explained, "he's just a big dog." LeClair certainly had taken some bites out of the Kings.

The winning play actually began with the Kings in possession of the puck in the Canadiens zone. Carson passed it to Donnelly, whose shot sailed wide, struck the boards and caromed all the way to center ice. Because the puck came out so far, four Kings were trapped in the Montreal end. The result was a two-on-one Canadiens rush, led by LeClair. He moved down the left side and intended to pass the puck to Stephan Lebeau, but was forced to shoot by Zhitnik.

Hrudey made the save as he came out to cut down LeClair's shooting angle, but LeClair regained possession and shot again, striking Hrudey's stick. Whether the puck would have hopped out of harm's way after that will never be known. Darryl Sydor, believing Hrudey was in trouble, made a mad dash to join the play, went down to block LeClair's second shot, and inadvertantly knocked the puck into the net.

"I really feel sorry for the kid," Jacques Demers said. "He played a great game and was just trying to help his goaltender." Sydor was unconsolable. "I saw Kelly was out of the net, I tried to go down and block it, and it went off my shin pad and in," he said quietly. "I saw Kelly was out and I reacted, that's all. It was my own instinct. Obviously it was the wrong instinct. We got robbed again."

But by a Roy, not a rulebook. The Kings took their best shots, 10 in the overtime and 42 for the game, and they weren't enough. Sandstrom, Gretzky and Granato combined to take 18 shots, all repelled. Hrudey was solid, as usual. He made six saves in the overtime and 36 for the game, and they weren't enough, either. Three consecutive overtime losses for the Kings, it didn't get much tougher than that. A record 10 consecutive overtime wins for the Canadiens, it didn't get any better. Roy had been in the net for all of them, all 96 minutes, 39 seconds.

"We must have an overtime god," Canadiens defenseman Mathieu Schneider said, "and I think it's Patrick Roy." When Roy won a Stanley Cup seven years earlier, he was a flaky, fuzzy-faced rookie who talked to his goalposts. "My friends," he called them then. Now the Kings were talking, but to themselves. "It doesn't matter to me whether it's the first period, the second period, the third period or overtime," Roy said. "This is the Stanley Cup playoffs. You don't get tired because it pumps you up. I just try to be comfortable out there. I want my teammates to believe in me."

If the Kings were convinced Roy was infallible, or that their rollicking, incredible, magical ride was destined to end in disappointment, they wouldn't admit it. "You always believe," Hrudey said. "We're not giving up. You've got to believe. Any loser can find an excuse. You don't play professional hockey for 12 years if you're a quitter. Quitters come and go, and I want to stay. The good part is we've played well enough to win. We just have to find a way to win, that's the only thing we're missing."

History was not on Los Angeles' side. Eleven teams since 1939, including the Kings, had rallied from a 3-1 deficit to win a playoff series, but only one team, the 1942 Toronto Maple Leafs, had accomplished the feat in a Stanley Cup final; Toronto lost the first three games and came back to whip the Detroit Red Wings that year.

Not that Demers wanted to hear about history. "They are competitive, these Kings. This team, the Kings, they are giving us the best battle in the playoffs," he said. "Wayne Gretzky's team is never a beaten team. They are a group of athletes that is very courageous. They are hitting, Kelly Hrudey has been outstanding and they have three kids on defense who are getting better all the time. No, as soon as you think you have beaten Gretzky, that's when he is going to beat you."

Apparently not all the Canadiens felt that way, though. *New York Daily News* reporter Frank Brown chided a few members of the team for failing to carry themselves with the dignity of former Montreal players after the Game 4 victory. This is how he described the scene in the dressing room:

"Ed Ronan, a wing whose main claim to fame this series has been a goal Wayne Gretzky tipped into his own net in Game 1, felt the need to ask, at the top of his lungs, 'What excuse are (the Kings) going to come up with for this one?' Kirk Muller, a few wickets down the locker line, hissed at his teammate. 'Eddie!' he snapped, adding a withering look to silence the bigmouth. Then Gilbert Dionne let out a whoop and vanished in the hiss of the shower room, after which someone — I am presuming it was Dionne — treated visitors to a few bars of 'America the Beautiful,' mocking the anthem of choice at Kings' games. The singer's contempt was unmistakable and more than a little brash for someone with only 15-16ths of a Stanley Cup ring. When you respect Stanley, you respect the team giving blood to try to win it."

The Kings might have been inclined to stop off at a blood bank once they arrived in Montreal because they didn't have much of their own left to give. No one was questioning the team's heart, not after all it had been through since training camp. But gearing the Kings up even one more time after three consecutive gut-wrenching losses promised to be a difficult task even for Melrose.

"All year, when we were battling through adversity, Barry kept telling us that we would be a better team because of it," Tony Granato said. "At first I remember we would all sort of look at him and say, 'Right, Barry.' But he was right, and those are the kind of things we need to draw on now."

But in the end, which came in the form of an anticlimactic 4-1 Montreal victory, the Kings simply didn't have enough of whatever it takes to skate around and drink from a Stanley Cup. NHL commissioner Gary Bettman presented it to the Canadiens' eagle-eyed captain, Guy Carbonneau, as the words *"Le Canadien champion de la Coupe Stanley""* flashed on the Montreal Forum scoreboard and the crowd of 17,959 rose to salute its conquering heroes. It was the 24th such presentation for a Canadiens team but the first to take place in Montreal since 1986.

In what amounted to a no-brainer, goaltender Patrick Roy was voted the Conn Smythe Trophy as the most valuable player of the playoffs. Roy joined Gretzky, Mario Lemieux, Bobby Orr and Bernie Parent as the only two-time winners of the trophy after registering a 16-4 record and 2.13 goals-against average. His numbers against the Kings were even more impressive: 4-1 record, 2.02 average.

Coaches aren't eligible for the Conn Smythe, but if Roy had his way, Demers would have won it. "He was our key player," Roy said. "The call he made on Marty McSorley in the second game was the turning point of the series. Without that, we would have gone to L.A. down 2-0 and our chances of winning would have been small."

It was hard to imagine the Kings holding any opponent to a measly 15 goals in a five-game stretch, as Hrudey did in the Stanley Cup final, and winning only one of them. Three of the goals came in overtime and another was Gretzky's infamous tip-in, which tells you something about Hrudey's play and even more about Roy's.

But Roy had a considerably easier time in the clincher than in any of the preceding games, especially after Stephan Lebeau completed a pretty passing play with Keane and LeClair to score a power-play goal at 11:31 of the second period. The goal staked Roy to a 3-1 lead and his defense held the deflated Kings to seven shots over the final 28 1/2 minutes.

Dipietro sandwiched first- and third-period goals around one by Kirk Muller, who slipped Rob Blake's check and poked a loose puck under Hrudey after Damphousse fanned on a wrap-around attempt. Melrose called Muller's goal "the one that killed us." It came came at 3:51 of the second period, just 71 seconds after McSorley tied the game, 1-1, with a wicked 30-footer that sailed over Roy's left shoulder.

As you can imagine, the Kings dressing room was not the happiest place on earth after the game. They had lost the series and now it looked like they might be losing their captain. Gretzky, physically exhausted and mentally drained, announced he would seriously ponder retirement. He'd had a remarkable season considering how it started, even finished as the leading playoff scorer with 15 goals and 40 points in 24 games, but he couldn't have been pleased with his Game 5 performance, which didn't include a single shot.

"It's the hardest loss I've ever had," said Gretzky, who hurried off the ice after the traditional handshaking ceremony. He had stopped briefly to chat with Demers, whom he handed his stick. "The last time I lost in the final I was 22 years old and I knew I'd get there again. I'm 32 now and I'm not sure. Listen, I would have killed for this Cup. I'm more proud of this team than some of the teams that did win because those teams should have won. This Cup would have meant so much to win because we were such underdogs. We were so close. We lost three overtime games . . . unbelievable. Montreal is a better team, but not a dominant team. The breaks could very easily have gone our way.

"I've always thought of what's good for the team, what's good for the league, what's good for hockey. It's time I thought of what's good for me. And this isn't a negotiating tool. Bruce has already put a blank piece of paper in front of me and said, 'Fill in the amount.' There's a lot of money for me to be made next year, but I'm not sure that's the best decision to make."

Gretzky's announcement appeared to catch owner Bruce McNall off-guard. "My suspicion is you're dealing with a guy whose emotions are speaking," McNall said of his star player and business partner. "But it wouldn't really be right for me to try to sway him one way or the other. He's a big boy, he'll do the right thing. Whatever he does, we'll support him."

Melrose, and the rest of the Kings players, expressed similar sentiments. But this was also a time when they needed to rally around each other. "These guys played their hearts out for me," Melrose said. "I have never been prouder to be associated with a group of players in my life." The hurt and the pain was etched on Melrose's face, on his players' faces. The Kings had talked bravely of winning the Stanley Cup nine months before, when no one else believed it was possible, and they had come within three overtimes and two controversial rulings of fulfilling that dream. Now the dream was over. Reality can be hard.

"It was fun while it lasted," said Dave Taylor, whose shoulder injury kept him out of the last two games. "But we really would have liked to have hoisted that Cup." Like Gretzky, Taylor had a career decision to make. "I have to talk to the Kings and see what they're thinking," he said.

McSorley was certain to reflect on Game 2 for a while, to think about that extra quarter-inch curve on his stickblade, on the effect it had on the series, on his place in Stanley Cup history. Well, perhaps not. "I'm not going to carry that around," he said. "I know what happened and I'm not going to kid anybody. I'm nobody's fool. Certainly it didn't help our hockey club, but what do I say? What do I do? I'm not fearful of anything. I'm responsible for what I do, but I'm going to take everything in stride and try to be a better player for it. That's all I can do."

And then McSorley was gone, headed up a dim hallway to join the rest of his teammates for the bus ride to the airport and one last flight home.

Seventeen

A New Beginning?

There was no Stanley Cup victory parade through Los Angeles' downtown streets, no extravagant Hollywood party, no celebration of any kind. The Kings enjoyed a glorious season in many respects, went where no previous team in franchise history had dared to go, and they were unquestionably champions in the hearts and minds of their fans. But the Montreal Canadiens knocked them off where it counted most, on the ice, and that was the end of that.

A parade did take place in Montreal, though on a much smaller scale than originally planned. City officials decided to cancel a postparade party at the Forum after rampaging fans celebrated the Canadiens' victory by swarming the downtown area, smashing windows, looting stores, overturning parked cars and setting at least one on fire. A pack of fans even surrounded the Kings' team bus before it departed, shaking it violently, breaking two windows and ripping off a side-view mirror.

The Kings were frightened but unharmed. And happy as hell to get out of Montreal in one piece, even without the Stanley Cup. The Insurance Bureau of Canada estimated the vandals' damage to property and goods, which stretched for 30 blocks along Ste. Catherine Street, at $10 million. Officials reported 115 people were arrested and 168 injured, though none seriously.

More dollars than damage control were needed clear across the continent to keep the Kings together. "I hope we all come back," Tony Granato said, "but we probably won't. Very seldom does a team end a season and have exactly the same players come back the next year. That's the part of it that stinks, but it's also a part of the business."

Now, more than ever, economics are being factored into the player personnel decisions that are made in front offices throughout the NHL. General managers who once wondered "Can he help us?" are starting to ask another question first. "Can we afford him?" Hockey salaries are modest when compared to the other major sports, but they are skyrocketing and the Kings have had one of the league's higher payrolls since Bruce McNall became sole owner in 1988.

McNall can count on a full house at the Forum almost every night now, and the Kings are very adept at marketing and merchandising, but McNall's deep pockets do have bottoms and his general manager, Nick Beverley, does have a budget. True, when Wayne Gretzky announced in July that he would be returning for at least one more season, McNall repeated his promise to restructure the Great One's contract. Gretzky, who made $3 million in 1992-93, would pass Pittsburgh's Mario Lemieux as the highest paid player in the league.

But McNall's generosity with Gretzky, who was given a three-year, $25.5 million contract, didn't necessarily apply to every other member of the team. McNall sees Gretzky's situation as unique; he is a player whose economic value in terms of box office and publicity supersedes anything he accomplishes on the ice. You might say Gretzky is a living, breathing cash register for the Kings.

Marty McSorley, as much as the Kings wanted to keep him, was not viewed in the same manner. McSorley is a unique player in his own right, a charismatic fellow off the ice and an intimidating presence on it. But when the St. Louis Blues signed him to a five-year offer sheet in August that would pay him in the neighborhood of $10.6 million, the Kings balked. Rather than lose McSorley, a Group III free agent, to the Blues without being compensated, they matched the offer and traded him to the Penguins for Shawn McEachern, a center-left winger who scored 28 goals in 1992-93, his rookie season.

"It's hard to move anybody we care about," said coach Barry Melrose, who called McSorley "the best defenseman in hockey" during the playoffs. "If we accepted (the offer), it destroys our salary structure." But agent Michael Barnett said McSorley, who made $650,000 in what proved to be his final year with the Kings, could have been re-signed earlier in the season for considerably less than what he is receiving in Pittsburgh.

McSorley said he requested a four-year, $5 million contract in December 1992 and was rebuffed. Then, he said, the Kings agreed to those terms and notified Barnett with a memo on the day of the fifth and deciding game of the Stanley Cup final. "(But) the actual dollar value of the contract they sent me in July was worth less," McSorley said. "Look, I drive a pickup truck and I live in a rented house. We went to the Stanley Cup finals and I was not prepared to throw that away quickly just to grab cash and run. If anything, I'd love to take all the fans with me, and all the friends I've acquired on the ice and off."

McSorley's departure was fascinating in another regard. A *Los Angeles Times* report following the Montreal series claimed Gretzky's future with the Kings hinged on their complying to a list of demands he had submitted to McNall. The story said Gretzky would not return to the Kings unless McSorley, rugged free-agent winger Warren Rychel, and assistant coach Cap Raeder, whose contract was expiring, were re-signed. Raeder was given a new three-year contract in June. Rychel, who was being wooed by the Detroit Red Wings, was signed to a three-year, $1.6 million deal, a nice piece of change for a guy coming off a six-goal, 314-penalty minute season.

But no McSorley. And, according to Gretzky, no demands. "If anybody in this organization asked me about Dave Taylor or Warren Rychel or Pat Conacher, I'd be honest with them. I would say, 'Yes, they are important to the team,' " Gretzky said. "But I don't sign the checks. I don't lie down in front of Mr. McNall's office and say, 'If you don't sign them, you can't get out of your office.' I just want to win. The biggest reason I'm returning is that we have a chance to win. I would like to win one more championship, and I really believe this group can do it."

On the other hand, it is certain Gretzky would have preferred that McSorley remained. They have been friends for many years, and Gretzky had a difficult time coping when Paul Coffey was traded to Detroit. But business is business. He didn't *like* that, necessarily, but he understood. And didn't this particular transaction lend further proof that Gretzky's influence with the boss is greatly exaggerated?

Other changes were made, but with the notable subtractions of McSorley and center Corey Millen, the Kings were likely to take another run at the Stanley Cup with essentially the same cast of characters that took the Canadiens to overtime three times. Millen, a postseason flop with two goals and four assists in 23 games, was traded in June to the New Jersey Devils for a fifth-round draft pick. Also cut loose were wingers Lonnie Loach and Jim Thomson; they were claimed by the Mighty Ducks of Anaheim in the expansion draft.

Dave Taylor, still hungry after all these years, signed a one-year contract and returned for a 17th season, and another greybeard, Pat Conacher, signed a two-year deal. Jimmy Carson, a Group II free agent who was not deluged with offers from other teams, was anxious to forget his troubled season and reported to training camp without a contract; he eventually signed a three-year, $3.3 million deal.

Brent Thompson, his abdominal problems corrected through off-season surgery, was being counted on to add toughness to the young, mobile defense that eventually will be the backbone of the team. Thompson is 22. Rob Blake, 23, should contend for the Norris Trophy, which is awarded to the NHL's best defenseman. Darryl Sydor and Alexei Zhitnik, both 21, were expected to flourish as sophomores.

Melrose, whose own contract was extended through 1996-97, remained positively positive. Some things won't ever change. "Our goal every year that I coach here will be to win the Stanley Cup," he said. "The more pressure you can put on yourself, the better. I don't think people think we're out of our minds to think about winning it."

Returning to the Stanley Cup final one year after finishing second is even rarer than defending a championship. No runner-up has made it back the following season since 1984, when the Edmonton Oilers won their first Cup and were in the process of building a dynasty.

Los Angeles still has a lot of ice to cover to reach that point. Perhaps it never will. But isn't progress often marked by the smallest of strides? At least now, the Kings' skate marks are pointing in the right direction.

Epilogue

I waited 20 years to see Southern California sports fans embrace hockey the way they did in the spring of 1993. Oh, there had been a few other times when the Kings seemed like they were just on the verge of capturing their enthusiasm, only to fall short.

In 1975, after their best regular season ever, the Kings were eliminated by the Toronto Maple Leafs in a best-of-three series. In 1976, they forced the Boston Bruins to a seventh game in the quarterfinals, only to lose and be eliminated. Then there was the great playoff comeback game in 1982, the "Miracle on Manchester" game against the Edmonton Oilers in which the Kings rallied from a 5-0 third-period deficit to win in overtime, 6-5. The Kings managed to win that series, but they were beaten in the next round by the Vancouver Canucks.

So, obviously, nothing matched the sustained interest and excitement of the 1993 Stanley Cup playoffs.

For me, the most memorable series of the four the Kings played was the Campbell Conference final against the Maple Leafs. Kings fans were finally going to see their team play beyond the second round, and the enthusiasm in the Los Angeles area for hockey and the Kings was steadily building. Never before had I seen so many newspaper reporters and television stations following the Kings on the road.

Game 7 at Maple Leaf Gardens was one of the greatest games I've ever had the pleasure of broadcasting. There was so much tension knowing the Kings were so close, just one victory, from advancing to the Stanley Cup final.

Toronto's captain, Wendel Clark, almost scored 30 seconds into the game, but his shot just slid wide. Had he scored that early, it might have given the Maple Leafs great momentum and changed the outcome of the game. Of course, the Kings' captain, Wayne Gretzky, was outstanding.

I'll never forget the third period. The Kings had a 5-3 lead with three minutes left when Dave Taylor took a pass from Jari Kurri . . . and missed a wide-open net. Taylor is such an outstanding person, has been such a credit to the Kings organization for 16 years, that everyone was hoping he would somehow get an opportunity to win a Stanley Cup before his career ended. So when Toronto scored with a minute to play, cutting the Kings' lead to a goal, I was thinking, "Don't let them tie and win it, or Taylor will never live down missing that empty net."

The last minute of that game was really hectic, on the ice and in the television booth. Several times I had to tell myself to settle down. "Just call the game," I thought. "You have a job to do, don't get involved like a fan."

At one point in the third period, I had the weirdest feeling I have ever experienced during a broadcast. The Maple Leafs were buzzing around the Kings net, and for about five seconds I had a sort of shiver come over my body. I felt as if I wouldn't be able to speak. I also felt, if any words did come out, they would be something like, "Don't let them score!" Now that's hardly what you would want to hear from a professional announcer.

Finally, with about five seconds to play, the Kings cleared the puck from their zone and I could say something I had waited 20 years to say: "The Los Angeles Kings are going to the Stanley Cup finals, the Kings are Campbell Conference champions."

Several Kings fans have told me they recorded those last lines and have put them on their telephone answering machines. I remember thinking this is why we have all been working so hard for so many years, to experience a Stanley Cup final in Southern California, to turn the whole area on to hockey. Hopefully, to recruit thousands of new fans.

I called my wife, Judy, at our home in California after the

game. She had invited a couple of friends, Randy and Dona, who are Kings season ticketholders, over to watch the game. I talked to Randy, asked him what he was doing, and he replied, "Jumping up and down on your furniture!" That sort of symbolized what was going on all over Southern California.

I heard from people who said fans were cheering and screaming while they drove in their cars, that the sports bars were packed. Had it been that long ago when people said no one in Los Angeles would ever care about hockey this way? The only frustrating part for me was not being able to experience it all first-hand.

Several Toronto policemen came into the locker room after the game and said that anyone leaving the arena on the Kings bus should wait for a police escort. What now? As we left the building to board the bus, people lining the sidewalk pelted us with eggs, paint, and who knows what. Gee, that was fun.

When we got to Montreal, the papers were reporting that a Stanley Cup final in that city was hardly anything new and certainly nothing to get *too* excited about. The folks who lived in Los Angeles, meanwhile, were really getting into it.

When I went to the Montreal hotel that was being used as press headquarters and picked up my credentials, a woman walking beside me said, "Excuse me, please. Can you tell me, what is the Stanley Cup?" I nearly fell down. Hey, this was Montreal. No kidding, I began to look for Allan Funt; this had to be a set-up for "Candid Camera." Well, as it turned out, the woman was from the United Kingdom. So I guess she could be excused.

I couldn't believe how many radio interviews I did in the days leading up to the series against the Canadiens. I literally sat in my hotel room much of the time and did interviews with radio stations from Miami, Washington, New York, St. Louis, Minneapolis, Seattle, Denver, San Diego, and Sacramento. Oh, did I forget to mention Los Angeles?

One thing I noticed was the distinct contrast to the manner in which the Kings and Canadiens behaved during their separate press conferences before the series actually began. The Canadiens were favored to win and yet they seemed to be uptight and serious. I'll never forget how loose the Kings appeared to be. They were all laughing and joking. The Montreal writers, and I imagine a lot of the other reporters from around the league, were looking at the Kings as if to say, "Do these guys know this is the Stanley Cup final, or do they think it's the All-Star Game?"

But that's how coach Barry Melrose prepared his team. He told them in their very first meeting at training camp, if you're afraid to talk about winning the Stanley Cup, you will never win it. The Kings weren't afraid to talk about the Cup, and they were going to have some fun playing in the final.

After the Kings won Game 1 handily, I ended the telecast with the words, "The Kings are three wins away from the Stanley Cup." But as fate would have it, they never got any closer.

The teams were tied, 1-1, at the end of the second period in Game 2, which is when Montreal broadcaster Dick Irvin said to me, "If the Kings win tonight, they will sweep the series." Well, with under two minutes left in the game and the Kings ahead, 2-1, we showed a shot on our telecast of the Montreal bench. The Canadiens were hanging their heads and they looked like a defeated team. Then came the turning point of the series, Marty McSorley's illegal stick. When referee Kerry Fraser grabbed the stick to measure it, my telecast partner, Jim Fox, shook his head. He knew the stick was illegal.

As you know, McSorley was given a penalty and the Canadiens scored a power-play goal to tie the game. Then they won it in overtime. Now, the Kings didn't necessarily lose the series because of McSorley's penalty. Montreal still had to play well to win. But the infraction certainly opened the door and the Canadiens skated through. Later, I was told that the Maple Leafs suspected McSorley was using an illegal stick. I wondered why they never called him on it.

We experienced another frightening situation in Montreal after the Canadiens won Game 5 and were presented with the Stanley Cup. Mobs outside the Forum were rocking the Kings bus. Concerned that someone might throw a rock, I moved away from the windows but could hardly stand in the aisle; the bus was being rocked that violently. The side-view mirror on the driver's side was torn off and the people outside barely got out of the way when the bus began to move. I kept thinking, "Their team just won the Stanley Cup and these idiots are acting like this. Imagine if the Canadiens had *lost*."

It is astounding to me that Montreal could win 10 overtime

games in the playoffs. The odds on that must be astronomical. Sure, the Canadiens played well, but they also continued to get all of the right bounces.

Eric Desjardins' winning goal in Game 2 was a perfect example. He took a shot that rocketed high and wide of the Kings net and, usually in an instance like this, the puck will ricochet around the glass out toward the blue line or skip out of play into the stands. This time, the puck hit a metal brace that holds the glass in place and dropped right down behind the net to Montreal's Benoit Brunet. I lost sight of the puck for a moment because I was looking for it to come toward the blue line. Then, suddenly, I saw Desjardins wind up again off a pass from Brunet and score.

Before Game 3, the first-ever Stanley Cup final game to be played in Los Angeles, we had to do a live cut-in on our television pregame show. I was asked to comment on the atmosphere. Just before I went on, I looked below our broadcast location and saw what apparently were four season ticketholders opening a bottle of champagne. The fans raised their glasses in a toast. They obviously had waited a long time for this, and I bet there were times they doubted they'd ever see it.

I remember there was such a feeling of excitement and electricity in the building when the Stanley Cup was brought to center ice before the player introductions. The crowd stood and just roared.

The Stanley Cup and the other NHL trophies were on display in Los Angeles, just as they were in Montreal. On the off-day between Games 3 and 4, my wife and I, and two other couples, went to see the display at the Westin hotel, which is near the airport. I ran into Dick Irvin as we entered the lobby, and he was simply amazed that there had been such a steady stream of people for two days. We were there for about two hours and the fans never stopped coming. They had video cameras and still cameras and were standing about four-deep to get a glimpse of the Stanley Cup.

Hockey was hot, no doubt about it. The television ratings proved that. In 1973, when I started my career with the Kings, we televised a total of 15 games. Last season we televised 105 games. The Stanley Cup final produced all-time record ratings for cable TV in the Los Angeles area with a 22 percent share of the audience. In fact, more viewers were watching the Game 4 overtime than any other competing program; peak viewership topped 725,000 homes. There were more first-time TV viewers than at any time in Kings history.

No question about it, we Southern Californians really do care about our hockey.

— Bob Miller

Key Dates

KEY DATES FROM THE 1992-93 SEASON

1992

June 25 — Kings owner Bruce McNall replaces himself with Roy Mlakar as team president. Nick Beverley is named to replace Rogie Vachon as general manager. Vachon becomes McNall's special assistant. McNall had been elected chairman of the NHL Board of Governors on June 22. Barry Melrose is named head coach, replacing Tom Webster, who was fired May 4.

September 12 — Training camp opens at Lake Arrowhead, California.

September 13 — Defenseman Alexei Zhitnik, a fourth-round draft pick in 1991, signs a four-year, $1.7 million contract. Captain Wayne Gretzky leaves camp to be with his wife, Janet, who is due to give birth to the couple's third child.

September 14 — Janet Gretzky gives birth to Trevor Douglas, who weighs in at eight pounds, seven ounces.

September 16 — Wayne Gretzky is admitted to Centinela Hospital Medical Center with what Kings officials describe as an upper-back strain. Beverley says, "We're just taking this one day at a time. I certainly don't see this as being a time to panic."

September 18 — Gretzky remains hospitalized as the Kings open preseason play with a 3-3 tie in Vancouver. According to back specialist Dr. Robert Watkins, Gretzky is receiving medication for significant back pain.

September 22 — The Kings call a news conference at the Forum to announce that Gretzky is suffering from a herniated thoracic disk in his back and will remain out for an indefinite period. Watkins says the chances of getting such a career-threatening injury are "one in a million."

October 3 — The Kings close out the preseason by defeating the San Jose Sharks, 8-5, giving them a 3-3-2 exhibition record.

October 5 — Melrose picks Luc Robitaille to replace Gretzky as captain. Paul Coffey and Tony Granato are named assistant captains.

October 6 — The Kings kick off the regular season with a 5-4 victory in Calgary, thanks to a goal by Granato late in the third period and one by Tomas Sandstrom in overtime.

October 8 — The home opener is spoiled by the Detroit Red Wings, who capture a 5-3 decision.

October 17 — Jari Kurri collects the 500th goal of his career, an empty-net job, with 53.7 seconds remaining to seal an 8-6 win over Boston.

October 31 — Marty McSorley is suspended for six (non-game) days and fined $14,130 by NHL president Gil Stein for cross-checking Boston's Darren Banks in the face in an October 29 game at Boston Garden. The Kings respond by closing out the month, along with a six-game road trip, with a 7-1 rout of Hartford. The Gretzky-less Kings are 7-4-1.

November 5 — The Kings swap defensemen with the Pittsburgh Penguins, dealing Peter Ahola in exchange for Jeff Chychrun.

November 7 — Gretzky, in an interview on "Hockey Night in Canada," says he isn't certain if he will be able to play again. His back still hurts and he isn't ruling out surgery, a last resort. The Kings, meanwhile, have fashioned a 9-4-1 record.

November 8 — Mike Donnelly, Jari Kurri and Luc Robitaille each collect hat tricks in the Kings' 11-4 pounding of the San Jose Sharks at the Cow Palace.

November 14 — Edmonton's Louie DeBrusk crashes into Dave Taylor, who bangs his head on the Forum ice and suffers a concussion, headaches and vertigo. Taylor, in his 16th season in Los Angeles, will miss 18 consecutive games.

November 17 — San Jose registers the first shutout in its history, pinning a 6-0 loss on the stunned Kings.

November 19 — Miraculously, Gretzky's back pain disappears. He anticipates resuming skating within two months. Rookie goaltender Robb Stauber goes the distance in a 4-1 win over Chicago for his sixth consecutive win and the team's ninth in a row at home.

November 21 — Winger Tomas Sandstrom fractures his right arm when he is slashed by Doug Gilmour of the Toronto Maple Leafs in the Kings' 6-4 win. Sandstrom goes on to miss 23 of the next 24 games.

November 28 — The Kings spend the better part of a 3-2 defeat in Toronto attempting to make Gilmour pay for his slash of Sandstrom. The NHL already had decided to make Gilmour pay in the form of an eight (non-game) day suspension and $28,984 fine.

December 7 — Gretzky skates for 40 minutes without pain at the team's Culver City Ice Rink practice facility under doctors' supervision.

December 8 — Montreal's Vincent Damphousse scores three goals in the final eight minutes to give the Canadiens a 5-5 tie with the Kings in a neutral-site game at Phoenix. As it turns out, these teams will meet again when the stakes are much higher.

December 10 — A listless 5-4 defeat to Quebec at the Forum snaps the Kings' club-record home winning streak at 12 games. Still, they own an impressive 19-8-3 record overall.

December 15 — The Kings embarrass themselves with a 3-2 loss to the Tampa Bay Lightning, an expansion team. Stauber's seven-game winning streak comes to an end when Mikael Andersson scores against him on a penalty shot with 33 seconds remaining in the third period. The penalty shot was awarded after Stauber threw his stick at a loose puck.

December 19 — Center Corey Millen, on a tear with 20 goals in his first 30 games, goes down with a groin injury in the Kings' 5-3 loss in Calgary. Millen will miss the next 38 games.

December 20 — Forward Bob Kudelski, upset because coach Barry Melrose won't play him, wants out and finally is traded. Kudelski, who averaged 23 goals in each of his previous three seasons as a King, is shipped to the expansion Ottawa Senators along with minor-league center Shawn McCosh. The Kings receive forwards Marc Fortier and Jim Thomson.

December 22 — Gretzky claims he will be able to begin practicing with his teammates within a few days and make his season debut within two or three weeks.

December 26 — Gretzky practices at the Cow Palace, then the Sharks chew up the Kings, 7-2, as San Jose goaltender Jeff Hackett makes 59 saves.

December 29 — The situation deteriorates for the Kings, who are steamrolled by the Philadelphia Flyers, 10-2, at the Forum even though Flyers rookie star Eric Lindros is sidelined with a knee injury. The loss is the Kings' fourth in a row. Dave Taylor, his dizzy spells gone, plays for the first time since November 14.

1993

January 3 — Gretzky takes part in a Kings scrimmage after passing a physical exam and expresses optimism that he will return to the lineup soon.

January 4 — The Kings hold a news conference at the Forum and announce that Gretzky will play in the team's next game — two days later against Tampa Bay.

January 5 — Luc Robitaille gives up the team captainship to Gretzky.

January 6 — Gretzky's first game of the season is the 1,000th of his career. He is nearly great with a pair of assists, but the Kings lose to the Lightning, 6-3, and stretch their winless streak to nine games. They are 1-8-3 since Gretzky resumed skating. The Kings were 20-14-5 during the 39 games Gretzky missed.

January 8 — A 6-3 loss in Winnipeg extends the Kings' winless streak to 10 games (0-8-2), the fifth-longest winless streak in franchise history.

January 10 — Tony Granato scores two goals and picks up an assist as the Kings win in Chicago, 5-4. It is their first victory since December 12. Charlie Huddy and Jari Kurri are benched by coach Barry Melrose. The Kings have completed the season's first half with a record of 21-16-5.

January 18 — The losses continue to mount and general manager Nick Beverley suggests it may be necessary for him to shake things up if the Kings continue to stumble. "You get to the point of wondering how long you can go without doing something," he says.

January 21 — Tomas Sandstrom celebrates his first full game in two months by scoring three goals against Vancouver. His effort is wasted because the Kings still lose, 5-4.

January 23 — Melrose fumes and accuses his players'of quitting on goalie Robb Stauber after an 8-3 loss to the New York Rangers, who score five consecutive third-period goals. The Kings had battled back from a 3-0 deficit to tie the game.

January 28 — Club owner Bruce McNall has had it with his floundering Kings. "We're playing horribly," McNall says. "There are times when I want to put a paper sack on my head and be the anonymous owner." McNall feels even worse after a Paul Coffey slap shot catches Tomas Sandstrom in the face. Sandstrom will miss 21 games with a broken jaw.

January 29 — Management runs out of patience during a protracted slump that reaches 4-13-2. Beverley's first major trade is somewhat controversial. He deals Coffey, rookie winger Jim Hiller and minor-league center Sylvain Couturier to the Detroit Red Wings in exchange for center Jimmy Carson and two minor-league wingers, Marc Potvin and Gary Shuchuk. Wayne Gretzky, upset because Coffey is one of his closest friends, leaves practice without commenting.

January 30 — The Kings respond to the trade by tying Chicago, 2-2, at the Forum. Blackhawks star Jeremy Roenick scores with 5:27 remaining to drop the Kings into fourth place in the Smythe Division, one point behind the Winnipeg Jets. The Kings are 1-8-2 in their past 11 games at home. Meanwhile, Gretzky responds to Coffey's departure. "It was a tough day for me," he admits. "But I've got to come here with a smile on my face and try and give the young guys some direction."

February 3 — The Canadiens clobber the Kings, 7-2, in Montreal in the final game before the All-Star break. Gretzky, who earlier was added to the Campbell Conference team by league president Gil Stein, remains in town with Jari Kurri and Luc Robitaille. The three will represent the Kings in the midseason classic in three days.

February 5 — McNall is forced to call a news conference before the NHL All-Stars skills competition in Montreal to shoot down rumors Gretzky is angry about the Coffey trade and wants to be dealt to the Toronto Maple Leafs.

February 9 — The Kings are drilled by Edmonton, 6-3, in their first game after the break and skid to .500 (24-24-6) for the first time since the second game of the season. Defenseman Brent Thompson misses his fifth consecutive game with an abdominal strain he hid from the medical staff for three weeks.

February 10 — Beverley denies published reports that say the Kings are interested in obtaining Brett Hull from the St. Louis Blues. "We just made a major deal (for Carson) and we're looking for some stability," Beverley says. He adds the Kings could use an experienced defenseman, but he won't give up much to get one.

February 11 — Carson produces his first goal for the Kings and Coffey is blanked in a 6-6 tie with Detroit in the first meeting between the teams since the blockbuster trade.

February 15 — In what is seen by some as an act of desperation, the Kings announce that they have signed career minor-league goalie Rick Knickle, 33, for the remainder of the season. Knickle had rolled up a 33-4-4 record with a 2.17 goals-against average for the San Diego Gulls of the International Hockey League but had never played in an NHL game since turning pro in 1980.

February 17 — Gretzky scores his first goal in 17 games, a 40-day span, and adds four assists in a 10-5 blowout of Minnesota. It proves to be the final Met Center appearance for Gretzky and the Kings because the North Stars move to Dallas when the season ends.

February 18 — Fighting dehydration from a two-week-old bout with food poisoning and unable to overcome the sloppy play of his teammates, Rick Knickle permits four third-period goals on the way to a 7-2 loss at Chicago Stadium in his NHL debut.

March 4 — The Kings struggle to hand Ottawa its 33rd consecutive road loss, 8-6. Former King Bob Kudelski collects a goal and two assists for the Senators.

March 9 — Bruce McNall decides to allow the team to use the private jet he bought three years earlier for the remainder of the season. He took away the $5 million luxury plane following the first-round playoff exit the preceding spring.

March 13 — Fierce winds powering a mighty blizzard along the Eastern seaboard blow out a pane of glass at the Spectrum in Philadelphia during the first period of a game with the Flyers, forcing building officials to suspend the final two periods.

March 14 — The Kings are stranded inside their grounded plane for five hours at snow-bound Philadelphia International Airport before they leave for Buffalo, where a game is scheduled that afternoon. The Sabres game is postponed until the next evening, prompting several Kings players, including Wayne Gretzky, to criticize Los Angeles management.

March 15 — Gretzky scores a goal and sets up two others in a 4-2 win over Buffalo, then the team takes a cross-country flight home for its home game against Winnipeg the next night.

March 16 — Gretzky and his linemates, Tony Granato and Luc Robitaille, combine for four goals and five assists as the Kings demolish the Jets, 8-4, expanding their lead over Winnipeg to three points in the race for third place.

March 22 — The Kings beat the trading deadline with a few hours to spare, dealing center John McIntyre to the Rangers in exchange for defenseman Mark Hardy, who spent his first eight NHL seasons in Los Angeles.

March 26 — A 4-1 win in Edmonton clinches a Stanley Cup playoff berth for the Kings and eliminates the Oilers, who had punched out Los Angeles in the first round of the tournament the year before.

March 28 — Robitaille and coach Barry Melrose scream at each other following a 3-3 tie in Winnipeg. The Kings blew a two-goal lead in the third period and Melrose calls Robitaille "selfish."

March 31 — NHL commissioner Gary Bettman announces that the league's Board of Governors has approved the first major realignment plan since 1981-82. The Kings will play in the Pacific Division and Western Conference in 1993-94 rather than in the Smythe and Campbell, respectively. They will be joined in the Pacific Division by the expansion team Mighty Ducks of Anaheim, Calgary, Edmonton, San Jose and Vancouver.

April 1 — The Kings return to the Spectrum and ground the Flyers, 3-1, in the makeup game of the match suspended from the great blizzard. They finish 3-1-2 on a grueling six-game, nine-day trip.

April 3 — Defenseman Rob Blake bruises his lower back in a 3-0 loss to Minnesota at the Forum. He will miss the final five regular-season games.

April 8 — Robitaille breaks Steve Shutt's NHL record for goals by a left winger in a season with his 60th and 61st in a 2-1 decision over San Jose.

April 13 — Despite a 7-4 defeat in Vancouver, third place in the Smythe Division is clinched, along with a first-round playoff series against Calgary.

April 15 — An 8-6 loss to the Canucks at the Forum leaves the Kings with a 39-35-10 regular-season record.

April 18 — Blake doesn't play because of his ailing back and Wayne Gretzky suffers what the team calls a charley horse in the first period, but the Kings win the opening game of their playoff series in Calgary, 6-3, before an ABC-TV audience.

April 21 — The Flames score five times in the second period on the way to a 9-4 blowout.

April 23 — Calgary takes a 2-1 lead in the series with a 5-2 victory at the Forum.

April 25 — Robb Stauber, who sat in the stands both games in Calgary, starts in goal and plays brilliantly with 28 saves in a 3-1 win that evens the series at two games each.

April 27 — Gretzky, Tony Granato, Luc Robitaille and Tomas Sandstrom all score their first goals of the series in a 9-4 cakewalk at the Olympic Saddledome in Game 5.

April 29 — Jari Kurri sparks an entertaining 9-6 shootout decision at the Forum that clinches the series and propels the Kings into the Smythe Division final against Vancouver, a team that took seven of nine decisions between the clubs in regular-season play.

May 2 — Playing past April for the first time in franchise history, the Kings are flat in a 5-2 loss to the Canucks. Media reports out of Vancouver all but assure the Kings will go down quietly.

May 5 — Kelly Hrudey plays in goal for the first time since Game 3 of the Calgary series and watches teammate Mark Hardy deliver a goal 19 seconds into the game. After getting a goal and two assists in the Kings' 6-3 victory, Gretzky tells ESPN commentator John Davidson that he actually cracked a rib in the opening game of the Flames series. Gretzky says he was taking pain-killing injections before games but that he is now healthy.

May 7 — Gretzky looks healthy as he scores two more goals in Game 3, a 7-4 victory. The Kings rattle Canucks goalie Kirk McLean for four goals in the third period, then Gretzky hits an empty net with one second to play.

May 9 — Vancouver hits everything in sight and overcomes a 2-1 deficit with six unanswered goals in a 7-2 win at the Forum that ties the series at two games apiece.

May 11 — On a hunch, coach Barry Melrose puts wingers Gary Shuchuk and Marc Potvin in the lineup and benches Mark Hardy and Corey Millen. Potvin never leaves the bench, but Shuchuk scores 6 minutes and 31 seconds into the second overtime period for a 4-3 win at Pacific Coliseum. It is the longest game in Kings history.

May 12 — The Kings pepper McLean with 50 shots and five different players hit paydirt in a 5-3 victory at the Forum. The Kings take the series, four games to two, for their first-ever Smythe Division playoff championship.

May 15 — The Toronto Maple Leafs defeat the St. Louis Blues, 6-0, to clinch the Norris Division final and earn a berth in the Campbell Conference championship series against the Kings, who pack their bags to begin their third straight series on the road.

May 17 — Marty McSorley smashes Leafs' star Doug Gilmour to the ice with an elbow to the head late in the Kings' 4-1 series-opening defeat and immediately becomes Public Enemy No. 1 in Toronto. McSorley's hit triggers a brawl on the ice and prompts Leafs coach Pat Burns to leave his bench and scream at Melrose.

May 19 — Sandstrom beats rookie goalie Felix Potvin with a 30-foot laser-beam type shot at 12:20 of the third period to snap a 2-2 tie and give the Kings a 3-2 win at Maple Leaf Gardens. The series is tied heading to Inglewood.

May 21 — Shorthanded goals by Jari Kurri and Dave Taylor enable the Kings to crumple the Leafs, 4-2. McSorley, sporting a black eye from his Game 1 fight with Wendel Clark, receives a standing ovation from the Forum crowd when his face is shown on the scoreboard screens.

May 23 — Home-ice advantage doesn't help in Game 4, a 4-2 Toronto win that evens the series.

May 25 — Kurri and Gary Shuchuk produce first-period goals, but the Kings collapse and drop a 3-2 overtime decision that includes Glenn Anderson's goal with only 40 seconds to play in the first sudden-death overtime.

May 27 — Wayne Gretzky's second goal of the series comes 1:41 into overtime and gives the Kings a 5-4 win at the Forum, forcing a seventh and deciding game in Toronto.

May 29 — Stung by criticism that he has been badly outplayed by Gilmour, Gretzky lights up the Leafs with the ninth playoff hat trick of his career. The 5-4 victory puts the Kings into their first Stanley Cup final. They'll meet the Montreal Canadiens.

June 1 — The underdog Kings dominate a Canadiens team that had been off for eight days after taking out the New York Islanders in the Wales Conference final. Gretzky has a goal and three assists while Montreal native Luc Robitaille scores twice in a surprisingly-easy 4-1 win.

June 3 — The Kings are nursing a 2-1 lead with 1:45 remaining and threatening to take a 2-0 series lead back to California when the Canadiens ask referee Kerry Fraser to measure McSorley's stick blade. It turns out to have an illegal curve and McSorley is given a minor penalty. Montreal coach Jacques Demers yanks his goalie, Patrick Roy, for an additional skater and Eric Desjardins scores the tying goal during the two-man advantage with 1:13 to play. Desjardins scores again 51 seconds into overtime for a 3-2 Canadiens win.

June 5 — Robitaille, Granato and Gretzky score second-period goals as the Kings rally from a 3-0 deficit in the first Stanley Cup final game ever played in Inglewood. But John LeClair's goal 34 seconds into overtime gives Montreal a 4-3 victory and a 2-1 series lead. The Kings complain that Montreal's Guy Carbonneau covered up a puck in the crease late in regulation and that they should be awarded a penalty shot. Referee Terry Gregson disagrees.

June 7 — The Canadiens win their record 10th consecutive overtime game in the playoffs when LeClair banks the puck off sliding Kings rookie defenseman Darryl Sydor into the net at 14:37 of the first extra period. The 3-2 victory gives Montreal a commanding 3-1 advantage in the series.

June 9 — The Kings are limited to 19 shots and lose, 4-1, in Montreal. The Canadiens are presented with their 24th Stanley Cup and Roy is awarded with the Conn Smythe Trophy as the playoffs' most valuable player. Gretzky makes even bigger news, saying he is seriously considering retiring.

Transactions

MAJOR TRANSACTIONS IN 1992-93 SEASON

1992

May 4 — Head coach Tom Webster is fired. His three-year record in Los Angeles was 115-94-31, a .544 winning percentage that is the highest in franchise history. Webster's record in the Stanley Cup playoffs was 8-10, a .444 percentage.

June 11 — Center Robert Lang, a seventh-round draft pick in 1990, signs a three-year, $515,000 contract.

June 20 — Defenseman Justin Hocking of the Western Hockey League's Spokane Chiefs is selected as the team's first pick (second round, 39th overall) in the entry draft in Montreal.

June 22 — Kings owner Bruce McNall is elected chairman of the NHL Board of Governors.

June 25 — Roy Mlakar replaces McNall as team president. Nick Beverley replaces Rogie Vachon as general manager. Barry Melrose replaces Tom Webster as head coach. Vachon is named McNall's special assistant.

August 1 — Assistant coach Cap Raeder is retained. Assistant coach Rick Wilson is not. Wilson moves on to the Minnesota North Stars as an assistant to GM-coach Bob Gainey.

September 3 — Center Pat Conacher is acquired from the New Jersey Devils in exchange for future considerations.

September 13 — Defenseman Alexei Zhitnik, a fourth-round draft pick in 1991, signs a four-year, $1.7 million contract.

September 21 — Defenseman Rob Blake signs a two-year contract.

September 29 — Left winger Jay Miller is cut with two years and $640,000 remaining on his contract.

October 3 — Left winger Warren Rychel signs a one-year, $175,000 contract.

October 5 — Melrose names left winger Luc Robitaille to replace injured center Wayne Gretzky as team captain. Defenseman Paul Coffey and right winger Tony Granato are named assistant captains.

October 13 — Defenseman Tim Watters is assigned to the Phoenix Roadrunners (IHL).

October 19 — Right winger Ed Kastelic and defenseman Brent Thompson are assigned to Phoenix for conditioning.

November 2 — Thompson is recalled from Phoenix.

November 5 — Kastelic clears waivers and is loaned to Phoenix. Defenseman Peter Ahola is traded to the Pittsburgh Penguins in exchange for defenseman Jeff Chychrun.

November 14 — Lang is assigned to Phoenix.

November 23 — Center Guy Leveque and right winger Sean Whyte are recalled from Phoenix.

December 4 — Leveque is reassigned to Phoenix.

December 14 — Leveque and right winger Frank Breault are recalled from Phoenix.

December 16 — Right winger Jim Hiller is assigned to Phoenix.

December 20 — Right winger Bob Kudelski and center Shawn McCosh are traded to the Ottawa Senators in exchange for center Marc Fortier and right winger Jim Thomson.

December 21 — Hiller is recalled from Phoenix.

December 24 — Breault is reassigned to Phoenix.

1993

January 7 — Leveque is reassigned to Phoenix. Goaltender David Goverde is recalled.

January 11 — Goverde is reassigned to Phoenix. Left winger Lonnie Loach is assigned to Phoenix for conditioning.

January 16 — Fortier is assigned to Phoenix. Loach is recalled.

January 21 — Whyte is reassigned to Phoenix.

January 29 — Defenseman Paul Coffey, center Sylvain Couturier and Hiller are traded to the Detroit Red Wings in exchange for center Jimmy Carson and right wingers Marc Potvin and Gary Shuchuk.

February 8 — Chychrun is assigned to Phoenix. Defenseman Rene Chapdelaine and Watters are recalled.

February 12 — Goverde is recalled from Phoenix.

February 15 — Goaltender Rick Knickle's rights are acquired from the San Diego Gulls (IHL) in exchange for future considerations and he is signed for the remainder of the season. His contract is worth $68,000 plus bonuses. Goverde is reassigned to Phoenix.

February 16 — Thomson is assigned to Phoenix.

February 19 — Fortier and Lang are recalled from Phoenix.

February 24 — Fortier and Lang are reassigned to Phoenix.

March 1 — Right winger Brandy Semchuk and left winger Darryl Williams are recalled from Phoenix.

March 2 — Loach, Semchuk and Williams are reassigned to Phoenix.

March 4 — Loach and Williams are recalled from Phoenix.

March 5 — Williams is reassigned to Phoenix.

March 7 — Thompson is assigned to Phoenix for conditioning.

March 16 — Thompson is recalled from Phoenix.

March 18 — Thompson is assigned to Phoenix.

March 22 — Center John McIntyre is traded to the New York Rangers in exchange for defenseman Mark Hardy. Chapdelaine is loaned to San Diego to complete the future considerations portion of the Feb. 15 deal involving Knickle.

April 12 — Thompson is recalled from Phoenix.

April 15 — Leveque, Thomson and Semchuk are recalled from Phoenix.

June 19 — Melrose receives a one-year contract extension through the 1996-97 season. Assistant coach Cap Raeder receives a new, three-year contract.

June 24 — Loach and Thomson are selected by the Mighty Ducks of Anaheim in the NHL expansion draft.

June 26 — Right winger Shayne Toporowski of the Western Hockey League's Prince Albert Raiders is the team's first choice (second round, 42nd overall) in the entry draft in Quebec City. Center Corey Millen is traded to New Jersey in exchange for a fifth-round pick.